RESOLVE IN INTERNATIONAL POLITICS

PRINCETON STUDIES IN
Political Behavior

Edited by Tali Mendelberg

RECENTLY PUBLISHED IN THE SERIES:

Democracy for Realists: Why Elections Do Not Produce Responsive Government by
Christopher H. Achen and Larry M. Bartels

RESOLVE IN
INTERNATIONAL POLITICS

JOSHUA D. KERTZER

Princeton University Press
Princeton and Oxford

Library of Congress Cataloging-in-Publication Data

Names: Kertzer, Joshua D., 1984– author.
Title: Resolve in international politics / Joshua D. Kertzer.
Description: Princeton, New Jersey : Princeton University Press, 2016. |
Series: Princeton studies in political behavior | Includes bibliographical
references and index.
Identifiers: LCCN 2016012451 | ISBN 9780691171609 (hardback : acid-free paper)
Subjects: LCSH: International relations–Psychological aspects. | Political psychology. |
Economics–Psychological aspects. | War–Decision making–Psychological aspects. |
BISAC: POLITICAL SCIENCE / International Relations / Diplomacy. |
POLITICAL SCIENCE / International Relations / General. | SOCIAL SCIENCE / General.
Classification: LCC JZ1253 .K47 2016 | DDC 327.101/9–dc23 LC record available at
https://lccn.loc.gov/2016012451

British Library Cataloging-in-Publication Data is available

CONTENTS

TABLES

FIGURES

ACKNOWLEDGMENTS

If the aphorism is true, and all books are autobiographical, I have a number of issues with resolve.

When they began is an open question, but the book itself began as a dissertation written at the Ohio State University under the tutelage of Rick Herrmann, Bear Braumoeller, Kathleen McGraw, and Chris Gelpi, who were more generous with their time and more thoughtful in their feedback than they had any need to be, and who patiently let me pursue a riskier project than I had any right to pursue. Most of the book's redeeming qualities were likely incepted from them.

I also appropriated liberally from the remarkably helpful and constructive comments I received presenting parts of the project to audiences at Binghamton University, Dartmouth College, Harvard University, McGill University, New York University, Ohio State, Princeton University, UCLA, UC San Diego, UC Santa Barbara, the University of Illinois at Urbana-Champaign, the University of Kansas, the University of North Carolina, the University of South Carolina, the University of Southern California, Yale University, and the annual meetings of the International Studies Association and the Peace Science Society. To this end, I'm grateful to too many people to name, including Bentley Allan, Scott Althaus, Burcu Bayram, Adam Berinsky, Daniel Bessner, Bill Boettcher, Jake Bowers, Jan Box-Steffensmeier, Steve Brooks, Zoltan Buzas, Austin Carson, David Carter, Dave Clark, Giacomo Chiozza, Mike Colaresi, Allan Dafoe, Alex Debs, Peter Feaver, Ben Fordham, Jeff Friedman, Stephen Gent, Emilie Hafner-Burton, Steph Haggard, Marcus Holmes, Ted Hopf, Mike Horowitz, Susan Hyde, Ben Jones, Luke Keele, Katja Kleinberg, Andy Kydd, David Lake, Debbie Larson, Brad LeVeck, Jason Lyall, Sebastien Mainville, Eleonora Mattiacci, Rose McDermott, Jennifer Mitzen, Nuno Monteiro, Neil Narang, Irfan Nooruddin, Barry O'Neil, Krzysztof Pelc, Maggie Peters, Paul Poast, Vincent Pouliot, Bob Powell, Katy Powers, Mike Poznansky, Brian Rathbun, Jonathan Renshon, Elizabeth Saunders, Randy Schweller, Patrick Shea, Harvey Starr, Janice Stein, Tricia Sullivan, Phil Tetlock, Alex Thompson, Rob Trager, Mike Tomz, Chris Twomey, David Victor, Srdjan Vucetic, Alex Wendt, Jessica Weiss, Bill Wohlforth, and Keren Yarhi-Milo.

The survey experiment in chapter 4 was made possible thanks to the National Science Foundation's Time-sharing Experiments for the Social Sciences (TESS) initiative; I am grateful to Jeremy Freese, Penny Visser, and the anonymous reviewers for their help in improving the experiment's instrumentation, and to Ben DiPaola and Poom Nukulkij at GfK for their assistance fielding the study. The project was also supported in part by a doctoral fellowship from the Social Sciences and Humanities Research Council of Canada, a dissertation-year fellowship from the Graduate School at Ohio State, and a wonderful year as a fellow at the Dickey Center for International Understanding at Dartmouth College under the intrepid leadership of Dan Benjamin.

The book was completed at Harvard, where I found a vibrant intellectual community in the Government Department, under the skilled stewardship of Tim Colton. I'm particularly indebted to Jeff Frieden, Iain Johnston, Steve Rosen, Beth Simmons, and Dustin Tingley for all of their guidance with the project, as well as all of the colleagues, faculty, and graduate students who sharpened my thinking along the way. I'm also beholden to Steve Bloomfield and Tom Murphy for giving me a home in the Weatherhead Center, and to Frankie Hoff, who knew the answer to every question I asked. An Undergraduate Research Scholars award from the Institute for Quantitative Social Science helped broaden the book's audience, and I'm grateful to Alice Hu, Aaron Miller, and Nathan Williams for their helpful research assistance.

At Princeton University Press, Eric Crahan was willing to gamble on a manuscript probably more conceptual than most quantitative books, and probably more quantitative than most conceptual books; I am thus thankful for his risk preferences, as I am for Tali Mendelberg's time horizons, and for the improbably helpful comments procured from three anonymous reviewers.

Finally, for raising my costs of backing down, my deepest thanks to Adrienne, Jonathan, and Nicholas Kertzer, Nick White, Ryan Brutger, Amy Catalinac, George Ibrahim, Eleonora Mattiacci, Brian Rathbun, Jonathan Renshon, Elizabeth Saunders, Keren Yarhi-Milo, and Thomas Zeitzoff, all of whom cathected the project in different ways, and whose support and encouragement made it possible. The book is dedicated to Sam and Miriam Kertzer, and Olga and George Haas, who knew much more about resolve than I do.

RESOLVE IN INTERNATIONAL POLITICS

CHAPTER 1.

Resolve in International Politics

Desire, wish, will, are states of mind which everyone knows,
and which no definition can make plainer.

—William James (1950 [1890], p. 486)

On January 12, 2010, an earthquake struck the island nation of Haiti, reducing much of the capital city of Port-au-Prince to rubble. In the days afterward, as the casualty estimates grew by the hundreds of thousands and the international community turned its attention toward rebuilding the ravaged country, pundits pontificated on the uphill battle faced by a country that had suffered as many man-made disasters as natural ones. Bob Herbert, writing in the *New York Times*, struck an optimistic note: the Haitians would succeed, he argued, because they had shown "resolve among the ruins."[1]

Herbert is not alone in positing resolve and its synonyms—willpower, self-control, dedication, tenacity, determination, drive, and so on—as a solution to political problems. The collapse of the Mubarak regime in Egypt has frequently been attributed to the resolve of the protesters in Tahrir Square ("their determination is unshakeable," noted the editor of the *Egyptian Daily News*), while the same attribute has been used to account for the opposite event in neighboring Libya, where Moammar Qadaffi clung to power despite months of NATO airstrikes and armed insurrection ("War is largely about willpower," wrote an analyst for the DC-based Washington Institute for Near East Policy, "and Qadaffi currently holds the upper hand on this front").[2] When militants from the Islamic State regained control of Ramadi in May 2015 despite being outnumbered by Iraqi Security Forces, American Secretary of Defense Ashton Carter blamed the Iraqis' defeat on their lack of a "will to fight."[3] Writing several years prior in *The Weekly Standard*, Charles Krauthammer dismissed prophecies of American decline by arguing that "decline is a choice" rather than "a condition," and that the slide toward multipolarity can therefore

---

1 Herbert 2010.
2 Michaels and May 2011; White 2011.
3 Williams 2015.

be reversed through "moral self-confidence and will."[4] Similarly, when the Canadian government was deliberating over whether to renew its deployment in Afghanistan in 2008, the independent panel it convened to issue recommendations released a report arguing that Canadians must exhibit "sustained resolve" in order to allow the mission to succeed.[5]

This is a book about resolve in international politics. Sometimes, scholars of world politics write books to draw attention to a crucial concept or phenomenon that has been problematically ignored by policymakers, or prematurely neglected by political scientists, showing us how we gain a much more vivid understanding of the world once we bring this concept "back in" to our models of world affairs. This is not one of those books, and resolve is not one of those concepts.

After all, resolve is already a ubiquitous ingredient in the study of international relations, used to explain everything from why states win wars to how they prevail at the bargaining table during foreign policy crises, thereby preventing conflict from breaking out.[6] Rationalist approaches to the study of international conflict revolve around resolve: in a dispute between two actors, if both sides can be made aware of each others' levels of motivation to fight, the less resolute side backs down before a crisis can even take place.[7] Likewise, it is motivation, not muscle, that is used to explain why great powers fare so poorly in asymmetric conflict, and why the United States was never able to push the North Vietnamese to their "breaking point" during the Vietnam War.[8]

These types of arguments about resolve are made not just by those who study war, but also by those who wage it. Napoleon Bonaparte famously declared that "in war, the moral is to the physical as three to one," while Marshall Foch, the commander of the French Ninth Army at the Battle of the Marne in 1914, went even further, proclaiming in his lectures at the École de Guerre that "in a material sense no battle can be lost."[9] This belief in the power of resolve formed a major part of the "cult of the offensive" that reigned supreme in military academies across Europe by the time of the First World War: prewar British training manuals pronounced that "moral force in modern war preponderates over physical force," while in Germany in 1916, Paul von Hindenburg, then Chief of the German General Staff, declared that "victory will go to him who has the best nerves."[10]

---

4 Krauthammer 2009. The article, influential in conservative quarters, was later cited by the Republican Congressman (and later, Vice Presidential nominee) Paul Ryan in his June 2, 2011 speech to the Alexander Hamilton Society. See Warren 2011.

5 Manley et al. 2008, 8.

6 Maoz 1983; Pape 1996; Schelling 1966; Snyder and Diesing 1977; George and Simons 1994.

7 Powell 1987; Morrow 1989; Fearon 1995.

8 Mack 1974; Mueller 1980; Arreguín-Toft 2001.

9 Chandler 1966, 155; Recouly 1920.

10 Van Evera 1984, 61; Travers 1979, 274; Watson 2008, 1.

Given that exhortations of resolve routinely punctuate politicians' press conferences, and invocations of resolve drive many of our theories of world politics, the aim of the book is not to "bring resolve back in," but rather, to *lend it microfoundations*, to help us understand what resolve is, and how—and whether—it works. At its broadest level, the book is motivated by three puzzles: one conceptual, one methodological, and one theoretical.

First, what *is* resolve, conceptually? Is it related to an actor's capabilities, as it was for the classic international relations theorists who wrote about the "national will" as a source of power?[11] Is it equivalent to an actor's intentions or preferences, as in rational choice approaches that equate resolve with utility?[12] And if resolve is the same as capabilities or intentions, why should we go to the trouble of using the term in the first place? Building on a diverse array of literature across the social sciences, I sweep the conceptual minefield and suggest that resolve is something different altogether: a state of firmness or steadfastness of purpose, a "second-order volition" that is neither reducible to an actor's intentions, nor isomorphic with its capabilities.[13] Akin to the idea of willpower, resolve is not *what* an actor wants, but rather, the extent to which she maintains this intention despite contrary inclinations or temptations to back down.

Second, how should we study resolve? How do we know resolve when we see it? Precisely because resolve is not directly observable, I suggest that IR scholars have ended up in a paradoxical position, where although many of us would agree that resolve matters, we have had less success marshaling empirical evidence to test whether this assumption is true. As a result, although resolve is perhaps one of our favorite explanatory variables in our theoretical models, we tend to either explicitly avoid measuring it, or implicitly risk tautology by inferring it from the same outcomes we use it to explain: we assume, for example, that because the United States lost in Vietnam, it must have been less resolved than the North Vietnamese, and attribute the Iraqi Security Forces' defeats at the hands of militants from the Islamic State to the absence of a "will to fight." Studying resolve in this manner problematically turns the concept into a catchall residual category used ex post to explain outcomes we were unable able to explain ex ante, making it difficult to subject our theories about resolve's effects to rigorous empirical testing. The problem is not that resolve has no explanatory power in these cases, but that we would not be able to tell either way.

In an era when politicians and pundits routinely posit a kind of "Green Lantern" theory of foreign policy in which every geopolitical challenge can be overcome with a sufficient application of willpower, this methodological

---

11 E.g., Wright 1964.
12 E.g., Fearon 1994.
13 Frankfurt 1971.

challenge bears real political consequences. If we merely infer resolve from victory and irresolution from defeat, it becomes difficult to argue against the axiom that to win wars, one needs to be more resolved, or to push back against the claim suggested at General Mark Milley's confirmation hearing before the Senate Armed Services committee in July 2015, that "one of the most central tasks that the new army has" is the question of how the United States can "teach the will to fight" to the foreign troops it supports.[14]

Third, where does resolve come from? In the context of military interventions, why do some leaders and publics display remarkable persistence—the British in the Malayan emergency, for example—while others cut and run, like the United States in Somalia in 1993? Although we often explain behavior and outcomes in international politics by pointing to variation in actors' levels of resolve, we have trouble explaining this variation itself. In short, we lack microfoundations, and with them, a *theory of resolve*. The task I take up in this book is how to address these three lacunae, which are, course, interconnected: as long as we disagree on what resolve is, we will not be able to agree on how to measure it, and by gaining leverage on the determinants of resolve, we are better able to explore its consequences.

In this book, I address these challenges by offering a behavioral theory of resolve, suggesting that variation in time and risk preferences, honor orientation, and self-control shape how actors respond to the situations they face. In this sense, I argue we should think about resolve as an interaction. Contrary to its usual portrayal in IR, resolve is neither a simple cost-benefit calculation nor an invariant "type" of actor, but a contingent state, a function of both dispositional and situational causes, both traits and stakes, both mind and matter. Importantly, the dispositional characteristics I focus on here are among the traits that social scientists turn to when trying to explain willpower in our daily lives. Building on a growing body of research on willpower and self-control from elsewhere in the social sciences, I suggest that "political will" is more than just a metaphor or figure of speech, in that the characteristics that behavioral decision-making scholars turn to when modeling our tendencies to choose carrots over cheesecake, take gambles, and pick fights with people who bump into us, also spill over into the political domain, and can tell us something about why certain types of actors are more or less sensitive to different types of costs of war. In fact, it turns out that dispositions matter so much that it is difficult to understand how we respond to conflict without them: how we think about time and risk, how we feel about honor, and how much perseverance we display in our daily lives all shape how much resolve we display in political contexts.

14 C-Span 2015.

In this sense, this is a book about the political psychology of international politics, showing how we gain a richer understanding of global affairs when we focus not just on the macro-structural forces "shaping and shoving,"[15] but also on the properties and characteristics of actors themselves. In positing that characteristics or attributes from our daily lives spill into the political domain and can tell us something about international affairs, the book is also part of a broader movement in IR scholarship pushing back against the notion of international politics as an autonomous sphere of inquiry.[16] Perhaps paradoxically, much of the progress in IR theory over the past 40 years has come from the discipline chipping away at its own distinctiveness: just as earlier work showed that politics does not stop at the water's edge and that domestic politics bleeds into the international realm, my aim here is to go a step further, and illustrate some of the ways in which the personal spills over into the political.

Like the structural realists they sought to supplant, the rationalist approaches that have been prominent in mainstream IR over the past several decades have tended to privilege structure over agency, based on a "methodological bet" that greater theoretical progress can be made in International Relations by focusing on environmental features rather than actor-level characteristics.[17] Although this tendency has fostered many rich and remarkable contributions, it has also stymied our attempts to understand phenomena like resolve, frequently reducing it to an actor's costs of war, and leading to a number of both empirical and conceptual conundrums. Looking at how dispositional features moderate the effects of situational factors is critical in explaining how two actors can face the exact same situation, but respond in strikingly different ways. As the British historian James Joll put it when reflecting on the causes of the First World War, "it is only by studying the minds of men that we shall understand the causes of anything," and it is in this tradition that the book is situated.[18] While couched in a different language, the motivating premise of the book—that structural theories of action are indeterminate unless we also have a theory of how actors come to define their situation and make sense of their environment—is thus also one to which many constructivists would likely be sympathetic.[19] Although the discussion in the following chapters is often critical of how resolve has been studied in rational choice approaches—in particular, the tendency to reduce resolve to the cost of war—I should note that there is little about the framework I advance here that is inherently antithetical to rationalism, particularly if

---

15 Waltz 1986, 343.
16 See Morgenthau 1985; Wight 1966.
17 Lake and Powell 1999.
18 Joll 1968, 24.
19 Wendt 1999.

rationality is understood simply as actors making choices under constraints.[20] As pioneering work by McDermott, Mercer, and others has shown, rationalist approaches rest on particular sets of psychological assumptions, which are often left unarticulated.[21] The book is thus intended less as a riposte to rationalism, and more as a reimagination: turning to insights from the behavioral sciences about the systematic ways that actors differ from one another affords us the opportunity to revisit some of the classic assumptions that animate our theories, show that the constraints shaping choices are not simply external, and improve our explanatory power in the process.

Just as the book builds on theoretical frameworks from elsewhere in the behavioral sciences, it also borrows methodological tools. To try to avoid some of the pitfalls that ensue from inferring the presence or absence of resolve from the same outcome I am using it to explain, I employ a two-stage research design, at multiple levels of analysis, that studies resolve first as *explanandum* and then as *explanans*. Each half of the research design asks and answers a different question. First, I employ a series of original laboratory and embedded survey experiments to probe the individual-level microfoundations of resolve in the context of public opinion about military interventions. By manipulating the costs of war, these experiments offer control and the ability to engage in causal inference, model strategic choices directly, and avoid the concerns about endogeneity that plague the use of observational data. They also confer critical measurement advantages, measuring the resolve displayed by the studies' participants in a manner that would not be possible in a natural setting. Moreover, the controlled nature of the studies enables me to borrow instruments from social psychology and behavioral economics to measure participants' dispositional characteristics in domains unrelated to that of military interventions, therefore letting me test how these characteristics spill over into politics. Altogether, these experiments offer a chance to build theoretical microfoundations and explain individual-level variation in resolve, all while enriching our understanding of the dynamics of public opinion toward the use of force.

The experiments show that there is considerable variation in how much resolve individuals display, that this variation can be explained theoretically as a function of situational and dispositional factors, and that these factors interact in coherent ways. In the lab experiment, more patient individuals are more sensitive to casualties, and more risk-averse individuals are more sensitive to both the human costs of fighting and the reputational costs of backing down. These results not only remind us of the importance of disaggregating the costs of war and indicate the public is less beholden to casualties than cynics often assume, but also suggest we can turn to

20 Snidal 2002.
21 McDermott 2004; Mercer 2005.

dispositional characteristics to explain why certain types of costs of war loom larger for certain types of actors.

Having employed experiments as theory-building exercises to study resolve as a dependent variable, I then shift both the focus and the level of analysis to study resolve as an independent variable. The chief difficulty political scientists face in studying resolve in the historical record is that it is not directly observable, which makes it difficult to subject our theories of its effects to empirical testing without tautologically inferring it from the same outcomes we are using it to explain. Rather than infer resolve from its consequences, I do so based on its causes, using the experimental findings to build composite situational and dispositional measures of resolve at the leader- and country-level for the great powers from 1945 to 2003. This novel analytic move allows me to test whether resolve has the effects we often claim, without lapsing into tautology. Using Boolean statistical models, I investigate whether resolved great powers were indeed more likely to prevail in their military interventions in the postwar era and explore the interplay between leader- and country-level factors. The results suggest that resolve matters: great powers who are more resolved are indeed more likely to attain their desired objectives in their military interventions. The effect of resolve is less than its boosters might hope—contrary to Napoleon's proclamation, for example, the moral does not outweigh the material by a ratio of three to one—but more than its skeptics might assume. In addition to presenting a novel strategy for studying unobservable phenomena, I also find different patterns of effects for the dispositional and situational sources of resolve: for situational variables, the most relevant level of analysis appears to be the country- rather than the leader-level, whereas for dispositional variables, leaders matter more than the country as a whole, and overall, these dispositional factors outweigh situational ones. Assessing resolve in military interventions thus requires paying attention to leader-level dispositional features, country-level situational ones, and the interactions between them.

As Sartori argued, "concept formation stands prior to quantification," so before proposing or testing a theory of resolve, it is important to clearly specify why we need one in the first place, and discuss the problems confronting the field.[22] Thus, in this first chapter, I begin by defining resolve, discussing the variegated manner in which it has been understood in international affairs, and arguing that we have built mar*e* of our theories of world politics around a phenomenon that has been inconsistently theorized. I then offer a conceptual architecture I return to throughout the book, connecting the IR literature to a growing body of work on willpower from elsewhere in the social sciences to suggest that there have typically been two types of "stories" social scientists tell

---

22 Sartori 1970, 1,038.

about resolve: an inside, dispositional account that understands resolve to be a kind of trait, and an outside, situational one that perceives resolve to be a function of the costs or stakes an actor faces. Finally, I conclude by outlining the proceeding chapters of the book.

DEFINING RESOLVE

Any study of a phenomenon has to begin with a definition. I follow the *Oxford English Dictionary* in defining resolve as "firmness or steadfastness of purpose," maintaining a policy despite contrary inclinations or temptations to back down. In its emphasis on determined, sustained effort despite temptations to the contrary, resolve can therefore be considered synonymous with willpower, as well as related forms of self-regulation like self-control (the deliberate use of willpower to avoid undesirable actions) and self-discipline (the deliberate use of willpower to achieve desirable goals), and the opposite of weakness of will, irresolution, incontinent action, and other such antonyms.

Defining resolve in this manner has two advantages. First, it reflects the way we use these words in ordinary language: to describe an actor as "resolute" intuitively means the same thing as to argue the actor is persistent, motivated, committed, determined, and so on. Indeed, in his discussion of resolve, O'Neill notes that scholars seem to use a wide variety of terms, which "appear to be manifestations of one unnamed central quality."[23]

Second, it allows the analysis that follows to be grounded in an interdisciplinary fashion. The past several decades have witnessed a *Risorgimento* of resolve throughout the social sciences, most notably in the psychological literature on self-regulation and the economic literature on intertemporal choice and self-command, but also in fields as varied as the philosophy of action, education research, law and public policy, organizational theory, criminology, and even animal psychology.[24]

---

23 O'Neill 1999, 107.

24 On self-regulation in psychology, see Baumeister and Vohs 2004; Ryan and Deci 2006; Baumeister, Vohs, and Tice 2007; Galliot et al. 2007; Ackerman et al. 2009; Morsella, Bargh, and Gollwitzer 2009. For economists' growing interest in self-control and intertemporal choice, see Thaler and Shefrin 1981; Schelling 1984; Jolls, Sunstein, and Thaler 1998; Gul and Pesendorfer 2001; Bénabou and Tirole 2004; Fudenberg and Levine 2006. Philosophers of action have long been interested in weakness of will or *akrasia*; for recent developments in the literature, see Stroud and Tappolet 2003; May and Holton 2012. Beyond these approaches, we see similar interest in willpower in education research (e.g., Kohn, 2008), law and public policy (Posner, 1997; Fennell, 2009), criminology (Gottfredson and Hirschi, 1990; Tittle, Ward, and Grasmick, 2003; Pratt, Turner, and Piquero, 2004; Boutwell and Beaver, 2010), animal psychology (Tobin and Logue, 1994; Miller et al., 2010), as well as work on hardiness and resilience in military psychology (King et al., 1998; Bartone, 2006), gerontology (Ong et al., 2006; Trivedi, Bosworth, and Jackson, 2011), and a fertile interdisciplinary literature operating at the nexus of multiple fields (Logue, 1988; Ainslie, 1992; Elster, 2000; Ainslie, 2001; Kalis et al., 2008).

This growth has occurred in tandem despite each literature retaining its own nomenclature: IR theorists tend to favor "resolve," social psychologists typically adopt "self-regulation," economists choose "self-command," criminologists refer to "self-control," and philosophers invoke "willpower." Similarly, each discipline has predominantly applied the concept to different domains: political scientists frequently restrict resolve to military contexts by defining the term as "willingness to fight," whereas economists tend to define self-control purely in terms of consumption decisions, and developmental psychologists and criminologists focus on self-control in the realm of refraining from socially undesirable actions.[25] Despite these differences, however, if theorizing is about following Rosenau in asking "of what is this an instance?," I argue that the underlying construct remains the same in all cases: a resolute actor is engaged in what Young called "an intensity of feeling": a firmness or steadfastness of purpose, resisting temptations to the contrary.[26] In this sense, resolve is a *second-order* volition, in that it refers not to the substance or content of an actor's desire—whether to fight, quit smoking, save money, and so on—but to the steadfastness, dogged persistence, or "sticktoitiveness" with which it is being pursued.[27]

RESOLVE IN INTERNATIONAL RELATIONS

Resolve is a frequent protagonist in IR theory, arising in a wide variety of camps. The first is deterrence theory, whose advocates have long argued that it is essential for states to maintain "reputations for resolve" so that other actors will not try to take advantage of them.[28] While this line of argument has come under increased scrutiny since actors may not have as much control over their reputations as they think, its critics do not downplay the importance of perceptions of resolve so much as suggest that these perceptions are usually outside one's control.[29] The perception of resolve is an "emotional belief," such that there may be little that the United States can do to convince al Qaeda that it is not a "paper tiger"; for the same reason, despite the fears of US

25 E.g., Sartori 2002; Ameriks et al. 2007; Finkenauer, Engels, and Baumeister 2005.

26 Rosenau 1980; Young 1968, 33.

27 Frankfurt 1971. Because of the association between self-mastery and virtue in classical philosophy (Baumeister and Exline, 1999) the philosophy of action literature has traditionally viewed resolve in the context of upholding better judgments (Dunn, 1987), but if resolve merely refers to a firmness of purpose irrespective of its content, one can be as resolved to indulge as one is to abstain (Kivetz and Simonson, 2002; see also Rosen, 2005, 154). For more on this point, see the discussion of the "dark side of resolve" in chapter 6.

28 Jervis 1976, 1979; Powell 2003.

29 Mercer 1996; Tang 2005. For a potential exception, see Press 2005, although even here, the "current calculus" theory of credibility argues not that perceptions of resolve are irrelevant, but that they are more likely to stem from what I call situational.

policymakers, American defeats in the developing world during the Cold War did little to weaken Soviet perceptions of American determination.[30] Concerns about reputation for resolve have thus long outlasted the Cold War context in which early waves of deterrence theory were conceived.[31]

The second camp is the crisis bargaining literature more broadly, which argues that states embroiled in crisis negotiations are partaking in games of risk that are won not by strength, but by "nerve."[32] Crisis bargaining models rely on the same payoff structure as the game of Chicken, in which each side prefers to stand firm and induce its opponent to back down, but also prefers retreating over a situation where neither side relents and war emerges. As bargaining is a competition in risk-taking, an actor that is able to credibly signal its resolve— usually by taking risks that an irresolute actor would be unwilling to tolerate— will successfully avert war on its desired terms.[33] Since, however, resolve is an actor's "private information," and there are incentives to misrepresent resolve in order to secure advantages in negotiations, actors often have to rely on commitment mechanisms such as domestic audience costs to signal their resolve.[34] Thus, although rationalist models typically invoke incomplete information and commitment problems as two distinct causes of conflict—the former to be rectified by signaling (sinking costs), the latter via commitment devices (tying hands)—resolve figures prominently in both camps, not only because commitment devices are often used to draw inferences about resolve, but because, as will be argued below, it is precisely because of weakness of will that many commitment problems arise in the first place.[35]

In the third camp, international security scholars argue that resolve explains military outcomes.[36] Writing in the shadow of the Vietnam War, Rosen suggests that to understand which side wins the war, we need to pay attention to each party's "willingness to suffer," and Mueller points to the importance of the "breaking point" in determining who accepts defeat.[37] Similarly, Maoz finds that a "balance of resolve" model better explains outcomes of military interstate disputes than a balance of capabilities model does, while Stam points

---

30 Mercer 2010; Shannon and Dennis 2007; Hopf 1991b.

31 Lupovici 2010.

32 Schelling 1960; Iklé 1964; Schelling 1966; Young 1968; Snyder and Diesing 1977.

33 Jervis 1972; Morrow 1985; Powell 1987; Morgan 1990.

34 Fearon 1995; Becker 1961; Elster 1979, 2000; Fearon 1994.

35 Fearon 1997.

36 Recent rationalist scholars of conflict—what Powell (2004, 345) calls "the second wave of formal work on war" would reject this distinction between crisis bargaining models and models of military outcomes, envisioning war not as something that happens when bargaining fails, but rather, as a continuation of the bargaining process (Goemans, 2000; Wagner, 2000; Filson and Werner, 2002; Smith and Stam, 2004).

37 Rosen 1972; Mueller 1980.

to several domestic political factors that affect each side's sensitivity to costs and lower the war's net benefits, thereby making belligerents less resolute and more willing to settle for a draw.[38] Just as crisis bargaining theorists argue that war can be prevented if the parties recognize the true balance of motivation, military scholars suggest that wars will end once the combatants learn each others' levels of resolve, frequently inferred via events on the battlefield.[39] A similar mechanism is posited in the literature on conflict mediation as well, as third parties can prevent conflict from breaking out either by making their own resolve as a mediator known, or by providing information about the resolve of one of the potential belligerents.[40]

Finally, theories of conflict also give resolve a role at lower levels of analysis by examining the resolve of military units and the public at large. Reiter and Stam, for example, find that levels of troop morale are positively correlated with military victory, similar to classic findings in military sociology.[41] Similarly, although Schultz argues democracies are often able to avoid war because they are better at signaling their resolve, scholars of counterinsurgencies and asymmetric conflict frequently inquire as to whether democratic publics are too "soft"—John F. Kennedy called it "the slow corrosion of luxury"—or cost-intolerant to be resolute, and so are doomed to suffer what Morgenthau called a "paralysis of will."[42] Even if the public is not casualty-phobic, what makes the "rally around the flag" effect significant is that rallies end just as quickly as they begin, and support for conflict decays over time as the public loses heart.[43]

WILLFUL NEGLECT? CAPABILITIES, INTENTIONS, AND RESOLVE

As the preceding discussion illustrates, references to resolve permeate the international security literature, and are especially prominent in rationalist models of conflict. Indeed, a content analysis of three central pieces in this research tradition by James Fearon finds that resolve and willingness are invoked nearly 170 times, making it the sixth-most popular term across the

---

38 Maoz 1983; Stam 1996.

39 George and Simons 1994; Goemans 2000; Smith and Stam 2004; Ramsay 2008.

40 Walter 1997, 340–341; Kydd 2003; Rauchhaus 2006.

41 Reiter and Stam 1998a; Shils and Janowitz 1948; Baynes 1967.

42 Schultz 1998; Pape 2003, 349; Mueller 1971; Mack 1974; Merom 2003; Lyall 2010; Morgenthau 1951, 222.

43 Gartner and Segura 1998; Gelpi, Feaver, and Reifler 2005/06; Baum 2002; Kam and Ramos 2008; Reiter and Stam 2002, ch. 7; Sullivan 2008. Beyond the study of war, scholars of governance and state-building are increasingly interested in "resilience," the extent to which communities and institutions are able to "bounce back" in response to stresses and risks—a concept I set aside for most of the discussions that follow, but to which I return in chapter 6. See Joseph 2013; Chandler 2013.

three articles.[44] When rationalists talk about war, resolve is the language they use.

However, despite the popularity of resolve, it is not clear that rationalist models of war in fact need resolve at all, not just because many incomplete information models of war do not directly model resolve,[45] but also because, as Sartori notes, the term has been used in a variety of different ways by different scholars, such that it is unclear that many of the models that invoke resolve are in fact referring to the concept as properly understood.[46]

Realist approaches to international security often argue that states have three pieces of private information: capabilities, intentions, and resolve, yet resolve is often presented in a manner that renders it analytically indistinct from the other two. This definitional ambiguity is all the more surprising given that capabilities and intentions mean rather different things.[47] Capabilities refer to the material resources—military might, a population base, territory, economic clout, and so on—from which an actor's relative power is drawn. Intentions, in contrast, refer to an actor's goals and desires, and therefore, govern how capabilities are used: whether a state is revisionist or status-quo-seeking, for example. Thus, while capabilities dictate what an actor *can* do—you cannot fight wars if you cannot afford to pay for them—intentions refer to what an actor *wants*.[48] Historically, capabilities and resolve were thought of as conceptually distinct: during the French Succession Crisis in the sixteenth century, for example, Queen Elizabeth's advisor Lord Burghley calculated the threat posed by Philip of Spain by evaluating his regime on the dimensions of "potestas," or power, on the one hand, and "voluntas," or will, on the other.[49] Many IR theorists, though, lump in resolve with capabilities, an approach that comes in three variants. First are those who

44 Fearon 1994, 1995, 1997. For more details, see appendix A.1.

45 Filson and Werner 2002; Fey and Ramsay 2007. These works are notable not because they are bargaining models of war that do not invoke resolve, but because they are incomplete information bargaining models of war that make no direct mention of the concept. In a complete information game, uncertainty about the other player's level of resolve cannot be a cause of war—Fearon (1994, 583) shows that when states have complete information about resolve, no foreign policy crisis occurs— so it is therefore unsurprising that models of bargaining in war that do not rely on incomplete information (e.g., Wagner, 2000) would have no need for resolve. It should be noted as well that while these models do not feature references to resolve, they do model the cost of war—a concept some rationalists treat as equivalent to resolve, but which I argue below is distinct.

46 Sartori 2005, 7.

47 Tang 2008.

48 Schweller 1994; Kennedy 1987. Although these attributes are conceptually distinct, scholars of folk psychology note that we frequently draw inferences about one of these attributes based on our perceptions of the others. For example, if we know a task is difficult and that someone's capabilities are low, we assume that their resolve is high; likewise, if we see actors give up easily, we not only make inferences about their lack of resolve, but also revise our initial assumptions about their intentions. See Heider 1958, ch. 4.

49 Owen 2010, 107.

view resolve as a source of capability—for example, the classic IR theorists who wrote about "national morale" or "national will" as a component of power.[50] Second are those who invert the relationship and propose that capabilities are a source of resolve.[51] These two approaches are less definitional than causal, although the fact that the causal arrow points in different directions in each approach invites further attention toward resolve's relationship with capabilities, causal or otherwise.[52] Finally, another common approach is to use the terms indistinguishably: Slantchev's argument about when strong states will feign weakness treats resolve and strength interchangeably (a resolute state is a "strong type"), while Smith and Stam discuss Saddam Hussein's view of the US public as casualty-sensitive during the Gulf War as an instance of "Iraqi beliefs about US *capabilities*."[53] The very idea of will*power* in ordinary language similarly captures the extent to which resolve and capabilities are often seen as intertwined.

For others, resolve is used synonymously with aims or intentions: Jervis suggests the two cannot be separated from one another, and Fearon uses the terms interchangeably, referring to audience costs both as a device for signaling resolve and as a tool for signaling intentions, as do Rosato and Trager.[54] Schultz, Walter and Snyder and Borghard treat resolve as synonymous with "preferences," and although Starr', notion of "willingness" has been operationalized any number of ways, it tends to be treated less about will as a second-order volition and more about first-order intentions or preferences, a distinction similarly blurred by Morrow, who makes an offhand reference to "national preferences (i.e. the political will)."[55] Indeed, uncertainty about an actor's resolve is often framed as ambiguous or misperceived intentions: whether Berlin knew if St. Petersburg wanted war or not in 1914, the veracity of Saddam Hussein's assumption that the United States would stand idly by during the 1990 Iraqi invasion of Kuwait, the United States trying to convince Argentina that Great Britain's threats of war in the Falklands Crisis were not bluffs, and so on.[56]

Ultimately, if resolve is the same as intentions or capabilities, it is unclear why we should go to the trouble of using the word "resolve" in the first place.

---

50 Wright 1964; Organski 1968; Cline 1975; Morgenthau 1985; Cline 1994.

51 Snyder and Diesing 1977; Morrow 1989; Meirowitz and Sartori 2008, 329, fn. 4. Recent debates about nuclear crisis outcomes between the "brinksmanship" and the "nuclear superiority" schools similarly hinge on whether we think of capabilities as a source of resolve or not. See Kroenig 2013; Sechser and Fuhrmann 2013.

52 For example, it is also possible that the two properties are in a constitutive relationship. On causation and constitution, see Wendt 1998.

53 Slantchev 2010; Smith and Stam 2004, 808, emphasis added.

54 Jervis 1976, 48; Fearon 1994, 578, 587; Rosato 2003, 598–599; Trager 2011, 469–472.

55 Schultz 1999, 327; Walter 1997, 341; Snyder and Borghard 2011, 3; Starr 1978; Morrow 1988, 82.

56 Copeland 2000, 90–91; Mearsheimer 2001, 38; Kydd 2003. See also Yarhi-Milo 2014.

Yet the issue goes beyond lexical inconsistency, as innovative work by Smith and Stam illustrates.[57] In their model, war consists of a series of negotiations: if a round of negotiations fails, then the two sides fight a battle in which the victor takes a "fort" from the opposing side, the two parties update their beliefs, and negotiations resume; the cycle repeats itself until one side's supply of forts has been depleted, or their beliefs have sufficiently converged that they are able to reach a negotiated agreement. Their approach is innovative, particularly because it permits belligerents to have heterogeneous beliefs even when exposed to the same information.[58]

However, resolve in their game is operationalized as the supply of forts, one of which changes hands at the end of each battle. In this respect, there is nothing here that sets resolve apart from any other resource exchanged or depleted in war—as the authors acknowledge in their assessment that forts in modern war represent "units of resolve or strategically important pieces of land," but could be "any particular form of military resource that is necessary for the two nations to continue to fight and that can trade hands."[59] Indeed, the "fort" metaphor is derived from an earlier work that never directly mentions resolve, referring to forts instead as "a discrete approximation of what nations are fighting over."[60] Since resolve functions in their approach as a generic type of resource, it is unclear what the model gains from labeling the resource "resolve" rather than cannonballs or horses, both of which are also subtractable resources that can change hands, but which actors need in order to continue to fight.[61] After all, the strength of formal theoretical approaches is the extent to which they force scholars to clearly define their concepts and specify the assumptions needed for a theory's predictions to hold.[62] Even outside the realm of rational choice, if resolve is simply doing the work that capabilities or intentions can do, then our theories of world politics are less parsimonious than they otherwise could be. Instead of portraying states as grappling with uncertainty over others' capabilities, intentions, and resolve, we could simply substitute the last property with the first two. To answer this question, I step back and adopt a broader view, contextualizing resolve in light of how the phenomenon is understood elsewhere in the social sciences.

57 Smith and Stam 2004.
58 For a critique, see Fey and Ramsay 2006.
59 Smith and Stam 2004, 788–789.
60 Smith 1998, 303.
61 In this sense, like it does in many models, resolve functions here as what Alfred Hitchcock called a "MacGuffin": the object that motivates all of the action, but whose intrinsic properties are irrelevant (the microfilms in *North by Northwest*, the statue in the *Maltese Falcon*, the briefcase in *Pulp Fiction*, and so on).
62 Bueno de Mesquita 1985; Martin 1999.

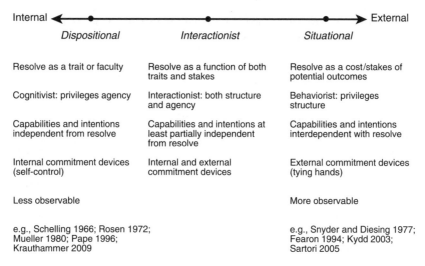

FIGURE 1.1. A spectrum of theories about resolve.

TWO STORIES ABOUT RESOLVE

There are two types of stories social scientists have told about resolve: an inside story, and an outside one.[63] The outside or situational story, popular in behaviorist branches of psychology and economics, understands resolve as the costs or stakes that an actor faces in a particular situation; the inside or dispositional story, more common in philosophy and social psychology, views resolve as something internal to the actor itself. As a heuristic device, I array these two poles on a spectrum shown in figure 1.1, with an interactionist perspective in between. The poles are ideal types, and many IR scholars adopt positions that veer away from these two extremes,[64] but as demonstrate, it is notable just how much of the IR literature can be characterized as residing at one of the two ends of the spectrum. In the section that follows, I briefly introduce each perspective and show how they differ from one another, both in terms of second-order questions of ontology and first-order substantive questions in IR theory. One of the reasons why our understanding of resolve in IR is so muddled is because we have borrowed assumptions from various

---

63 I borrow this framing device from Hollis and Smith (1990), but whereas their two sets of stories are epistemological—referring to how we know of or come to understand social phenomena—mine are ontological, referring to assumptions about what the phenomena *are*.

64 For example, Powell (1987) and Morgan (1994) treat resolve as a function of both situational features (e.g., cost-benefit calculations about the stakes) and dispositional ones (risk orientation), although they do not incorporate them into the kind of thicker interactive framework I describe in chapter 2.

points across the spectrum, making it difficult to produce a coherent account of what resolve is and how it works.

Situational Theories of Resolve

Starting at the right-hand side of the spectrum, one can imagine a situational theory of resolve, which argues that actors will display resolve when the stakes are high, and will be irresolute when the stakes are low. Situational theories of resolve were briefly ascendant in economics and experimental psychology during the movement toward behaviorism: operant conditioning studies with pigeons and early delayed gratification studies with young children emphasize the importance of *external reinforcement*, observing the extent to which people and pigeons alike respond predictably to external stimuli.[65] Behaviorists argue that self-control is primarily a function of two phenomena: the magnitude of the reinforcement, and the delay involved; by manipulating the size of the reinforcer and the length of the delay, actors will display self-control problems, and reverse their choices.[66] In the behaviorist paradigm, self-control is therefore situational rather than dispositional: the higher the level of abstraction a reward is, the greater we discount it, and what philosophers refer to as "weakness of will" is a consequence not of a lack of character, but of intersecting hyperbolic discounting curves.[67]

Hyperbolic discounting has yet to make much of an impact on IR,[68] but situational conceptualizations of resolve should nonetheless be easy to imagine for a political science audience, particularly amongst rational choice scholars. Consistent with rationalism's "methodological bet" that greater theoretical progress can be made in IR by focusing on structural features than actor-level heterogeneity, much of the IR literature has defined resolve situationally in terms of costs and benefits, especially in the study of crisis bargaining: an actor will be resolved in a crisis bargaining situation when the stakes are high relative to the costs, and irresolute when they are low, such that actors are systematically more resolute about some issues than about others.[69] As can be expected, there is some conceptual ambiguity here: as Pape notes, some approaches fully reduce the "balance of resolve" to the "balance of interests," thereby treating an actor's resolve as its cost of conflict.[70] Others treat an actor's

65 Herrnstein 1970; Rachlin and Green 1972; Mischel and Grusec 1967.

66 For a review, see Logue 1988, 1998.

67 Gifford 2002; Trope and Liberman 2003; Stroud and Tappolet 2003; Elster 2006; Hoffmann 2008; Green and Fisher 1988, 684; Ainslie 1992, 2001; Frederick 2006.

68 Although see Streich and Levy 2007; Krebs and Rapport 2012.

69 Snyder and Diesing 1977; Betts 1980; George and Simons 1994; Powell 2003; Trager 2011.

70 Pape 1996; Lebow 1998; Arreguín-Toft 2001; Snyder and Diesing 1977; Gartzke, Li, and Boehmer 2001; Kydd 2003; Rauchhaus 2006; Fey and Ramsay 2011; Lake 2010/11.

costs as one of several *determinants* of resolve.[71] Alternately, others model an actor's cost of war and level of resolve as distinct types of private information altogether.[72] These distinctions are not just semantic, especially for deterrence theorists: why bother maintaining a general reputation for resolve if resolve is merely a by-product of the particular interests at stake in a situation?[73]

Situational theories of resolve in IR raise an additional theoretical issue: how do actors weigh the different types of costs at stake? IR scholars have focused heavily on military fatalities as the "human cost" of war, but war also has economic costs, and is rife with opportunity costs as well.[74] After all, although fighting imposes a considerable burden, so too do defeat and withdrawal, which may bear reputational costs that will long outlast the immediate physical consequences of the conflict.[75] In this sense, one can imagine a wide range of situational theories of resolve based upon the particular types of costs that matter, whether reputational, economic, or otherwise. What all of the theories at this portion of the spectrum share, though, is the sense that it is more theoretically useful to explain variation in outcomes by pointing to variation in the strategic situations actors face, rather than to properties or characteristics of actors themselves.[76] Situational theories of resolve thus posit an automaticity through which these costs translate into action: sufficiently raise the costs, and all actors will back down, irrespective of political ideology, regime type, or any other internal factor inside the actor that might affect how they respond to these external stimuli.[77]

Dispositional Theories of Resolve

Situational theories of resolve carry many advantages: they are parsimonious, base their predictions on observable and manipulable factors (a point to which I return below), and correspond with much of what ordinary intuition tells us about how actors behave when the stakes are high. Ultimately, though, if we think of resolve as maintaining a policy *despite* contrary inclinations or temptations to back down, it implies that resolve involves resisting situationally induced pressures to retreat or reverse course; to reduce resolve to utility or a cost-benefit calculation is to purge it of its second-order quality, collapsing resolve into preferences or intentions. Moreover, when we talk about someone being resolved, we are usually referring to something that

---

71 Morrow 1985, 1987; Mattes and Morgan 2004.
72 Goemans 2000.
73 Jervis 1979. See also Press 2005.
74 Mueller 1971; Gartner and Segura 1998; Gelpi, Feaver, and Reifler 2005/06; Caverley 2009/10; Geys 2010.
75 Filson and Werner 2007b; Sullivan 2008.
76 Lake and Powell 1999.
77 Pape 1996; Sullivan 2007.

emanates from within rather than being dictated from without, a property of the actor itself rather than a feature of the situation. Foch and Napoleon contrasted resolve with material factors out of the assumption that resolve involves being unmoved by material disadvantages, and in the historical cases we associate with resolve—for example, the French persisting at the Battle of Verdun despite suffering nearly a third of a million dead, injured, or missing, the Guomindang's long and grueling fight against the Japanese during the second Sino-Japanese War, the Paraguayans pressing on in the devastating War of the Triple Alliance, and so on—we know that the French, Chinese, and Paraguayans were resolved not because they acted in accordance with the costs inherent in the situation, but because they persisted *despite* these costs. Our lay theories about resolve, then, are dispositional in nature.

This dispositional intuition is bolstered both by much of the literature on willpower and self-control throughout the social sciences as well as by work in IR itself. Sociologists and psychologists have tended to treat self-control or willpower as an "individual difference" similar to a personality trait, and like other such traits, possibly genetically inherited.[78] The ego-depletion model of willpower recently popular in psychology treats self-control as a trait activated in multiple spheres: attention control, emotion inhibition, thought suppression, volition and choice, and so on.[79] Regardless of whether the specific task at hand requires stifling emotional reactions, maintaining handgrip stamina, or eating radishes while facing a plate of freshly baked cookies, the findings suggest that the same psychological processes are at work, consistent with folk intuitions about willpower as a trait better developed in some individuals than others, which is depleted over time, strengthened through training, and so on.

Although these psychological findings are all at the individual level, IR scholars have made similarly dispositional arguments about resolve at the collective level. Sartori, for example, notes that although some deterrence theorists have viewed resolve solely as a function of the issues at stake in a particular crisis, others "maintain that it is an enduring, dispositional quality, that some states generally are more willing to fight than others."[80] Similarly, both formal theorists and empirical IR scholars have noted that collective actors vary in their sensitivity to costs: Mueller suggests that one of the American strategic failures in the Vietnam War was the assumption that sufficient costs would push the North Vietnamese past their "breaking point"; Pape similarly notes that states vary in their vulnerability to coercion, Jervis

---

78 Gottfredson and Hirschi 1990; Caspi 2000. On the inheritance of self-control, see Beaver et al. 2010; Boutwell and Beaver 2010.

79 Baumeister, Vohs, and Tice 2007; Galliot et al. 2007; Hagger et al. 2010. For a critique see Job, Dweck, and Walton 2010.

80 Sartori 2005, 45.

refers to states varying in their "willingness to pay," while Rosen argues that states vary in their "willingness to suffer."[81] Two of the dominant research traditions in the democracies in war literature—the "selection effects" work that predicts that democracies are more likely to win their wars because they are more cautious in choosing which wars are worth fighting, and the literature investigating whether the advantages of democracy in battle decline over time because democratic publics are too casualty-shy to sustain lengthy combat operations—both acknowledge the importance not just of costs, but of cost sensitivity.[82] In much of the literature, the issue is not whether democracies have higher costs of war than autocracies, but how tolerant they are of the costs.[83] Some states have more elastic demand curves for war than others: cost-sensitive actors will lose their appetite for conflict if the price is high, while other actors have relatively inelastic demand curves and will continue to support the conflict despite the raised costs. A recent wave of game theoretic work in IR has explicitly incorporated cost sensitivity into their models, which, even if relying on perhaps overly simplistic assumptions about the relationship between regime type and cost sensitivity, is nonetheless useful for our purposes, since cost sensitivity is portrayed in a manner that makes it inversely related to resolve.[84] Thus, like situational theories of resolve, dispositional theories of resolve are well represented in both IR theory and the social sciences more broadly.

81 Mueller 1980; Pape 1996; Jervis 1976, 51; Rosen 1972. Stam (1996, 19) suggests this variation occurs cross-temporally as well: France lost hundreds of thousands of troops at the Battle of Verdun yet remained in the First World War, but surrendered in the Second World War after having lost 50,000 soldiers over the course of five weeks.

82 On democratic selection into war, see Siverson 1995; Reiter and Stam 1998b; Valentino, Huth, and Croco 2010. On democratic discomfort with lengthy combat operations, see Bennett and Stam 1998; Gartzke 2001; Reiter and Stam 2002; Sullivan 2007, 2008; Gelpi, Feaver, and Reifler 2009; Lyall 2010.

83 Although see Schultz 1999. This literature varies as to where democratic cost-sensitivity comes from: some accounts point to a free press and open information environment (Johnson et al., 2006), others emphasize institutions promoting foreign policy accountability (Koch and Gartner, 2005), and others suggest that cost-sensitivity stems from political ideology, with left-leaning political parties being more sensitive to the costs of war than right-leaning ones (Palmer, London, and Regan, 2004; Koch and Sullivan, 2010). It may seem counterintuitive to characterize institutional explanations as being dispositional—particularly from the perspective of comparative politics, which characterizes domestic political institutions as contextual factors—but in the context of inter-*national* politics, "inside," dispositional accounts are those that refer to characteristics or attributes of states, while "outside," situational accounts involve the environment or context in which the state is operating. Thus, what Waltz (1959) called "second-image" accounts are dispositional rather than situational; *innenpolitik* is very much an inside story rather than an outside one. I return to this point in the discussion of the large-N analyses in chapter 6. The question of where we locate agency in collective actors like states is an interesting one (Wendt, 2004), but outside the scope of this project.

84 Stam 1996; Slantchev 2003; Filson and Werner 2004; Mattes and Morgan 2004; Filson and Werner 2007b; Maoz and Siverson 2008.

Comparing the Two Stories

As discussed above, dispositional and situational theories of resolve differ in the extent to which they conceptualize resolve as an internal or an external phenomenon. Dispositional theories of resolve treat it as an internal trait—part of the actor itself—whereas situational theories of resolve treat it as an external phenomenon—a feature of the environment in which the actor is operating. To a certain extent, the division between these two sets of approaches is merely analytic rather than theoretical, reflecting a disagreement over whether it is more interesting to demonstrate situationally induced convergence (very different actors responding to environmental features in exactly the same way: there are no atheists in foxholes) or dispositionally induced divergence (different actors responding to the exact same environmental features in very different ways: *de gustibus non est disputandum*).[85] Nonetheless, the two sets of theories offer strikingly different implications both in terms of second-order questions of ontology and first-order questions in IR theory.

The Agent-Structure Problem

First, they offer divergent approaches to the agent-structure problem.[86] Whereas situational theories treat resolve as a structural phenomenon, dispositional theories of resolve privilege agency instead. Perhaps reflecting the language of levels of analysis, the relationship between agents and structures has typically been portrayed in IR through the use of vertical metaphors in which agents are understood to be embedded in, but nonetheless, "below" structures that constrain and enable agents' choices, such that Wendt writes about "bottom-up" versus "top-down constitution."[87] This external vision of structure is the one adopted by situational theories of resolve, in which actors are impeded or encouraged to pursue particular goals by the costs or benefits imposed by the strategic environment. Structures, though, are not just external to the agent, and we can imagine agents constrained or enabled both externally and internally, in that agents also have interior organizational structures, internal dynamics of agency that mirror what psychologists call self-regulation— not just regulation of the self, but regulation of certain parts of the self by

85 This distinction is different from the traditional divide between theories emphasizing agency and theories emphasizing structure, because it is analytic rather than ontological, as suggested in the discussion below.

86 Wendt 1987. As Dessler (1989, 443) writes, the agent-structure problem "emerges from two uncontentious truths about social life: first, that human agency is the only moving force behind the actions, events and outcomes of the social world; and second, that human agency can be realized only in concrete historical circumstances that condition the possibilities for action and influence its course."

87 Singer 1961; Onuf 1995; Wendt 1999.

other parts of the self.[88] Dispositional theories of resolve focus on these internal moving parts: we call it "self-control" out of the assumption that the concept refers to a feature or faculty independent from the environment.[89] Studies of resilience in development and ecology treat it as an emergent systemic-level process rather than a fixed individual-level quality, but nonetheless adopt a similarly internal vision of structure.[90]

Commitment Problems

It is for this reason that advocates of dispositional and situational theories of resolve also have such opposing views of commitment problems, instances where actors are unable to maintain behavioral consistency over time.[91] The same rationalist IR theorists who define resolve situationally in terms of the costs an actor faces also perceive commitment problems through a situational lens: actors will experience commitment problems when a plan or agreement that was in their interests ex ante is no longer in their interests ex post due to changes in the environment in which an actor finds itself.[92] Thus, for situationalists, commitment problems are resolved through the use of external commitment devices—"tying hands," like Ulysses instructing his crew to bind him to the mast of his ship so that he will be unable to act on the Sirens' call— that render behavioral consistency incentive-compatible.[93] The dispositional accounts of resolve popular in psychology and parts of economics, on the other hand, lead to an understanding of commitment problems from an internal perspective, in which commitment problems involve a failure to resist temptation and engage in self-regulation, but can be rectified by internal commitment devices—the exercise of willpower or self-control.[94]

---

88 Todd and Gigerenzer 2003; Wendt 1987, 359; Baumeister and Vohs 2004.

89 Kuhl 1988. Philosophers from Plato onward called this feature the "will," a volitional faculty of the mind that translates thought into action (Arendt, 1971; Davenport, 2007). In this sense, resolve is central to many of the aspects we associate with agency: the sense of action being guided autonomously (Ryan and Deci, 2006), the ability "to have acted otherwise" (Doty, 1997, 372), and the capacity for second-order volitions (what Frankfurt (1971, 15) called the freedom for an individual "to want what he wants to want").

90 Bourbeau 2013.

91 Becker 1961.

92 Kydland and Prescott 1977; Powell 2006; Beardsley 2008.

93 Fearon 1997; Walter 1997; Elster 2000. This is also reflected in language suggesting that actors "create" resolve (Morgan, 1990, 283–284) through commitment devices; if resolve truly was purely dispositional, it would not need to be created in the first place.

94 Gifford 2002; Bénabou and Tirole 2004; Benhabib and Bisin 2005; Hofmann, Friese, and Strack 2009. See also Fessler and Quintelier 2013, on the distinction between objective versus subjective commitment, which mirrors the situational versus dispositional account I discuss here.

The Interdependence of Resolve, Capabilities, and Intentions

Similarly, the two bodies of theories espouse very different predictions about the relationship between (i) resolve and capabilities, and (ii) resolve and intentions. Dispositional theories of resolve see all three concepts as distinct: like in force activation models, actors can have sophisticated capabilities but lack the will to fully apply them, while weakness of will means that actors can intend to do something—commit to a war, push the other side to the brink in a crisis bargaining scenario—but lack the resolve to follow through.[95] As Sheeran notes, there is often a marked gap between our intentions and the actions in which we actually engage.[96] The three concepts may not be entirely independent of one another in dispositional accounts, but the automaticity found in the outside story is not present in the inside one.

Situational theories, on the contrary, see the concepts as highly interrelated, causally if not definitionally. First, as actors' relative capabilities increase, their cost of fighting will decrease, effectively rendering them more resolved, such that increases in relative capabilities produce increased resolve.[97] Second, if actors are self-interested utility maximizers, then inasmuch as we can overcome the problem of other minds and study motivations at all,[98] we can derive actors' intentions from the costs and benefits of particular policies: if the cost of a policy increases, actors will be less interested in pursuing it, and will act accordingly. For the outside story, then, cost, capabilities, intentions, and resolve all become highly intertwined.

The (Un)observability of Resolve

Dispositional and situational theories of resolve differ in another dimension as well, since situational features are generally observable to an extent that dispositional ones are not. Even if actors routinely get situational features wrong—e.g., British and German decision-makers miscalculating the offense-defense balance during the First World War, American concerns about the "missile gap" at the tail end of the Eisenhower administration, and so on— these situational features are nonetheless more easily observed than their dispositional counterparts. It is easier to know whether an adversary is likely going to be facing high costs of war, for example, than to overcome the problem of other minds and access some interior attribute belonging to decision-makers or domestic constituencies. Indeed, one of the main attractions of situational theories is the relative discernability of the factors they emphasize, which allow us to focus on observable causes rather than force us to wrestle

95 March 1966.
96 Sheeran 2002.
97 Snyder and Diesing 1977; Morrow 1985.
98 Morgenthau 1985, 5.

with "the ghost in the machine."[99] In contrast, although even relatively intangible dispositional features can have observable causes (as I suggest in chapter 6), they are still likely to be inferred with a great deal of noise. In the realm of cross-cultural psychology, for example, scholars have found that distributions of dispositional characteristics indeed vary across countries and regions, but our perceptions of these characteristics tend to be inaccurate; even when groups do differ from one another, the stereotypes they have about the way they differ tend to be wrong.[100]

This observability question raises some interesting conceptual issues—can resolve truly be "private information" if it does not implicate some component specific to the actor itself?—but two important substantive ones as well. First, the further we slide toward the dispositional side of the spectrum in figure 1.1, the less observable resolve is, and the greater the uncertainty actors should possess about each others' resolve. The character of international politics should therefore be different at this end of the spectrum than at its situational antipode. At the dispositional end of the spectrum, because of the difficulty in directly observing resolve, leaders should spend considerable efforts sending and deciphering signals of it. If resolve is dispositional, international affairs become characterized by an emphasis on perception and misperception; politics becomes more obviously psychological.[101] If resolve is strictly situational, on the other hand, we need not go to lengths to cultivate reputations for resolve, since our allies and adversaries should simply be able to infer it from features of the world around them, such as the balance of capabilities or the level of intrinsic interests at stake.[102]

Second, if we believe that decision-makers are strategic actors, they should take observable features into account when calculating and calibrating policy decisions, a "selection effect" that means that those features should play less of a role in shaping actual conflict and bargaining outcomes, because leaders already acknowledged them in their prior decision to escalate to crisis in the first place. The more dispositional resolve is, then, the more it should matter in crises. Rational choice treatments that reduce resolve to the "cost of war" therefore also reduce its potential explanatory power in the process.

---

99 Ryle 1949. Though, as I discuss in chapter 2, the aggregation problem posed by multiple types of costs of war may force us to wrestle with the ghost after all.

100 McCrae and Terracciano 2005; Rentfrow, Gosling, and Potter 2008; Terracciano et al. 2005.

101 Jervis 1976. Alternately, one might also imagine that the further we slide to the dispositional side of the spectrum, the more international politics becomes characterized not by uncertainty, but by *misplaced* certainty, as actors unable to directly access the inner attributes of others turn to schema and heuristics that lead them to make judgments with unwarranted confidence (Mitzen and Schweller, 2011). Note, however, that while distinct mechanisms, both uncertainty and misplaced certainty in this context, lead to similarly dour consequences, a point to which I return in chapter 6.

102 Press 2005.

CONCLUSION

It was argued in this chapter that although resolve is one of the most central concepts in the study of international politics, the term is often used in imprecise and incompatible ways. Yet the cost of this neglect goes beyond the usual slings and arrows of polysemy: resolve has been turned into a catchall residual category used to explain everything that our traditional theories cannot, threatening to reduce the concept to a set of "post-hoc explanations for otherwise perplexing conflict outcomes."[103] For resolve to be a theoretically useful construct, however, it cannot simply be a magic ingredient we turn to after the fact to explain events that our theories otherwise cannot. The motivating puzzle of the book, then, is to see whether it is possible to purge resolve of this magic—and, if successful, whether it has any explanatory power left. Integrating the IR literature on resolve with its counterparts in other fields, I argued that social scientists traditionally have told two types of stories about resolve: an inside, dispositional account in which resolve is treated as a trait, and an outside, situational account in which resolve is understood as the costs and stakes an actor faces.

The two stories differ not just in terms of metatheoretical assumptions, but also in their political implications. A world where resolve is dispositional looks very different than one in which it is situational. The neoconservative rhetoric of resolve evident in Krauthammer's declaration that "decline is a choice" understands resolve dispositionally, such that liberals who show a lack of resolve are displaying a kind of weakness of character to be rectified by self-discipline. Indeed, just as a lack of resolve is typically understood as a character flaw in the domestic realm, a lack of political will is typically understood as a sin in the political arena, responsible for genocides, defeats, and disappointments.[104] This dispositional understanding of resolve looms especially large in American political culture, in which wars are seen as won abroad but lost at home, exemplified by Lyndon Johnson's concern in 1967 that "If we lose the war, it will be lost here—not in Vietnam," and repeated American failures overseas are attributed to the premise that "the United States has more power; its foes have more willpower."[105] Indeed, this kind of dispositional explanation is frequently put forward whenever pundits are compelled to explain "why the US can't beat an army the size of a junior college."[106] The liberal pundit Matthew Yglesias goes so far as to suggest that contemporary American conservative foreign policy discourse is marred by a "Green Lantern theory of geopolitics," where all military obstacles can

---

103 Sullivan 2007, 497; March 1966, 61; Baldwin 1979; Jervis 1979, 316; Rummel 1975b, 275; Ray and Vural 1986.
104 Baumeister and Exline 1999; Power 2002.
105 Cited in Hilfrich 2004, 69; French 2015.
106 Rothkopf 2014.

be overcome with sufficient willpower, and the journalist Jonathan Chait, writing in *The New Republic*, argues that "in the neoconservative world, mighty declarations of willpower always trump puny arithmetic."[107] It is not coincidental that Senator Joseph Lieberman's retrospective on the tenth anniversary of the September 11th attacks published in *Foreign Policy* was entitled "A Decade of Resolve."[108]

If, on the other hand, resolve is purely situational, then it is less like a switch that can be flipped by "digging deep," and is instead more closely tied to the stakes, costs, and benefits that actors find themselves facing. Decline is no longer a choice, but the product of broader forces beyond any one actor's control, "the will to fight" is inconsequential, and the Churchillian romanticization of the heroic will overcoming structural constraints ("I believe in personality," he thundered in his 1934 "penny-in-the-slot" speech) is misguided.[109] As is the case with any structural theory, situational views of resolve leave less room for agency: actors may try to transform their cost-benefit calculus by engaging in various commitment devices to change the stakes, but these may come with other political costs attached. Leaders should spend less time worrying about maintaining reputations for resolve, since these judgments should stem not from innate traits of actors, but the situational features of individual crises. The "cult of reputation" should be disbanded, and decision-makers should focus more on the intrinsic stakes and less on the extrinsic ones. In the current-day political climate, then, situational arguments about resolve in the context of international security tend to be made by the political left, and dispositional ones by the political right.

Situational and dispositional theories of resolve therefore not only come to very different understandings of what resolve is, but also different beliefs about how it functions. Although each account offers some insight into how resolve operates, neither offers a satisfactory explanation by itself. If we intuitively believe that some actors are more resolute than others in general, but also acknowledge that an actor's level of resolve will vary based on the situation it finds itself in, then resolve seems to have both dispositional and situational components. This is the challenge I explore throughout the rest of the book.

Thus, in chapter 2, I suggest that neither dispositional nor situational theories of resolve are satisfactory by themselves, and that taking resolve seriously requires us to think about the concept in an interactionist manner that connects the two. After discussing the merits of interactionist theories, I point to four dispositional variables (time preferences, risk preferences, honor orientations, and trait self-control) and two situational variables (casualties,

107 Yglesias 2006; Chait 2011.
108 Lieberman 2011.
109 Churchill 1934.

and the costs of backing down), interactions between which can explain why certain types of costs of war loom larger for certain types of actors.

In chapter 3, I turn to experimental methods to engage in theory-building, exploring individual-level microfoundations of resolve using a novel laboratory experiment that models both the selection into, and duration of support for, military interventions. The experiment manipulates situational features of the military intervention while measuring dispositional variables using techniques developed in experimental work in behavioral economics and social psychology. Because of its two-stage structure, I can measure resolve cleanly as a dependent variable by focusing specifically on the extent to which participants who originally supported an intervention continue to do so in the face of mounting costs. In chapter 4, I further extend the experimental findings, employing a national survey experiment that borrows many of the features of the laboratory study from chapter 3 while also modifying others to probe the robustness of the results on a nationally representative sample. Studying resolve as a dependent variable, these experimental analyses offer further evidence of the interactionist nature of resolve.

In chapter 5, I switch the focus of the analyses. The long-standing obstacle to studying resolve with observational data is that resolve is not directly observable; political scientists have thus largely been unable to adequately test whether resolve has the effects we often claim, because we have been forced to infer resolve from the outcomes we also use it to explain. I propose a novel solution: rather than infer resolve via its consequences, we study resolve via its causes. Having already established evidence for situational and dispositional determinants of resolve with experimental data at the individual-level, I use these same variables with observational data at the country- and leader-levels to construct composite situational and dispositional measures of resolve for the great powers in the post–Second World War era. I then employ a set of Boolean statistical analyses to study the impact of situational and dispositional pathways of resolve on the probability of victory of great power military interventions from 1946 to 2003. These Boolean analyses with resolve as an explanatory variable allow me to test whether resolve has the positive effects on conflict outcomes that military practitioners and IR scholars often claim, but doing so using measures of resolve derived independently of the behavior and outcomes I am using them to explain. The results suggest that the situational and dispositional determinants of resolve also predict the probability of victory, but at different levels of analysis: conflict outcomes appear to be primarily a function of situational determinants of resolve at the country-level, and dispositional determinants of resolve at the leader-level, and the dispositional characteristics outweigh the situational ones. Finally, chapter 6 concludes by examining the ramifications of the findings, paving the way forward for future analyses.

CHAPTER 2.

An Interactionist Theory of Resolve

Why do some leaders and publics display more resolve than others? In the previous chapter, I suggested that there have been two ways IR scholars have tended to answer this question, reflecting two different types of stories that IR scholars have told about resolve: an "outside" or situational account, in which resolve is simply a function of the costs and stakes inherent in a particular environment, and an "inside" or dispositional account, in which resolve is a property of actors themselves. Although thinking about resolve in terms of inside and outside stories is compelling, neither account offers a full or otherwise satisfactory account of the phenomenon under investigation. If we intuitively believe that some actors are more resolute than others in general, but we also assume that an actor's level of resolve will depend on the situation it finds itself in, then resolve seems to have both dispositional and situational components; given the choice between an inside story and an outside one, the most attractive option would seem to be to choose both. And yet, since the two accounts are defined in opposition to one another, both ontologically (that is, they disagree on what resolve *is*) and substantively (that is, they present divergent predictions on how it operates), one cannot situate oneself at both positions simultaneously: if both accounts are correct, than neither one is. The solution I pursue throughout the following chapters is to adopt an interactionist approach that splits the spectrum down the middle, a *via media* that views resolve as a state shaped by both dispositional and situational factors.

This chapter begins with a brief introduction to interactionist theories, elaborating what scholars of world politics gain by thinking of resolve in an interactionist manner. I then use this framework to introduce two sets of situational variables (the human costs of fighting, and the costs of backing down) and four dispositional variables (time and risk preferences, honor orientations, and trait self-control) to propose an interactionist theory of resolve, presenting a series of hypotheses elaborating why certain types of actors define the situations they face differently, and are therefore more or less sensitive to certain types of costs of war.

THREE MOTIVATIONS FOR INTERACTIONISM

Before presenting an interactionist theory of resolve, it is worth noting what such a theory entails, particularly because interactionism is a term with multiple meanings, and the type of interactionism I discuss here differs somewhat from some of its homonyms (for example, symbolic interactionism in social theory). By interactionism I mean a type of theory that emphasizes *the interplay between actors and their environment*, and thus explains phenomena as a function of both unit-level attributes and situational constraints. Although interactionism is by no means foreign to political science—as evident in classic pieces in the study of foreign policy decision-making such as Harold and Margaret Sprout's work on "man-milieu interactions"—contemporary political science's emphasis on parsimonious theories with fewer moving parts has meant that the field is less self-consciously interactionist than disciplines like psychology, where interactionism emerged as a way of reconciling personality psychology's emphasis on traits and individual differences with social psychology's emphasis on the power of the situation in which individuals are immersed.[1]

As summarized in table 2.1, interactionist theories in the social sciences tend to be employed for three distinct motivations, each of which relies on a different set of assumptions about the causal mechanisms driving the phenomenon under investigation. First, social scientists are occasionally simply interested in partitioning variance between dispositional and situational variables: incorporating both types of factors into a model, and determining the relative contribution of each one. This approach was popular during the height of the person-situation debate, as psychologists attempted to determine just how important each type of explanation was in explaining behavior. Nonetheless, it represents the thinnest type of interactionism discussed here, since it is only interactionist in that it includes both situational and dispositional variables in an additive model, without necessarily featuring the more elaborate interplay between the two sets of variables found in the other types of interactionism discussed below.

The second type of interactionist theorizing, which I call *interactive theories*, are what most social scientists tend to think of when they think of interactionism. In an interactive theory, the effect of one set of variables upon the dependent variable of interest is conditional upon (or is "moderated by" or "interacts with") another set of variables.[2] As the preceding definition

---

1 Sprout and Sprout 1957. For the canonical celebration of parsimony in IR, see Waltz 1979. On the reconciliation of situation and disposition in psychology, see Endler and Magnusson 1976; Mischel 2004; Reynolds et al. 2010.

2 As in the form $Y = B_0 + B_1X + B_2Z + B_3XZ + \epsilon$, $B_3 \neq 0$, where X is the focal predictor, Z the moderator, and XZ the interaction term. According to the framework I outline here, the $B_3 \neq 0$ restriction is what differentiates interactive and non-interactive interactionist theories.

TABLE 2.1. Rationales for Interactionist Theorizing, from Thinnest to Thickest

MOTIVATION	CAUSAL PATHWAY	RESEARCH QUESTION
1. Partitioning variance	Main effects	How much variation in a phenomenon is due to situational factors rather than dispositional ones?
2. Interactive theories	Interaction effects	*Multiplier effects*: do certain situational factors enhance the impact of dispositional ones, or vice- versa? *Scope conditions*: under what disposition-situation combinations is a phenomenon more likely to occur?
3. Definition of the situation	Direct and indirect effects	How do dispositional factors affect how actors perceive their environment?

makes clear, interactionist theories and interactive theories are only partially overlapping categories, since not all interactionist theories are interactive,[3] and not all interactive theories are interactionist. After all, as in the partitioning variance case discussed above, interactionist theories can specify additive rather than interactive functional forms, in which both dispositional and situational variables affect behavior, but through independent pathways. For example, neoclassical realist theories are interactionist, since they look at how both domestic politics and the international system affect state behavior, but are not necessarily interactive, in that they do not specify that the impact of one level of analysis is conditional upon the other.[4] Conversely, not all interactive theories are interactionist: Zaller's model of political behavior posits that an individual's level of knowledge interacts with her partisan identification in affecting her political behavior, but since both of these variables are attributes at the same level of analysis, the theory is interactive but not interactionist, properly speaking.[5] Nonetheless, many theories in political science are both interactionist and interactive in that they specify that the impact of a set of variables at one level of analysis depends on the values of a set of variables at a different level.[6] As such, interactive interactionist models are especially desirable when seeking to model multiplier effects (e.g., when certain dispositional

---

3 E.g., Fordham 2009.
4 Schweller 2003.
5 Zaller 1992.
6 E.g., Walt 1985; Herrmann and Fischerkeller 1995. I temporarily set aside the question of whether some of these theories are better expressed by a Boolean formulation rather than an interactive one (Braumoeller, 2003), exploring this possibility in chapter 5.

and situational factors are both present, an actor will be even more resolute), or aiming to incorporate scope or boundary conditions (e.g., the idea of "trait activation," which examines the conditions under which certain traits are more likely to be expressed) into the theory.[7]

A third type of interactionist theorizing occurs when a social scientist is interested in studying the impact of what the early-twentieth-century sociologist W. I. Thomas called the "definition of the situation." Whereas the previous two approaches understood dispositional and situational factors as entirely separate independent variables, this third form of interactionist theorizing questions the existence of an objective external environment apart from the observer, and notes that actors' dispositions affect their perception of the context they find themselves in. In the mid-2000s, for example, Republicans and Democrats held fundamentally different beliefs not just about subjective questions such as whether the invasion of Iraq was worth the casualties American forces were sustaining, but also objective questions such as how many casualties there actually were.[8] Americans thus differed from one another not just in terms of their sensitivity to the costs of war, but also their perceptions about the more fundamental question of what those costs were.[9] Similarly, the strategic scripts that policymakers evinced in 2014 about how to respond to Russian actions in Crimea differed according to the mental models to which they subscribed: those who saw Crimea as the Sudetenland and Vladimir Putin as using Russian nationals abroad as a pretext for annexation favored a very different policy than those who saw Russia as merely reacting defensively to NATO's eastward expansion. As such, although there are some cases where situations impact behavior through direct pathways—Wolfers's example of a fire in a crowded theater—there are others where situations impact behavior through indirect (dispositional) pathways instead, and thus this third type of interactionist theorizing bears some similarities to mediation analysis, with its emphasis on direct and indirect effects.[10] Perhaps unsurprisingly, definition of the situation theorizing not only explicitly arises in much of the cognitive revolution in psychology, but is also implicitly present in constructivist IR theory, in which anarchy (the situation in which states find themselves) is what states (and their leaders' and publics' dispositions) make of it.[11] In the empirical tests in chapters 3 and 4, I employ all three of these approaches, looking at how dispositional traits and situational stakes work in tandem to shape the amount of resolve actors display, but also probing the extent to which

---

7 Tett and Gutterman 2000.

8 Berinsky 2007.

9 The Iraq War example raises the question of the role that elite cuegiving, and interactions between elites and publics more generally, plays here; I largely bracket the roles of elites in the discussion below, before returning to it in the discussion of honor orientations.

10 Wolfers 1962; Baron and Kenny 1986; Imai et al. 2011.

11 Herrmann 1988; Wendt 1992.

the effects of the latter are conditional on the former, such that different kinds of actors perceive the situation in fundamentally different ways.

Finally, it is important to note that from a philosophy of science perspective, these three sets of rationales for interactionist theorizing render interactionism desirable regardless of the "academic sect" to which one pledges allegiance.[12] For scientific realists, an interactionist *via media* is obviously attractive if we understand resolve as shaped by both situational factors and dispositional ones, since the essence of ontological realism is the premise that our theories should correspond to the phenomena about which we are theorizing.[13] Yet, even among positivists or methodological instrumentalists—who view assumptions as neither true nor false, but only more or less useful,[14] and thus might be tempted for the sake of parsimony to restrict their analyses to just one level of analysis—an interactionist approach is nonetheless advantageous, since modeling only one half of an interactive relationship produces omitted variable bias, diminishing our theories' predictive utility.

One obstacle to thinking about resolve in an interactionist fashion is a metaphysical one—how can resolve *be* both dispositional and situational? This challenge is particularly vexing from a dispositional perspective, since the very idea of a "heroic will" implies a self-motivated force independent of the environment, which raises questions about construct validity (namely, whether the phenomenon being studied in an interactionist account of resolve is in fact resolve at all).[15] The solution I employ, rather than viewing resolve as both a disposition and a situation, is to understand resolve as a *state* that has both dispositional and situational *causes*, just as psychologists coming out of the person-situation debate have come to view "mentalistic" concepts like emotions and personality traits as a series of successive states that are affected by both dispositional and situational triggers.[16] We know some people, for example, are systematically more anxious than others: personality psychologists suggest that Ronald Reagan was rarely prone to worry, while Richard Nixon required medication to control anxiety.[17] At the same time, however, we also know that anxiety varies with features of the environment, and that different types of people experience different types of situational stressors. This cross-situational variation does not mean anxiety does not exist, nor that we should not think of it as an actor-level characteristic—it merely means we should think about it as an interaction.[18] I make similar claims

---

12 Lake 2011.
13 Joseph and Wight 2010.
14 E.g., Friedman 1953.
15 Smith 2001; Davenport 2007.
16 Dennett 1987.
17 Rubenzer and Faschingbauer 2004.
18 In appendix A.2, I offer a further discussion of this point, using the person-situation debate in psychology to make the above discussion more concrete, revisiting it again at the end of chapter 6.

here about resolve: that it varies both dispositionally and situationally, and that certain dispositional traits moderate the impact of different situational stakes in shaping the amount of resolve actors display over time.

AN INTERACTIONIST THEORY OF RESOLVE IN MILITARY INTERVENTIONS

Although resolve manifests itself in any number of domains (from crisis bargaining to international trade negotiations to counterterrorism campaigns), in this book I focus specifically on resolve in the realm of military interventions, a move that is advantageous for three reasons. First, although much of the social science literature on willpower treats resolve as cross-situational rather than domain-specific,[19] this is less likely to be the case if, as an interactionist theory expects, resolve has strong situational underpinnings: an actor may display strong political will in one issue, but very little on the next, and the determinants of resolve in each case may be different. By restricting the study of resolve to a single domain, I therefore gain greater leverage over the mechanisms that underlie it in this specific area.

Second, if resolve is conceptualized as something akin to persistence—a steadfastness of purpose that maintains a policy over time despite contrary inclinations or temptations to back down—international interventions are a perfect illustration of resolve at work, as leaders and their publics frequently intervene only to seek an exit option as the pressure mounts.[20] Third, military interventions represent one of the defining issues of the past decade, with questions about the sustainability of the US missions in Afghanistan and Iraq—and the shadow they have cast on other prospective interventions—occupying a prominent position in most Western countries' foreign policy agendas. Understanding the factors that make some leaders and publics in intervening states stay the course, and others cut their losses, is therefore of both theoretical interest and practical importance.

As a phenomenon driven by both situational and dispositional factors, resolve is ultimately likely to have a large number of causes. Our task as political scientists, however, is not simply to amalgamate all of the factors that could plausibly affect actors' resolve and insert them into a "garbage can" model, but rather, to focus on the workings of a small number of variables selected on theoretical grounds.[21] The interactionist theory of resolve I propose below is thus not intended to capture the universe of potential causes of resolve, but rather, seeks to integrate research on resolve in IR with a parallel body of work elsewhere in the social sciences, opening up the black box

---

19 E.g., Baumeister, Vohs, and Tice 2007.

20 Sullivan 2008; Polsky 2010; Koch and Sullivan 2010.

21 Achen 2002. As Achen 1977 argues, the purpose of quantitative social science is not merely to maximize an R^2 statistic. I return to this point in chapter 6.

of "costliness" by identifying two situational features—the costs of fighting, and the costs of backing down—and linking them with four dispositional characteristics–time preferences, risk preferences, honor orientations, and trait self-control–interactions between which can explain why certain types of actors are more or less sensitive to certain types of costs of war.

Situational Determinants of Resolve: Opening Up the Black Box of "Costliness"

Situational theories of resolve, like all rationalist theories of war, argue that leaders are motivated by a logic of consequences and therefore seek to make choices that maximize utility, weighing the perceived costs and benefits of options when deciding which ones to enact.[22] According to this argument, actors confronted with low costs of war will be more resolved than those with high costs of war; states with high stakes on the line will be more resolute than those with low stakes. As is the case with many structural theories, however, a purely situational view of resolve is indeterminate, since cost-benefit calculations are not always obvious. Although the IR literature has focused considerable attention on how uncertainty and overconfidence lead rational actors to pursue policies that are nonetheless inefficient ex post, less attention has been directed toward a different complication: how do actors decide which costs of war count as costly?[23]

Classical models of utility theory rely on unidimensional utility functions based on a single metric; actors can be assumed to have complete preferences because utility acts as a common denominator that enables direct comparisons of the value derived from any pair of alternatives.[24] Particularly in IR contexts where decision-makers weigh options using multiple criteria, however, it is often analytically useful to rely instead on *multiattribute utility functions*.[25] As Simon argued, our theories of rational utility maximizers are only as useful as our auxiliary assumptions about where actors derive their utility from; although situational theories of resolve appear parsimonious and clear in their predictions, some of this clarity comes from a sort of "iceberg parsimony," where much of the theory's mass is hidden under water.[26] It is one thing to say that actors will be resolved when their payoff structures tell them to be, but another to specify where these payoffs come from in the first place.

---

22 March and Olsen 1998.
23 Fearon 1995; Powell 2004; Blainey 1973; Johnson, Wrangham, and Rosen 2002.
24 von Neumann and Morgenstern 1944; Etzioni 1986.
25 Dorfleitner and Krapp 2007.
26 Simon 1985. This charge is similar to the constructivist critique of structural realism for basing its explanatory power on implicit assumptions about the "distribution of interests." See Wendt 1999, ch. 3.

After all, the costs of war come in many forms—economic costs, human costs in the form of casualties, reputational costs, personal political fortune, opportunity costs, sunk costs, and so on—but leaders have to come to some sort of decision about which costs outweigh others.[27] For example, models of war in political economy suggest that states make conscious decisions about sheltering capital or labor when fighting, implying that some states will be more sensitive to the human costs of war, while others will be more concerned about economic costs.[28] It is frequently argued that the United States has been so enamored with the capital-intensive warfare favored by the Revolution in Military Affairs (RMA) because of concerns that the American public is willing to spend money, but not lives.[29] Similarly, a number of scholars of international conflict have argued that states deciding whether to continue to prosecute a war must pay attention both to the cost of continuing to fight and to the costs of terminating the war, the latter of which involves a sunk cost argument, concerns about how withdrawal will affect reputation for resolve, and an acknowledgment of the greater concessions that must be made at the bargaining table.[30] The question, then, is not just about how attentive leaders and publics are to costs—the notion of cost-sensitivity—but how they weigh different kinds of costs, an aggregation process sufficiently complex that Schultz deems it a particularly "vexing" source of asymmetric uncertainty,[31] which chips away at the observability implied by the situational theories presented in chapter 1. Even if each type of cost of war *individually* represented an objective, observable feature of the world, the coexistence of *multiple* types of costs of war that shape and shove in different directions renders situational theories of resolve indeterminate without some sort of auxiliary assumption about how "costliness" is constructed.[32]

As illustrated by the left-hand panel in figure 2.1, I focus on two different types of costs of war as situational determinants of resolve in the context of military interventions: the costs of fighting—measured chiefly by casualties— and the costs of backing down, which include the intrinsic stakes of the mission and the reputational costs of withdrawal.

27 Geys 2010; Mueller 1971; Gelpi, Feaver, and Reifler 2009; Bueno de Mesquita and Siverson 1995; Nincic 1997; Boettcher and Cobb 2009.

28 Gartzke 2001; Caverley 2009/10.

29 Smith 2005.

30 Filson and Werner 2007a; Sullivan 2007, 2008; Koch and Sullivan 2010.

31 Schultz 2001, 34. The judgment and decision-making literature has focused on this subject in considerable detail; work on *mental accounting*, for example, focuses on the role that mental categorizations play in coding joint or multiple outcomes. See Thaler 1985.

32 For example, one research tradition in political psychology tells us that one way actors evaluate these types of tradeoffs is by denying they exist, downplaying the costs associated with their desired policy and focusing instead on the benefits (Snyder, 1978; Jervis, 1985b). Yet the fact that many people fall prey to these biases does not tell us anything about their directionality, or how people come to choose which cost counts as costly in the first place.

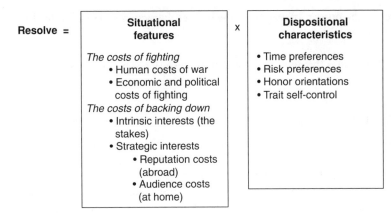

Resolve = | Situational features | x | Dispositional characteristics

The costs of fighting
- Human costs of war
- Economic and political costs of fighting

The costs of backing down
- Intrinsic interests (the stakes)
- Strategic interests
  - Reputation costs (abroad)
  - Audience costs (at home)

- Time preferences
- Risk preferences
- Honor orientations
- Trait self-control

FIGURE 2.1. Thinking about resolve as a dependent variable: a heuristic framework.

The Costs of Fighting: Casualties

Once a war or military intervention has begun, the first situational cost likely to affect an actor's resolve is casualties,[33] frequently argued to be the dominant indicator decision-makers use to judge a war's progress, as well as one of the major factors in the public's decision-making calculus when determining support for continued use of force.[34] Although casualties are not the only cost of fighting—both economic and political costs come to mind—they typically loom the largest in the public's consciousness. To be sure, the economic costs of war are often enormous—Bilmes and Stiglitz call the recent war in Iraq a "three trillion dollar war"—but the human costs figure more prominently in how we think about war, presumably because human life is understood as sacred in a way that money is not.[35] Although economists and accountants are comfortable calculating the value of a human life, the general public is far less sanguine, precisely why survey research shows the public to be extremely uncomfortable providing acceptable casualty levels for military scenarios.[36] Similarly, although war has political costs, these are often endogenous to casualties, since casualties increase the salience of military operations, which are then more likely to engender political opposition. I therefore expect that

33 Although "casualties" is often used in military circles to refer both to the number of dead and the number of wounded, I follow the rest of the casualty sensitivity literature in using casualties to refer to deaths alone.

34 Gartner 1997; Mueller 1971; Larson 2000; Gelpi, Feaver, and Reifler 2009.

35 Bilmes and Stiglitz 2008; Tetlock 2003. Moreover, most of our estimates of the economic costs of war actually hinge on the immediate-term *budgetary* costs of a conflict reflected in appropriations bills, rather than including macro-level effects like changes in the price of natural resources or the rate of investments. See Stiglitz and Bilmes 2012.

36 Viscusi and Aldy 2003; Boettcher and Cobb 2006.

the greater the human costs of war, the less resolve actors will display, leading to my first hypothesis:

> H1: The higher the number of casualties, the less resolve actors will display.

The Costs of Backing Down: The Issues at Stake, and Reputation

The second type of costs likely to affect an actor's resolve are the costs an actor incurs by backing down, either during a conflict or in a crisis situation.[37] An actor's commitment to a policy is in large part dependent upon how satisfying the alternatives are, so an actor is more likely to remain resolute when terminating a conflict or backing down on a threat would produce relatively unsavory consequences.[38] When an actor backs down or terminates a conflict, she pays two types of costs, which we can understand using Jervis's distinction between intrinsic and strategic (or extrinsic) interests.[39] First, the actor backing down inevitably sacrifices the *intrinsic interests*—the tangible objects or issues at stake in the conflict—since surrendering means accepting your opponents' demands. How much is at stake in a conflict depends on the nature of the issues under dispute: for example, humanitarian operations are less salient than operations that implicate core national security interests, especially those concerning threats to the territorial homeland.[40] The stakes are frequently emphasized in game theoretic models in which resolve is reflected in an actor's payoff structure, and is thus a function of the benefits of fighting relative to the costs.

Second are *strategic interests*, or the reputational costs that are incurred when an actor backs down, which for the sake of symmetry we might classify as *extrinsic interests* instead. There is a lively debate in the IR literature as to whether reputations are formed or broken in the manner that deterrence theorists assume,[41] but more important for our purposes is the fact that reputations are frequently formed for resolve, out of the belief that an actor who backs down from a threat or surrenders in a conflict will gain the reputation of being a "weak type" and therefore be more likely to end up in costly conflict in the future.[42] Domestic audience costs also fall in this

---

37 Filson and Werner 2007a.
38 Hoffman et al. 2009.
39 Jervis 1979.
40 Jentleson 1992; Gibler 2010.
41 Huth 1997; Tang 2005; Tingley and Walter 2011.
42 Schelling 1966; Alt, Calvert, and Humes 1988; Huth 1997; Walter 2006. Reputations are of course also formed for reasons other than resolve: states wish to maintain reputations for honesty (Sartori, 2005), reliability (Crescenzi et al., 2012), sovereign debt repayment (Tomz, 2007b), and so on.

extrinsic category, in that leaders who back down in a crisis situation then have to contend with the costs of punishment imposed by the electorate or their domestic constituency.[43] Thus, for all these reasons we can expect that the higher the costs of backing down, the more resolve an actor will display.

H2: The higher the costs of backing down, the more resolve actors will display.

H2A: The greater the intrinsic interests at stake, the more resolve actors will display.

H2B: The greater the reputational interests at stake, the more resolve actors will display.

Situational theories that link resolve to the costs of war also have an additional ambiguity: *whose* costs of war count as costly? Traditional rationalist models of IR assume the existence of unitary state actors pursuing policies that minimize costs and maximize benefits.[44] If we relax this assumption, however, we are faced with the question of whose costs of fighting and costs of backing down matter in affecting a state's resolve. After all, the cost of war is typically unevenly distributed, borne more heavily by some constituencies than others.[45] The choice between a conscription- and volunteer-based military, for example, has significant implications for who is "shouldering the soldiering," and analyses of the effects of local casualties in the Vietnam War suggest that the distribution of the conflict's costs also affects attitudes toward the mission in general.[46] In addition to cost asymmetries between different segments of the public, there also may be asymmetries between the public and its leaders; Chiozza and Goemans find that whether war is costly for leaders in terms of reduced time in office depends in large part on the political system in which they operate, such that leaders are often insulated from the costs of war imposed on their publics.[47] If a state's resolve is inversely related to the

---

43 Fearon 1994; Weeks 2008.

44 The accuracy and utility of the unitary actor assumption is frequently contested in IR (Allison, 1971; Keohane and Nye, 1977; Moravscik, 1997), but what matters for our purposes is that a divide exists in the rationalist literature between theories of resolve with unitary actors (Morrow, 1989; Morgan, 1990; Slantchev, 2005) and those that incorporate domestic politics, whether in the form of audience costs (Fearon, 1994), agent-principal problems (Downs and Rocke, 1995), selectorate theories (Bueno de Mesquita and Siverson, 1995), or two-level games (Putnam, 1988). In fact, much of the literature on the signaling of resolve explicitly requires non-unitary state actors, in that a state's ability to signal its resolve depends on the nature of the relationship between a government and its opposition (Schultz, 1998; Levy and Mabe Jr., 2004), or between the government and the public (Fearon, 1994).

45 Koch and Gartner 2005; Levy 2006.

46 Vasquez 2005; Horowitz and Levendusky 2011; Gartner, Segura, and Wilkening 1997.

47 Chiozza and Goemans 2004.

costs of war, it is therefore important to clarify whose costs of war matter. The experimental tests carried out in chapters 3 and 4 sidestep this level of analysis question by focusing specifically on individual-level microfoundations of resolve in the context of public opinion. I therefore defer the level of analysis question to chapter 5, when I use observational data to operationalize some of these situational variables with reference to leaders and to their countries at large.

Dispositional and Interactionist Determinants of Resolve

If casualties and the costs of backing down serve as the two situational determinants of resolve, the next task for an interactionist theory is to look for unit-level attributes or dispositional characteristics that produce resolve. We can envision dispositional determinants of resolve operating through each of the three causal pathways outlined in table 2.1. In the main effects approach, dispositions affect resolve independently of casualties and the costs of backing down, and we are interested simply in determining how much of the variation we observe in resolve is due to dispositional factors rather than situational ones. In the interactive approach, dispositions and situations have an interactive rather than an additive relationship: certain dispositions will amplify or attenuate the impact of casualties and the costs of backing down. Finally, the thickest interactionist approach blurs the distinction between the two sets of variables, suggesting that certain dispositions affect actors' perceptions of casualties and the costs of backing down.

As suggested in chapter 1, rational choice models of conflict have displayed a growing interest in the extent to which actors vary in their "cost sensitivity,"[48] but although cost sensitivity is certainly a dispositional variable, it makes for a dissatisfying explanation for resolve in that it suffers from "the problem of interiority": it explains resolve as a result of actors being less sensitive to the cost of war, but this merely pushes the causal story downward, leaving unanswered the question of why some actors are more sensitive to the costs of war in the first place.[49] Thus, the task I undertake here is to go beyond cost sensitivity, and point to specific actor-level characteristics that explain where cost sensitivity comes from. The attraction of the characteristics I focus on—time preferences, risk preferences, honor orientation, and trait self-control—is that they are routinely invoked as predictors of resolve, willpower, or self-control in other disciplines; following James Rosenau, if theorizing is about asking the question "of what is this an instance?," turning to these traits allows us to link research on resolve in IR with work on resolve more

---

48 Slantchev 2003; Filson and Werner 2004; Mattes and Morgan 2004; Filson and Werner 2007b.
49 Reus-Smit 2003.

generally.[50] In this sense, whereas the situational determinants of resolve discussed earlier are specific to the study of war, the dispositional sources I look at here also figure prominently elsewhere in the social sciences. The question I investigate below is how these characteristics might also spill over into the political domain.

Time Preferences

The first interactionist variable that influences which types of costs are perceived as costly is time preferences. Although there has been growing interest on time horizons in IR, the term has been used to refer both to the length of the time window in which leaders must act and to the idea of *time preferences*, a variable measuring the extent to which actors value the future compared to the present.[51]

A theory of resolve based on time preferences is in many ways intuitive, since the two factors are frequently conceptualized in relation to one another. We inherently think of someone who is resolved as being "in it for the long haul"; Bénabou and Tirole define a lack of willpower as "excessive preference for the *present*," Velleman portrays the will as a faculty that allows us to pursue our ends over *time*, Fennell defines willpower as "an individual's efforts to resist a *presently* attractive course of conduct," and Ainslie frames the "breakdown of will" in terms of hyperbolic *discounting* functions.[52] Similarly, one of the most popular ways of modeling willpower or self-control problems in the behavioral sciences is through "dual-self" models, in which choice decisions are made as the result of a bargaining process between a present- and a future-oriented self, buttressed by work in neuroscience suggesting that immediate gratification and long-term considerations activate different parts of the brain.[53] For these reasons, I argue that longer time horizons

---

50 Rosenau 1980.

51 Russett et al. 1994; Barkin 2004; Rosen 2005; Toft 2006; Streich and Levy 2007; Kreps 2008; Frederick 2006. A large body of research has been conducted on the impact of time on decision-making. We know that actors generally discount future benefits compared to present ones (Loewenstein and Elster, 1992; Elster, 2000; Frederick, 2006), although there is no consensus on whether this discounting occurs because of impulses and passions (Palacios-Huerta, 2003), evolutionary pressures in favor of immediate gratification (Moore, 1988), the implications of psychological distance (Trope and Liberman, 2003; Eyal et al., 2004; Fujita and Roberts, 2010), or because our future selves are in fact different from our present ones and thus do not merit the allocation of our utility (Parfit, 1971). For my purposes, though, the origins of time preferences are less important than the fact that resolve has such a clear temporal component to it, as reflected in the definition presented in Chapter 1.

52 Bénabou and Tirole 2002, 879; Velleman 2007; Fennell 2009, 93; Ainslie 1992, 2001, emphases added).

53 Thaler and Shefrin 1981; Elster 1986; Posner 1997; Ainslie 2001; Bénabou and Tirole 2004; Fudenberg and Levine 2006; Benhabib and Bisin 2005.

are associated with greater resolve. Suicide bombers, for example, are usually deemed resolute precisely because they have long time horizons: carrying out an attack requires sacrificing oneself in the present either to confer benefits on future generations or in order to enjoy rewards in eternity.[54]

Moreover, we can also think of time preferences in an interactionist framework, since an actor's time preferences affect sensitivity to costs and benefits that occur in the future relative to those that occur in the present. Decision-makers and members of the mass public typically face costs and benefits occurring at multiple points in time. Just as choosing between carrots or cheesecake, for example, requires managing tradeoffs between present and future costs and benefits (cheesecake provides immediate gratification but negative long-term consequences, while carrots typically provide fewer benefits in the short term, but greater benefits in the long term), choosing between continuing to prosecute a war or to terminate it short of victory involves a similar set of temporally arranged tradeoffs.[55] Although the topography of the intertemporal tradeoff varies across issues and domains, many military interventions are characterized by a temporal configuration in which the human costs of war are paid upfront, whereas reputational benefits are incurred in the future. As the literature on cooperation under anarchy suggests, the more actors discount the future, the less reputational costs matter.[56] Thus, all else being equal, once actors with longer time horizons enter into a war, they should outlast those with shorter time horizons, since they should be more willing to pay the short-term human costs of war in exchange for the longer-term benefits victory is posited to bring.

H3A: Actors with longer time horizons (more patient time preferences) will display more resolve.

H3B: Actors with longer time horizons (more patient time preferences) will be relatively less sensitive to casualties and relatively more sensitive to the costs of backing down.

Risk Preferences

Second are risk preferences. In IR, we frequently think of risk attitudes as a source of resolve, and the most influential work on coercion in international politics calls coercive bargaining "competition in risk-taking."[57] Given the literature equating resolve with an actor's level of "critical risk," the greatest

54 Azam 2005; Toft 2006.
55 The same is true for a host of other decisions—spending versus saving, smoking versus quitting, watching television versus writing your book manuscript, and so on. See Gifford 2002.
56 Axelrod 1984; Oye 1985.
57 Morrow 1985, 1987; Schelling 1966.

risk of disaster a state will tolerate in order to prevail in a crisis, one might expect resolve to increase with risk acceptance: the more tolerant actors are of risks, the more resolute they should be.[58] Yet there are two reasons to be skeptical of this hypothesized relationship. First, although IR scholars tend to see risk-acceptant behavior as an indication of a high level of resolve, sociologists have typically understood risk-seeking behavior as an indication of a lack of self-control; if resolve is indeed related to willpower and self-control, this contradiction is some cause for concern.[59] Second, whereas both rationalists and constructivists frequently rely on assumptions of common knowledge and intersubjectivity, one of the key insights of psychological approaches has been to emphasize the importance of modeling how actors perceive the situations they face, rather than assuming agreement and taking perceptions for granted.[60] Similar to Knight's distinction between risk and uncertainty, much of the political domain is not characterized by the kind of objective, measurable probabilities that would facilitate a clean relationship between risk attitudes and specific policy choices, without also taking actors' *risk perceptions* into account.[61] Many public debates, whether on nuclear power or genetically modified organisms (GMOs), center not on whether we should accept risk, but rather, on contesting which choices count as risky in the first place.

This dynamic is especially likely to be the case with military interventions. IR scholars who have thought about risk have often done so in a dovish way, associating risk with fighting. This is consistent with the liberal way we as a discipline tend to think about war in general, whether in the form of realists focusing on exculpatory causes of war like the security dilemma, or rationalists representing war as a form of market failure.[62] Yet, just as actors vary in their causal beliefs about threats, both fighting *and* backing down can be perceived as risky.[63] Military interventions are typically characterized by ill-structured decision environments, where there is little intersubjective agreement about what the relevant probabilities are. As the civil war in Iraq dragged on in 2004, for example, hawkish neoconservatives argued that the reputational consequences of withdrawal made "cutting and running" riskier than pressing onward, whereas dovish opponents of the war suggested that sinking into a quagmire was far riskier than a quick exit. If two actors facing

---

58 Jervis 1972; Snyder and Diesing 1977; Powell 1988.
59 Grasmick et al. 1993.
60 Jervis 1976; Herrmann 1988; Fearon and Wendt 2002; Grynaviski 2014.
61 Knight 1921; Slovic 1987. For a recent application of this distinction to IR, see Nelson and Katzenstein 2014.
62 Rationalist mechanisms for peace thus involve making the market more efficient. On realism's "status quo bias," see Schweller 1996. On the liberal politics of IR scholars more generally, see Rathbun 2012, 615.
63 Saunders 2011; Kertzer and Brutger 2016.

the same situation nonetheless espouse contradictory risk perceptions, the relationship between risk and resolve becomes nonlinear, and more complex than our standard theories assume, as risk-averse individuals display more sensitivity both to the risks of fighting, and to the risks of backing down. In appendix A.3, I demonstrate this point more formally, showing how the presence of countervailing risk perceptions leads to a curvilinear relationship between risk and resolve, the precise shape of which depends on the distribution of risk perceptions among the actors, and the strength of the relationship between risk perceptions and attitudes towards risk in general.

H4A: Risk aversion is associated with decreased resolve. (Linear hypothesis)

H4B: Risk aversion has a nonlinear relationship with resolve. (Nonlinear hypothesis)

H4C: Risk aversion increases sensitivity to both the costs of fighting and the costs of backing down.

Honor Orientations

Third, honor orientations offer another explanation for variation in sensitivity to different types of costs. During the era of "national character" explanations in anthropology and political science, cultural factors were commonly held to be the chief source of resolve: Organski, for example, argued that cultural identifications were a primary determinant of "national morale," while Cline argued that "cultural uniformity" was one of the main ingredients of "national will."[64] Although these types of analyses have largely fallen out of favor, a growing body of work in both cross-cultural psychology and political science has expressed interest in honor cultures (or honor orientations, their instantiation at the individual-level), ideological systems that place a strong emphasis on honor or face, maintaining reputations for toughness, and standing up to perceived slights.[65] In the Spartan debate in his *History of the Peloponnesian War*, Thucydides notes that "fear, honor, and interest" are "three of the strongest motives" for war, and this emphasis on protecting one's honor by not appearing weak in the eyes of others is manifested in what Mead (2002) refers to as the Jacksonian element in US foreign policy—traces of which are still evident in present-day neoconservatism.[66] Honor cultures are by no means

---

64 Charlesworth 1967; Morgenthau 1985; Organski 1968, 189; Cline 1994.

65 Nisbett and Cohen 1996; O'Neill 1999; Osterman and Brown 2011. The rise of constructivism has brought renewed attention to the impact of cultural factors like honor on international security (Johnston, 1995), but increased interest in culture has not been restricted to constructivists: game theorists treat culture as common knowledge used to solve games with multiple equilibria (see the discussion in Wedeen, 2002).

66 Thucydides 1998, 176; Mead 2002; Haglund and Kertzer 2008.

limited to the American context: a parallel literature on political violence has noted that concerns about honor play a significant role in the mobilization of insurgents, hence the seeming intractability of many counterinsurgency conflicts.[67]

Indeed, the psychological literature on sacred and protected values suggests that at the extreme, when principles like honor or face are endowed with sufficient significance within a belief system, actors may not be willing to entertain tradeoffs altogether, and will act out of a sense of duty rather than according to instrumental rationality.[68] If actors maintain a policy out of a sense of moral obligation completely divorced from prospects of success, they display the kind of intransigence we associate with a resolute actor maintaining its policies despite inclinations to the contrary.[69]

In this sense, we can think about honor orientations shaping resolve through multiple pathways, based on whether we are interested in exploring the effect of honor on resolve for publics, leaders, or both. First, if actors with high honor orientations are more likely to embrace a "cult of reputation" that causes them to perceive greater costs of backing down, they should display more resolve.[70] In this perceptual pathway, we can think of cultures of honor as helping construct actors' definition of the situation, whether these actors are elites or the public at large.[71] Certainly we see actors vary dramatically in the extent to which they are fixated on reputation: in 2015, Governor of Wisconsin (and, briefly, Republican presidential candidate) Scott Walker declared that the most consequential foreign policy event in his lifetime was Ronald Reagan's decision to fire 11,000 air traffic controllers during the 1981 PATCO strike, because of the positive consequences he believed it had on America's reputation for resolve.[72] That he would deem a domestic labor dispute to be more consequential than the Iraq War (which upended the regional balance of power in the Middle East), or the fall of the Berlin Wall (which heralded the end of the Cold War), shows just how large reputational concerns can loom in foreign policy belief systems; if honor culture helps

---

67 Atran, Axelrod, and Davis 2007; Atran 2010; Ginges and Atran 2011.

68 Tetlock 2003; Ginges and Atran 2011.

69 Atran, Axelrod, and Davis 2007. Rationalist models of conflict have made a similar argument, but couched in the language of issue indivisibility (Fearon, 1995; Toft, 2006): if an object under dispute is viewed as all-or-nothing, inviolable, or otherwise sacred, the lack of a bargaining range means that no amount of side payments can compensate for its loss. However, this literature has focused predominantly on indivisible parcels of territory (Hassner, 2003; Goddard, 2006)—for example, Jerusalem may be physically divisible in a literal sense, but is treated as indivisible by both Israelis and Palestinians, such that neither side is willing to entertain tradeoffs—whereas we can understand it as part of a more general phenomenon, an instance of actors with heightened sensitivity to certain types of costs compared to others.

70 Tang 2005.

71 Dafoe and Caughey 2016.

72 Rucker 2015. In her biography of Ronald Reagan and reflections on her time in the White House, Peggy Noonan attributed a similar statement to George Schultz. See Noonan 2002, 226.

predict the likelihood of individuals' subscribing to this "cult of reputation," we can explain some of this variation theoretically.

However, thinking about cultures of honor is also helpful because of the extent to which they delineate degrees of freedom in the "two-level games" leaders play against their domestic and foreign audiences. Leaders facing domestic audiences high in cultures of honor are likely to be punished more severely for incurring reputation costs than leaders facing domestic audiences that place less of an emphasis on honor or face. Indeed, it is telling that when rational choice scholars seek to explain how publics can tie leaders' hands, concern for national honor is one of the key mechanisms they cite.[73] Similarly, it is precisely because of the existence of cultures of honor that some authoritarian leaders are posited to be able to fan the flames of nationalist protest in order to credibly signal their resolve.[74] In this sense, although honor orientations are sometimes contrasted with rationalist theories of action, the former can easily be incorporated into the latter.[75] In the experimental investigations in chapters 3 and 4, I bracket the question of the role that cultures of honor play in constraining leaders, and return to it in chapter 5.

H5A: Actors subscribing to cultures of honor will display more resolve.

H5B: Actors subscribing to cultures of honor will be more sensitive to the costs of backing down.

Trait Self-control

One of the rationales in looking for specific dispositional sources of resolve is the premise that when IR scholars are talking about resolve, they are actually studying the same phenomenon that social scientists in other fields refer to as willpower or self control. The psychological literature on willpower—often emphasizes the extent to which willpower is not domain-specific, and is instead an individual-level characteristic activated in multiple spheres.[76] As such, it is worth investigating whether individuals high in what psychologists call "trait self-control" also display more resolve in their foreign policy preferences.[77]

---

73 E.g., Fearon 1994.

74 Weiss 2014.

75 Incorporating honor orientation into a rationalist framework is, of course, more difficult if one assumes it operates through a logic of appropriateness, or perhaps a non-reflexive logic of action—a distinction about which I am agnostic for the purposes of this discussion. See, e.g., Hopf 2010; Holmes and Traven 2015.

76 Hagger et al. 2010; Baumeister, Vohs, and Tice 2007.

77 Gibbs, Giever, and Martin 1998; Whiteside and Lynam 2001; Tangney, Baumeister, and Boone 2004; Duckworth and Kern 2011; de Ridder et al. 2012.

The point is not trivial. On the one hand, much of the popular discussion of resolve in contemporary foreign policy discourse is based on the notion that resolve generalizes beyond the political domain: both that willpower in our daily lives can aggregate upward (John F. Kennedy securitizing obesity by linking the diameter of American midsections to the stamina necessary to defend American liberties in the Cold War), and that a failure of political will can trickle downward (the American journalist Anthony Harrigan warning that "If we are defeated in Vietnam and elsewhere in Asia, we will be defeated in our own minds").[78] Certainly Churchill's emphasis on the transcendent power of resolve in his foreign policy views mirrors the endurance he displayed in his own personal life: overcoming a physical disability produced by a war injury to become one of the top polo players in the British army in India despite playing with his right arm strapped to his side, for example.[79] On the other hand, it is unclear how seamlessly personal characteristics like self-control translate into politics: Rubenzer and Fachingbauer, for example, argue that Lyndon Johnson was highly impulsive while Jimmy Carter was not, a diagnosis that would undoubtedly surprise both left-wing critics of the former (who see Johnson's obsession with resolve as reckless) and right-wing critics of the latter (who see Carter's putative lack of resolve as feckless).[80] The relationship between trait-self control and resolve in political contexts thus merits a closer look: if trait self-control spills over into the political domain and is indeed a significant predictor of resolve in military interventions, it offers further justification for linking the psychological literature on willpower with IR scholarship on resolve.

H6: Actors high in trait self-control will display more resolve.

Finally, it is important to note that, like their situational counterparts, these dispositional variables confront a levels of analysis question: when we model resolve as a function of dispositional characteristics like time and risk preferences, whose time and risk preferences are we talking about? Classical bargaining models in game theory acknowledge the possibility of unitary actors having different time horizons, but it is also possible that leaders and publics *within* a state will have different time preferences.[81] Much of the pessimism expressed by postwar realists about the instability of the foreign policy opinions of the American public stemmed from an image of the public as being as impatient as it was mercurial, reinforced by contemporary arguments that democratic war

---

78 Dean 1998; Harrigan 1965.
79 Pearson 1991, 82.
80 Rubenzer and Faschingbauer 2004.
81 Rubinstein 1982; see also Barkin 2004.

performance declines over time as the public loses the will to fight.[82] It is not necessarily clear, though, that leaders will always have longer time horizons than their publics. Given the extent to which time preferences, risk preferences, and honor orientation are frequently posited to be shaped by cultural factors, domestic or unit-level constructivists would express skepticism at the prospect that elites' characteristics are completely divorced from those of the mass public.[83] Perhaps impatient publics elect impatient leaders—or, in an autocratic context, leaders with short time horizons have an upper hand in seizing power in political environments that reward these shorter time horizons.[84] As is the case with the situational variables, I set this level of analysis question aside for the experimental analyses in chapters 3 and 4—which focus exclusively on individual-level microfoundations of resolve in members of the public—returning to it in chapter 5 in the large-N analyses with observational data.

CONCLUSION

I thus propose an interactionist theory of resolve that models it as a function of two situational features—the cost of fighting, and the cost of backing down—and four dispositional ones (time preferences, risk preferences, honor orientations, and trait self-control). Given that IR scholars have discussed all of these phenomena before, what is new about this approach?

First, it disaggregates the costs of war, explicitly modeling the competing incentives of fighting and backing down. Much of the rational choice literature reduces resolve to the costs of war relative to the benefits—that is, an actor's payoff structure—but the framework advanced above goes a step further, investigating the complex process through which these payoffs are calculated. In this sense, the theory follows Simon's encouragement to strengthen

---

82 Holsti 2004; Bennett and Stam 1998.

83 E.g., Hopf 2002. A large body of research links time preferences to cultural explanations: economists frequently argue that time preferences stem from cultural factors (Rogers, 1994; Offer, 2006), while Gifford (2002) suggests that time inconsistency problems stem from a divergence between a biologically derived preference for immediate rewards, and cultural preferences for future ones. Classic arguments in sociology make similar claims: the Weberian notion of a "Protestant work ethic" invokes a particular cultural framework that both lionizes long time horizons and promotes insensitivity to certain types of costs (Weber, 1904/1984), as is also true for most forms of utopian political thought, whose appeal rests on the promise of benefits that can only be realized in the future (Noyes, 1980). Risk preferences are similarly held to have cultural origins (Weber and Hsee, 1998; Hsee and Weber, 1999), while much of the work on honor comes explicitly from cross-cultural psychology. See Nisbett and Cohen 1996; Rodriguez Mosquera, Manstead, and Fischer 2002; Izjerman and Cohen 2011; Leung and Cohen 2011. On explaining variation in these dispositional characteristics, see the discussion in chapter 6.

84 Rosen 2005.

theories of decision-making by being explicit about where actors derive their utility from.[85]

Second, it avoids the problem of interiority by turning to specific dispositional characteristics to explain variations in resolve, rather than simply pointing to cost-sensitivity as a trait in and of itself. Moreover, it selects these dispositional characteristics because of the roles they play in the study of willpower and self-control outside of political science, which encourages us to understand resolve as a more general phenomenon rather than an IR-specific one. In positing that characteristics or attributes from our daily lives spill into the political domain and can tell us something about international affairs, it also pushes back against the notion of politics as a separate or autonomous domain of inquiry, harkening back to an older way of understanding international relations as constructed not just from the top down, but also from the bottom up, a kind of upward projection of personal values or generalization of interpersonal relations that has long since fallen out of favor in the discipline, and has only recently attracted renewed attention.[86]

Third, it incorporates these factors into an explicitly interactionist framework, in which these dispositional features moderate the impact of situational phenomena. Game theoretic analyses of conflict are conducive to interactionist theorizing—actors' risk preferences are incorporated into the shape of their utility functions, and time preferences incorporated into their δ parameters— but to keep models tractable, most analysts treat these parameters as fixed and target their focus elsewhere, such that resolve and "the cost of war" end up being used interchangeably.[87] The theory outlined above, however, is equally interested in both situational and dispositional phenomena, rather than assigning the former pride of place. If the strategic choice approach makes a "methodological bet" that greater theoretical progress can be made in IR by focusing on structural features than actor-level heterogeneity, the approach I adopt here places a different bet altogether.[88]

In the next three chapters, I test this theory at the micro-level and at the macro-level. At the micro-level, I employ laboratory and embedded survey

---

85 Simon 1985.

86 On politics as a separate domain of inquiry, see Morgenthau 1985. On IR as a generalization of interpersonal relations, see Christiansen 1959; Etheredge 1978; Rathbun 2014; Rathbun et al. 2016. This shift also parallels the rise of "bottom-up" constructivism—for example, the notion that the plots of Russian romance novels can tell us something about the direction of Russian foreign policy, as in Hopf 2013.

87 Kirshner (2000), for example, points out that Fearon's (1995) rationalist explanations for war rest on the assumption that leaders are not risk-averse, or at most, risk-neutral. In this sense, risk attitudes are part of Fearon's model, but inasmuch as they are largely held fixed, it is difficult to see their inclusion as interactionist in spirit. Writing in the context of deterrence theory, Jervis (1985a, 11) similarly notes the extent to which rationalist approaches tend to favor situational explanations.

88 Lake and Powell 1999.

experiments, presenting military intervention scenarios in which I manipulate features of the situation (costs of war ex ante, costs of war ex post, and the costs of backing down), in a between-group factorial experimental design. I also measure participants' time horizons, risk preferences, honor orientations, and trait self-control using instruments developed by economists and social psychologists. At the macro-level, I then build upon the experimental results using observational data, studying the interaction of these same variables at multiple levels of analysis in the context of great power military interventions from 1946 to 2003.

CHAPTER 3.

Experimental Microfoundations for Resolve: I

Following his success leading the Eighth Army at the battle at El Alamein in 1942, Viscount Montgomery wrote that "the more fighting I see, the more I am convinced that the big thing in war is morale," and encouraged military scholars to "make a study of this subject."[1] If political scientists wanted to take Montgomery up on his challenge and study resolve, where should they start? The approach I adopt here begins with an experiment in which I simulate war in the lab, exploring resolve in the context of public opinion about military interventions. As I detail below, understanding the origins of resolve in a public opinion context is important both because of the substantive role that public opinion plays in decisions regarding the use of force, and also because it affords the chance to use experimental methods to build an individual-level theory of resolve from the ground up.

The results of the experiment suggest that although resolve is shaped by the costs of war—when the costs of fighting increase, or the reputational costs of backing down are less salient, individuals are less likely to stay the course—actor-level variation in dispositional characteristics is particularly important. Participants who are relatively impatient, moderately risk-averse, low in honor orientation, and low in trait self-control display significantly less resolve in the experimental scenario. I also find that time and risk preferences can help explain variations in sensitivity to the costs of war, with more patient respondents displaying less sensitivity to casualties, and more risk-averse respondents displaying more sensitivity to the human costs of fighting as well as the reputational costs of backing down. The discussion that follows has four parts. I begin by justifying the use of public opinion as the domain in which to construct a theory of resolve. I then discuss the study's experimental design, before presenting the experiment's findings. Finally, I conclude by discussing a number of implications of the findings, for the study of public opinion, and for theories of resolve more broadly.

1 Fennell 2011, 1.

49

WHY PUBLIC OPINION, AND WHY EXPERIMENTS?

The purpose of this chapter is to build theoretical microfoundations for resolve, a task that requires specifying a particular micro-level context in which to begin the excavation. I choose to ground the theory in the domain of public opinion. Public opinion is by no means the only micro-level context in which to study the dynamics of resolve in military interventions—another such starting point could be the determinants of resolve at the military unit-level—but represents a good point of departure for the investigation, for both substantive and methodological reasons.[2]

First, the historical record suggests that, especially in democracies, leaders carefully monitor public opinion when making decisions about potential military interventions, from instigating William McKinley's involvement in the Spanish-American War ("a war which he did not want for a cause in which he did not believe"), to impairing Dwight Eisenhower's brinksmanship in the Taiwan Crisis of 1958 once he realized the American public did not perceive the defense of Quemoy and Matsu as worth the risk of nuclear war.[3] Although policymakers have incentives to publicly downplay the impact of the public on their decisions, even leaders who claim to ignore public opinion are tacitly attentive to its demands: when his approval ratings soured, George W. Bush warned in media interviews that "if the military thinks you're making decisions based upon a Gallup poll, they're not going to follow the commander-in-chief," but his administration nonetheless spent a million dollars on polling in 2001 alone.[4] Bill Clinton displayed similar ambivalence, simultaneously announcing in a September 1994 press conference that he did not "believe that the president ... could conduct foreign policy by a public opinion poll," but also acknowledging that "any sustained endeavor involving our military forces requires the support of the people over the long run."[5] It is precisely because of concerns about maintaining public support that troop commitments in foreign military interventions tend to be correlated with electoral cycles; the average foreign troop contribution in the first decade of the war in Afghanistan, for example, fell by half during election periods.[6] A new body of research is also beginning to challenge the assumption that public opinion is irrelevant in non-democracies, the chief indicator of which is the pains non-democratic governments take to monitor it: in China, for example, more than two million citizens are now employed as "public opinion analysts," collecting opinions from Chinese social media platforms to report to decision-makers.[7]

---

2 E.g., Grauer 2014.
3 May 1961, 237; Eliades 1993.
4 CNN Larry King Live 2009; Holsti 2004, 276.
5 Foyle 1999, 195.
6 Marinov, Nomikos, and Robbins 2015. See Table A5 in their supplementary appendix.
7 Cited in Dafoe and Weiss 2015. On the role of the mass public in Chinese foreign policy more broadly, see Weiss 2014.

The causal pathways through which public opinion shapes foreign policy are varied and complex: even if decision-makers follow the dictates of Kennan and Morgenthau in trying to insulate themselves the whims of the public, public opinion can shape foreign policy choices through indirect means.[8] Domestic opposition groups, for example, are often highly attentive to the public's mood on foreign policy issues, and capitalize on public disapproval by capsizing the executive's broader legislative agenda, as Johnson found with his Great Society initiative; fear of this same dynamic explains many of the Obama administration's foreign policy choices as well.[9] Foreign observers are also attentive to domestic discontent; John Foster Dulles noted that "other nations are more inclined to listen to proposals or objections from the President and me if they know that the American people are thoroughly behind us."[10] Given the resonance of Johnson's remark that foreign military interventions tend to be lost at home rather than abroad, as well as the rise of military doctrines like the Powell Doctrine (and before that, the Weinberger Doctrine) that explicitly enshrine widespread public support as a necessary condition for the use of force, understanding the underpinnings of resolve in the general public is of considerable importance.[11]

Second, studying resolve in a public opinion context is also attractive because it affords me the opportunity to test and generate a theory of resolve using experimental methods. At their heart, the logic of experiments is simple and straightforward: manipulate elements of the environment, whether in a laboratory (as in this chapter), or in information provided in a survey (as in chapter 4), and observe how participants facing the environment respond.[12] The attraction of experiments here is twofold. First, experiments offer researchers control, and with it, the ability to engage in causal inference and avoid concerns about endogeneity and causal pathways running in unanticipated directions. Outside of the lab, it is difficult to disentangle the multiple costs of war and sidestep the strategic choices actors encounter. If actors seem unmoved by reputational concerns as a conflict progresses, is this because they do not care about reputation costs altogether, or because they already took them into account when initially deciding whether to support the intervention, such that reputational considerations matter ex ante but not ex post? If actors make assumptions about the costs of fighting when deciding whether to begin a conflict, is it really the case that casualties sap resolve, as anticipated by H1, or does resolve increase the number of casualties actors are willing to bear in the first place? Experiments offer a unique advantage in this regard: they enable

8 Kennan 1951; Morgenthau 1985.

9 Gelpi and Grieco 2015; Dueck 2015, 8, 54–66.

10 Foyle 1999, 41.

11 Weinberger 1984.

12 For accessible introductions to experiments in political science and International Relations, see Morton and Williams 2010; McDermott 2011b; Hyde 2015.

me to model strategic choices directly, and by presenting participants with identical information about the situational features of the military intervention apart from those factors being manipulated by the researcher, permit me to rely on random assignment to ensure that differences across groups are due to the situational manipulations themselves rather than potential unmeasured confounders. As Harrison and List argue, all empirical researchers are in some sense experimentalists whenever they model a change in one factor producing a change in another; this assumption is most plausible when it is built into the data-collecting process itself, which is one reason why experimental methods are becoming increasingly popular in political science.[13]

Moreover, and no less important, experimental methods offer critical measurement advantages over their observational counterparts. I argued in chapter 1 that we should think about resolve as a second-order construct, as a matter not of what actors' preferences are, but the sticktoitiveness they display with them. By enabling me to gather measures of actors' preferences at multiple points in time, experiments let me more precisely track how much resolve actors display in a manner that would be unfeasible with observational data. Similarly, the kinds of dispositional characteristics I am interested in here—time and risk preferences, honor orientations, and trait self-control—are difficult to measure at a distance. As one influential early investigation in political science asked, "how can we give a Taylor Manifest Anxiety Scale to Khrushchev during the Hungarian revolt, a Semantic-Differential to Chiang Kai-Shek while Quemoy is being shelled, or simply interview Kennedy during the Cuban Missile Crisis?"[14] Analysts who want to study the dynamics of these individual differences in a more naturalistic setting would be forced to rely on relatively indirect evidence, whether through qualitative studies at a distance, or the kinds of proxies I employ in chapter 5.[15] In contrast, experiments let me leverage survey instruments developed by behavioral economists and social psychologists to more directly capture variation in participants' dispositional traits, without needing to, as Neustadt and May caution against, practice psychological assessment of world leaders "without a license."[16]

RESEARCH DESIGN AND MATERIALS

To test the hypotheses delineated in chapter 2 in the context of public opinion about military interventions, a laboratory experiment was conducted on 317

---

13 Harrison and List 2004, 1009. On the increasing popularity of experiments in political science, see Druckman et al. 2006.

14 Brody 1969, 116.

15 George and George 1956; Saunders 2011.

16 Neustadt and May 1986, 160.

college students recruited from undergraduate political science classes at a large Midwestern research university in December 2011.[17] The study consists of three parts: a factorial experiment that manipulates the human and reputational costs of a hypothetical military intervention, a dispositional questionnaire that measures participants' time and risk preferences, honor orientations, and trait self-control, and a concluding questionnaire that includes a battery of additional individual difference measures and demographic characteristics. Participants randomly received either the dispositional questionnaire or the intervention scenario first, such that the entire study can be thought of as a 2 (ex ante human costs: low or high) × (ex post human costs: low or high) × 2 (reputation costs: implicit or salient) × 2 (order manipulation: scenario first or second) fully crossed factorial experimental design.[18] The structure of the experiment is summarized in figure 3.1, and the survey instrumentation is presented in appendix B.1.

Situational Manipulations

The experiment itself consists of a foreign policy intervention scenario that has two stages. In the first (pre-invasion) stage, participants are asked whether they support a hypothetical military intervention the president wants to carry out (modified from Herrmann, Tetlock, and Visser) on behalf of a US ally under siege.[19] The scenario manipulates the amount of force the White House expects the intervention to require (low, or high), as well as reputational costs: in the reputation condition, participants are reminded "of the consequences that failing to stand up to aggression will have on America's reputation," while in the control condition, reputational concerns are not discussed. Regardless of whether participants support the intervention or not, they then proceed to the second stage of the scenario, in which the United States has proceeded with the intervention. In this post-invasion stage, I manipulate the rate of casualties

17 Participants—61% of whom identified as men, 77% as white/Caucasian, 7% as having served in the US Armed Forces, and 91% as having been born in the United States—ranged in age from 17 to 59 (μ: 21.27), and participated in the study in exchange for extra credit. Although all participants were enrolled in a political science class at the time of participating in the study, only 41.5% of them identified as political science majors, and supplementary analysis suggests that these political science majors did not behave significantly differently than non-majors.

18 The order manipulation is included to avoid downstream effects, to avoid the possibility that presenting participants with a military intervention scenario changes measures of their dispositional characteristics, and vice versa.

19 Herrmann, Tetlock, and Visser 1999.

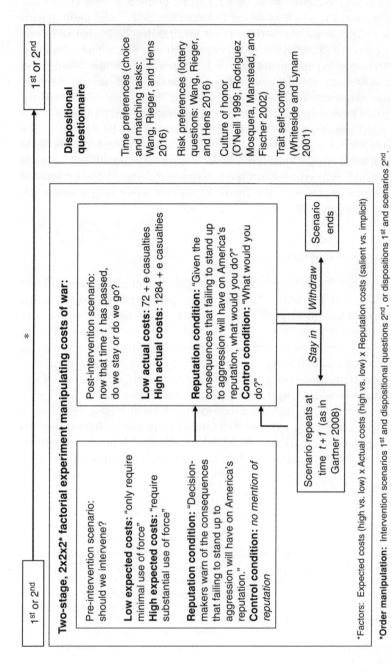

FIGURE 3.1. Laboratory experiment structure.

*Factors: Expected costs (high vs. low) x Actual costs (high vs. low) x Reputation costs (salient vs. implicit)

Order manipulation: Intervention scenarios 1st and dispositional questions 2nd, or dispositions 1st and scenarios 2nd.

the United States is experiencing (low or high), along with including the same reputation manipulation described above.[20]

Due to the two-stage structure of the experiment, it is necessary to restrict the number of situational manipulations in order to ensure statistical power and maintain a tractable experimental design. Thus, rather than manipulating the stakes of the intervention, I keep the stakes constant and focus specifically on reputation costs as the costs of backing down. I do so for three reasons. First, reputation costs clearly correspond to a dispositional counterpart (honor orientations), allowing for the study of interactionist mechanism, in that individuals who emphasize the importance of maintaining a reputation for resolve could potentially be more sensitive to reputational concerns. Second, a large literature in public opinion about foreign policy has already found evidence for the impact of the intrinsic stakes of a mission on levels of support, in that humanitarian operations tend to be less popular than conflicts where core national security interests are at stake, but the popularity also depends on individuals' underlying dispositions toward humanitarian rationales for intervention.[21] Third, what makes resolve such an engrossing phenomenon to study are the circumstances where we see actors behave in ways one would not expect from the stakes inherent in a situation: as social scientists, we are often less interested in people who flee a fire in a crowded theater than those who stay despite the fire, or who flee when no such fire exists.[22] In this sense, it is more theoretically germane to keep the stakes fixed and explore the impact of variation in the other situational factors.[23] I return to the stakes in the large-N analyses in chapter 5.

To explicitly capture the intertemporal quality of resolve, I employ what Gartner calls a "panel experiment": participants receive information about how the invasion has progressed in the past year (the nature of which depends on the participants' experimental condition), and are asked whether the United States should withdraw its forces or not.[24] If participants advocate withdrawal, the intervention scenario ends immediately; otherwise, the process repeats

20 In the low casualty condition, the US suffers $72 + \epsilon$ casualties a year; in the high-casualty condition, the US suffers $1248 + \epsilon$ casualties a year. These figures represent the annual equivalents of the 5th and 95th percentiles, respectively, of American monthly casualties in the Iraq War from March 2003 to January 2010, with an error term (ϵ) added so that casualties fluctuate within a narrow band from year to year.

21 Jentleson 1992; Klarevas 2002; Gelpi, Feaver, and Reifler 2009. For a contrary view on the former, see Mader 2015.

22 Wolfers 1962.

23 I also set aside the issue of audience costs. Audience costs are by definition paid by leaders rather than ordinary citizens, but since the experimental participants are exclusively the latter, I bracket this mechanism for the purposes of this experiment. See Tomz 2007a; Trager and Vavreck 2011; Kertzer and Brutger 2016.

24 Gartner 2008a.

up to seven times. The dependent variable is thus the number of periods participants supported the war, analyzed using an event history model, a type of statistical model used to analyze questions about *when* a phenomenon occurs.[25]

Dispositional Measures

As discussed above, experiments offer researchers two analytic advantages. First, the use of random assignment allows me to more cleanly engage in causal claims about the factors I am manipulating, which in this context are the situational features of military interventions. Second, they also offer measurement advantages for the study of dispositional characteristics. Importantly, I *measure* these characteristics rather than manipulate them, employing survey instrumentation derived from social psychology and behavioral economics to exploit natural variation in these traits across the respondents. Although this prevents me from making causal claims about these characteristics, it frees me from the burden of attempting to concoct treatments capable of rewiring participants' dispositional makeup in precise ways.[26]

To measure time preferences, I employ a set of hypothetical choice tasks. A growing volume of research in behavioral economics has found that the manner in which people make choices over time changes as we move into the future in a manner that deviates from classical theories of temporal discounting.[27] Samuelson's discounted utility model, for example—inherited by most game theoretic models in IR that deal with repeated games—assume that actors discount the future at a constant rate: if I prefer to receive X at time t to Y at time $t + d$, I should maintain this preference for all values of t.[28] Experimental evidence suggests, however, that although most people choose smaller rewards over delayed larger ones when t is small (most people would prefer to receive a check for $100 today instead of a post-dated check for $200 cashable three years from now), their preferences reverse when t is long (most people would prefer to receive a post-dated check for $200 cashable nine years from now than a post-dated check for $100 cashable in six years), even though the value of each option and the delay between them remains the same.[29] To capture this hyperbolic discounting dynamic, I turn to

25 As discussed below, I employ a Cox model, a semi-parametric event history model used to study duration data. See Box-Steffensmeier and Jones 2004.

26 After all, for randomization to facilitate causal inference about these quantities of interest, the treatments would need to manipulate one particular dispositional characteristic without affecting others; otherwise, the same concerns about potential unmeasured confounds arise in experimental work as they do with observational data.

27 Ainslie 1992; Loewenstein and Elster 1992; Frederick 2006.

28 Samuelson 1937.

29 Ainslie 2001.

"matching" tasks commonly used by behavioral economists who focus on time preferences as well as by social psychologists who study self-control, in which participants are presented with a hypothetical choice between receiving $1,000 today, or $X at some point in the future (e.g., a year from now), and asked how much $X would have to be in order for it to be preferred over the immediate payment.[30] By employing two different matching questions that vary the delay (e.g., one year versus ten years), I have enough information to construct hyperbolic discounting curves for each participant, and can calculate both the value of participants' long-term discount factor, δ (the length of their "shadow of the future"), and their present bias, B (the extent to which participants are more impatient than classical rational models of temporal discounting assume).

I solicit risk attitudes using a series of hypothetical lottery questions employed by economists, in which participants are asked how much they are willing to pay for a lottery ticket with a certain chance of receiving a particular prize.[31] The questions manipulate the value of the prize (e.g., a 60% chance of winning $100, a 60% chance of winning $400) in order to produce an estimate of participants' relative risk premium, a measure of whether participants are generally risk-averse, risk-acceptant, or risk-neutral.

There is a prominent literature on honor coming out of cross-cultural psychology, but it tends to assume the existence of cultures of honor based upon ethnic categories (e.g., southern Europeans have a culture of honor, while the Dutch have a "culture of dignity") or infer it from geographical origin (e.g., presidents born in southern states, rather than those born in northern ones), rather than measure it with survey instrumentation.[32] I thus constructed a new four-item scale measuring participants' honor orientations, derived from the discussion in O'Neill, and based off of items used by Rodriguez Mosquera, Manstead, and Fischer, described in greater detail in the discussion of the dispositional questionnaire later in the chapter.[33]

Finally, I also use the urgency and perseverance subscales of Whiteside and Lynam's trait self-control measure to study participants' levels of trait self-control.[34] Trait self-control is generally understood to be a multidimensional construct.[35] Whiteside and Lynam find that trait self-control has four factors, two of which are urgency and perseverance, both of which are related to what IR scholars mean by resolve—urgency implicating one's ability to control impulses, and perseverance referring to one's "sticktoitiveness" in carrying

---

30 Ameriks et al. 2007; Benjamin, Choi, and Strickland 2010; Wang, Rieger, and Hens 2016.
31 Wang, Rieger, and Hens 2016.
32 Nisbett and Cohen 1996; Izjerman and Cohen 2011; Dafoe and Caughey 2016.
33 O'Neill 1999; Rodriguez Mosquera, Manstead, and Fischer 2002.
34 Whiteside and Lynam 2001.
35 Grasmick et al. 1993; Arneklev, Grasmick, and Bursik 1999; Duckworth and Kern 2011.

out challenging or ungratifying tasks.[36] I also measure the usual assortment of demographic characteristics and individual differences (party ID, political ideology, and so on).

RESULTS

The results are discussed in four phases. First, I examine the dependent variables of interest—the extent to which participants supported the United States sending troops ex ante, and the duration they supported the mission ex post—demonstrating that some of the participants displayed far more resolve than others. Second, I analyze the impact of the situational manipulations to determine how participants' resolve was shaped by the human costs of fighting and the reputational costs of backing down, and how disaggregating participants based on their initial support for sending troops paints a finer-grained picture of resolve. Third, I describe the dispositional variables, and show how they are associated with resolve. Finally, I test the interactionist hypotheses, demonstrating how the impact of the situational determinants of resolve varies with certain dispositional features.

How Resolved Were the Participants?

As figure 3.2 shows, there was considerable variation both in participants' initial degree of support for the intervention and in how long until they advocated for withdrawal once the United States intervened. A total of 30.4% of respondents opposed the United States getting involved in the first place, compared to the 69.6% who supported deploying troops, but as the intervention progressed, the balance of support dropped precipitously: by the second anniversary of the intervention, nearly half (46.4%) of the respondents wanted the United States to leave. Two points are especially worth noting here. First, respondents displayed considerable variation in resolve: around a third (32.0%) of participants wanted the United States to cut and run by the end of its first year, whereas a fifth (20.4%) of participants continued to support the mission even when the scenario ended in its seventh year. Participants who persisted in supporting the mission at the end of seven years were given an open-ended question asking how many more years they would continue to support the intervention. Importantly, although 37.5% of the responses provided specific timelines (e.g., 13 of the 64 respondents mentioned 10 years as a suitable benchmark for withdrawal), the rest rejected the premise of the question, giving responses like "Until the job is done," "As long as it takes," "Until we win," and "Until the mission is completed." These responses

---

36 Whiteside and Lynam 2001. The other two factors—premediation (whether one thinks before acting) and sensation seeking (whether one is attracted to exciting or risky behavior)—are less obviously related to the construct under investigation here.

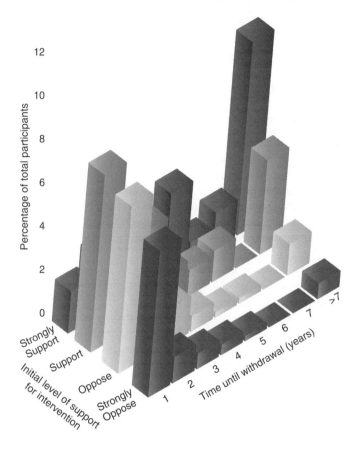

FIGURE 3.2. Distribution of the dependent variable. Do we go in, and how long do we stay? Initial attitudes toward the mission predict the duration of support ($\chi^2 = 103.6711$, $p < 0.000$). Results are pooled across all experimental conditions.

nicely illustrate the kind of variation we are trying to explain: why are some participants willing to persist eight years in, while others dip their toes in the water and want to leave immediately?

Second, how long people wanted US troops to stay was heavily dependent on their initial attitude toward the intervention: as figure 3.2 shows, individuals who did not want the United States to get involved in the first place were far more likely to advocate an earlier withdrawal than individuals who were initially strongly supportive of the mission. In this sense, although we see some evidence of sunk cost logic at work—a third of the respondents who were strongly opposed to the US intervening were nonetheless willing to stick it out for at least two years, and a number of the open-ended responses include comments about how "to withdraw before success would waste the lives and efforts of those before them"—in general, participants' initial attitudes toward the mission strongly predict their attitudes toward it once troops are deployed. Thus, my findings better support claims about how public opinion toward military operations is structured by perceptions of a conflict's rightness than they do arguments about sunk costs.[37]

Situational Determinants of Resolve

Thus far, the results show that some participants were highly resolved, advocating for the intervention many years after it had begun, whereas others were relatively irresolute, supporting the mission before it began but quickly favoring withdrawal as time passed. To what extent was this variation caused by the situational manipulations? I answer this question by estimating an event history, or duration model—a type of regression model designed to answer questions about *when* an event occurs—with each of the four treatments listed in table 3.1.[38]

Substantively, the most straightforward way to interpret the results of an event history model are by looking at its hazard ratios, which in the context of this experiment refer to the effect of each experimental treatment on the likelihood of participants advocating for withdrawal. Thus, positive hazard ratios indicate a treatment increases the hazard of withdrawal (or *decreases* the amount of resolve a participant displays), and negative hazard ratios indicate a treatment decreases the hazard of withdrawal (or *increases* the amount of resolve a participant displays). As the hazard ratios from table 3.1 suggest, casualties have a substantively large impact on participants' resolve, in a

37 Gelpi, Feaver, and Reifler 2009; Sullivan 2008. Importantly, though, when Gelpi, Feaver, and Reifler (2009) discuss beliefs about whether a war is justified, they are invoking a *retrospective* justification, which, as they acknowledge, may be endogenous to their other key independent variable, beliefs about the probability of success, since individuals are likely to update their belief as to whether an intervention was the "right thing" based upon how the intervention progresses. Here, though, the belief about whether the United States should intervene is measured at the beginning of the scenario, and thus is independent of the events on the ground that follow.

38 As Box-Steffensmeier and Jones (2004) note, duration data display a number of features that make them inappropriate to study with traditional linear regression techniques, chief of which is that they display *right censoring*: the dependent variable is the time until individuals call for troop withdrawal, but because a fifth of the participants want the mission to continue even after the time period ends, a traditional regression model would treat this part of the sample as missing, biasing coefficient estimates. Instead, I employ semiparametric Cox models, as presented in table 3.1, which, as a first cut, displays the results from a Cox model with each of the four treatments. Test results suggest no violations of the proportional hazards assumption. In lieu of presenting the higher-order interactions—which become difficult to substantively interpret, and suffer from a lack of statistical power—I focus solely on the main effects here, following the norm in large-scale experimental analyses in IR (e.g., Herrmann and Shannon 2001; Tomz 2007a). Table B.3 and figure B.3 in appendix B.1 display the hazard ratios (with 90% confidence intervals) for the full $2 \times 2 \times 2 \times 2$ model.

TABLE 3.1. Situational Determinants of the Duration of the Intervention

	β	SE	HAZARD RATIO	90% CI
Anticipated costs	−0.202	(0.128)	−18.28%	[−33.7%–0.81%]
Reputation costs	−0.192	(0.129)	−17.51%	[−33.3%–2.0%]
Casualties	0.277	(0.127)	31.9%	[7.0%–62.6%]
Order	0.037	(0.128)	3.8%	[−15.9%–28.0%]

N = 317. Main entries are Cox model coefficients. Positive coefficients indicate a greater likelihood of "cutting and running."

manner consistent with H1: when casualty levels are high, participants are 31.9% more likely to call for troops to be withdrawn at any given period of the intervention than when casualty levels are low. Interestingly, anticipated costs have the opposite effect: when participants were warned in advance that the intervention would require a substantial use of force, the respondents were 18.3% *less* likely to withdraw than if they were promised that the intervention would require only a minimal amount of force. Cost-sensitivity thus appears to partially stem from actors' expectations: participants were more patient when the intervention had been framed in advance as requiring a substantial amount of force than when it required only a minimal use.[39] In line with H2, reputation costs also bolstered actors' persistence: participants reminded of the costs of backing down were 17.5% less likely to withdraw than those who received no such reminder, thereby showing that participants were attentive to the cost of fighting and to the cost of backing down. These results are presented in visual form in the dark black lines in figure 3.3, which depict the hazard ratio with 90% and 95% confidence intervals illustrating our uncertainty around the effects of each of the situational manipulations; the greater the hazard of withdrawal, the less resolve participants display. Thus, the coefficient plot shows that the anticipated cost treatment and the reputation cost treatment bolster participants' resolve, while the casualty treatment lowers it, and the order manipulation has no significant effect.[40]

39 The expected cost manipulation may also have had this bolstering effect because participants perceived the amount of force the mission was expected to require as a proxy for how serious the stakes were for the intervention.

40 I present hazard ratio plots rather than survival curves because of the former's ease of interpretability, but the same conclusions hold. Since participants remain in the same casualty treatment as the intervention progresses, one might be concerned about the possibility of demand characteristics, in which participants become aware of the purpose of the study and attempt to behave accordingly (e.g., Orne 1962). Supplementary analyses presented in appendix B.1, however, suggest little concern is warranted, in that participants' predictions of future casualty rates do not become more accurate the longer they stay in the study.

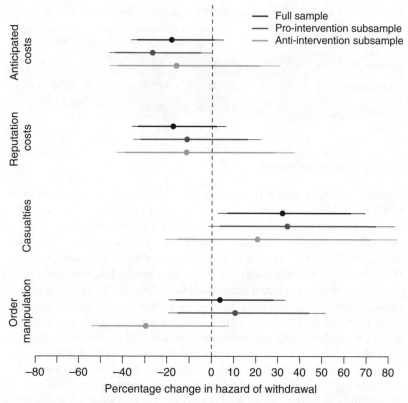

FIGURE 3.3. Coefficient plot of situational determinants of resolve. Point estimates of percentage change in the hazard ratio incurred by each of the four experimental manipulations, with 90% and 95% confidence intervals. Negative values indicate a decreased probability of withdrawal, and thus, greater resolve.

A More Precise Measure of Resolve

Given the two-stage nature of the experimental design—in which we have measures of participants' desire to intervene ex ante and how long they support the mission ex post, we have the opportunity to measure resolve in a manner that closely corresponds to our second-order definition of the concept. Thus, rather than simply inferring resolve based on the length of time individuals supported the mission (deeming participants who want to immediately "cut and run" less resolute than those who want the United States to remain involved for a longer period of time), we can also look more specifically at the duration individuals who *initially* supported the mission continued to do so. This analytic move allows us to study the *second-order* quality of resolve, preventing us from conflating the content of an actor's desire with the sticktoitiveness with which it is pursued. After all, we know that resolve involves maintaining a policy despite temptations to back down, and actors who never supported the mission in the first place can hardly be deemed irresolute for advocating for withdrawal. In the US political context, for example, Sen. John Kerry's evolving stance on the Iraq War caused him to be lampooned by his critics during the 2004 presidential election campaign, who seized on lines like "I actually did vote for [an $87 billion military appropriations bill] before I voted against it" as a sign that the presidential candidate was an irresolute "flip-flopper." In contrast, Sen. Dennis Kucinich, who voted against the Iraq War Resolution in October 2002, was never in favor of the war, and thus could not be criticized for lacking resolve by continuing to oppose it.

The first model in table 3.2 thus replicates the results from table 3.1, while the second and third models analyze the impact of the situational manipulations for the 220 participants who initially advocated that the United States intervene, and the 97 participants who initially preferred the country stay out, respectively.[41] Among participants who initially advocated intervening (whose hazard ratios and confidence intervals are illustrated by the dark grey lines in figure 3.3), both anticipated costs and casualties remain highly significant, with higher ex ante costs associated with a 26.9% increase in resolve, and higher casualties associated with a 34.2% decrease in resolve. However, the impact of reputation costs is no longer statistically significant, and is associated with only an 11.2% increase in resolve, although the magnitude of the change between the two models is not itself statistically significant.[42] Although the width of the confidence intervals suggests caution should be taken in comparing treatments between the full sample and the pro-intervention subsample,[43] it is nonetheless noteworthy that reputation costs are the only treatment effect

---

41 The decision to disaggregate the experimental results based on pre-intervention support (rather than include pre-intervention support as a control variable) stems from concerns about post-treatment bias (King and Zeng, 2007, 201–202): the treatments that shape the initial decision to intervene are also likely to affect the duration of the intervention, so controlling for the decision to intervene as an additional covariate in the model would thus bias the coefficient estimates of our treatments.

42 Both AIC scores and likelihood ratio tests comparing (i) an unrestricted model with an interaction between reputation costs and initial attitudes toward the intervention, to (ii) a restricted model without the interaction term find no significant improvement in model fit by varying the impact of reputation costs based on pro-intervention attitudes. Note that traditional tests of coefficient stability like the Chow test are inappropriate in a survival model context because they rely on the sum of squared residuals.

43 For this reason, it is also difficult to judge the impact of the treatments on participants who initially advocated staying out; the smaller sample size means that the standard errors increase in size (and thus the confidence intervals around the hazard ratios increase), but the order manipulation in this anti-intervention subsample is noticeably statistically significant, with participants who received the intervention scenario after completing the dispositional questionnaire being 29.7% more resolved than those who answered in the other order in this subsample.

TABLE 3.2. Treatment Effects Based on Initial Decision to Invade

	ALL PARTICIPANTS		GO IN		STAY OUT	
	β	HAZARD RATIO	β	HAZARD RATIO	β	HAZARD RATIO
Anticipated costs	−0.202	−18.28%	−0.314	−26.9%	−0.176	−16.1%
	(0.128)	[−33.7%, 0.81%]	(0.158)	[−43.7%, −5.2%]	(0.226)	[−42.1%, 21.6%]
Reputation costs	−0.192	−17.51%	−0.119	−11.2%	−0.122	−11.4%
	(0.129)	[−33.3%, 2.0%]	(0.162)	[32.0%, 15.9%]	(0.224)	[−38.7%, 28.0%]
Casualties	0.277	31.9%	0.294	34.2%	0.187	20.5%
	(0.127)	[7.0%, 62.6%]	(0.158)	[−3.4%, 73.9%]	(0.215)	[−15.4%, 71.6%]
Order	0.037	3.8%	0.101	10.6%	−0.352	−29.7%
	(0.128)	[−15.9%, 28.0%]	(0.161)	[−15.1%, 44.1%]	(0.217)	[50.8%, 0.6%]
N	317		220		97	

Main entries are Cox model coefficients; SEs in parentheses; 90% CIs around hazard ratios in brackets. Positive coefficients indicate a greater likelihood of "cutting and running."

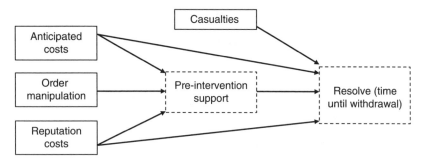

FIGURE 3.4. Mediation structure. Note: the order manipulation's direct effect on resolve is omitted here for presentational purposes.

whose magnitude seems to *decrease* in size when only those participants who initially advocated for the intervention are studied. One potential explanation for this change are *selection effects*: if participants already take reputation costs into account when deciding whether to initially support the mission, it should no longer exert an effect when deciding whether to stay or not.[44]

Nonparametric mediation analyses offer a formal means of testing this selection effect hypothesis for reputation costs, in which the effect of the reputation cost and anticipated cost manipulations on the duration of support for the mission is mediated through initial attitudes towards the intervention, as illustrated by figure 3.4. Since the results from the disaggregated analyses show that reputation costs appear to exert different effects on resolve depending on whether participants initially supported the intervention, mediation analysis is beneficial in its ability to trace this causal pathway and decompose each treatment's average total effect on resolve into two quantities of interest: the average direct effect, and the average causal mediation effect (ACME).[45] The ACME measures how much of the treatment effect operates through the mediator— in this context, how much of the reputation cost manipulation bolsters resolve by increasing the likelihood of initially supporting US involvement in the mission. The average direct effect measures how much of the treatment effect

44 For a series of analyses using manipulation checks to test the selection effects hypothesis alongside two alternative hypotheses—an escalation effects account, and a motivated reasoning account—see appendix B.1.

45 Imai et al. 2011. The average total effect is equivalent to the treatment effect we would estimate without mediation analysis; it is called the *average* total effect because in a potential outcomes framework, unit-level treatment effects are unobservable due to the fundamental problem of causal inference—that is, a unit can either be exposed to the treatment, or a control, but not both. Experimenters thus typically estimate causal effects by focusing on the average differences in the outcome variable between the treatment and control groups.

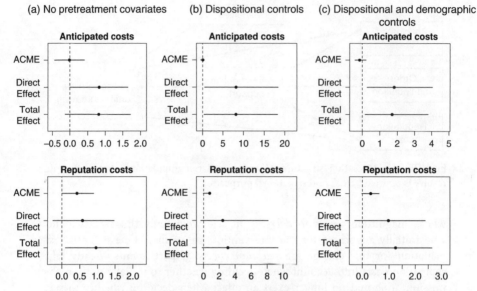

FIGURE 3.5. Nonparametric mediation effects: lab experiment. Mediation effects plotted using the mediation package from Tingley et al. (2014). All models are estimated using 1500 simulations with 90% quasi-Bayesian confidence intervals. Anticipated costs bolster resolve by making participants more patient after the intervention takes place, while reputation costs bolster resolve by making participants more likely to approve of the mission in the first place. To probe the robustness of the results, I run three iterations of the analyses: first, on a model with no pretreatment covariates, second, controlling for the dispositional factors of interest, and third, controlling for both the dispositional variables and demographic characteristics. I thus cannot eliminate the possibility that the results are an artifact of pretreatment confounders, but can test how robust they are to the inclusion of a large number of pretreatment controls.

operates through all other mechanisms by which the treatment might affect the outcome variable, rather than through the mediator.

The mediation analyses not only offer support for the selection effects hypothesis, but show that reputation costs and anticipated costs affect resolve through different pathways.[46] The results presented in figure 3.5 show that the impact of anticipated costs on resolve is not mediated by initial support for

---

46 The mediation analysis requires parametric duration models for computational purposes, so in the analyses that follow I estimate a series of Weibull models rather than the Cox models estimated in the main text. The results are similar to those from the Cox model estimated in table 3.1: anticipated costs raise resolve by 23.0%, reputation costs boost resolve by 22.3%, casualties lower resolve by 24.0%, and the order manipulation decreases resolve by a statistically insignificant 2.5%. Although the advantage of Cox models is that

the mission: across all three model specifications, the ACME lacks statistical significance, and no more than 5% of anticipated costs' effect on resolve comes through the mediator. The average direct effect of anticipated costs, on the other hand, is positive and statistically significant, and increases in significance (to $p < 0.01$) when pretreatment covariates are introduced. It is thus clear that anticipated costs raise resolve, but not by raising the likelihood of supporting the intervention ex ante. Instead, being warned in advance that an intervention is expected to require substantial use of force appears to make participants more patient when the United States does in fact encounter obstacles.

In contrast, the reputation cost manipulation displays a borderline statistically significant ACME ($p < 0.1$ with no pretreatment covariates, $p < 0.13$ with demographic characteristics), yet no significant average direct effect ($p < 0.23$ to $p < 0.30$, depending on the model specification). In a model with dispositional pretreatment covariates, a full 40.8% of reputation costs' effect on resolve goes through the mediator (although this percentage drops to 27.7% once demographic characteristics are also being controlled for). These results offer further support for the selection effects hypothesis, in that reputation costs bolster resolve by increasing the likelihood of wanting to intervene in the first place. In this respect, reputation costs and anticipated costs both exert a similar effect on resolve, but through opposite pathways: whereas anticipated costs bolster resolve by making participants more patient, reputation costs do not affect participants' patience, but rather, their desire to intervene in the first place.

Dispositional Determinants of Resolve

To measure participants' time preferences, participants were presented with two matching questions taken from Wang, Rieger, and Hens, where they were given the choice between receiving $100 today, or $X at either 1 or 10 years in the future, and asked to indicate how much $X would have to be to make it preferable to the immediate payment.[47] The lower the discount rate, the more the participant values the future relative to the present; an individual with a discount rate of 0 is indifferent between a payment today and an equal payment at time $t + 1$, whereas an individual with a discount rate of 5 values a payment at time $t + 1$ five times less than an equal payment today.

---

they do not force analysts to make assumptions about the shape of the baseline hazard (Box-Steffensmeier and Jones, 2004, 47–48), Bennett (1999) argues that there are some instances where the functional form of duration dependence can be theoretically important. In our case, the shape parameter (p) is positive ($p = 1.132$), which means the hazard is monotonically increasing with time, reflecting the tendency for participants to "lose heart" and be more likely to advocate withdrawal as time goes on.

47 Wang, Rieger, and Hens 2016.

If participants discounted time in the manner predicted by classical (expo-nential) theories of discounting, they would display identical discount rates regardless of whether \$X was being offered 1 year from now, or 10 years from now. Using participants' responses to the matching questions, I can derive these discount rates directly.[48] Although the two discount rates are correlated with one another ($r = 0.502$), participants tended to display a steeper discount rate for the 1-year payment than the 10-year one, consistent with behavioral economists' research on *present bias*: for 91.8% of participants, the one-year discount rate was greater than the ten-year discount rate, suggesting that respondents were disproportionately more impatient toward the value of the 1-year delayed reward than the 10-year delayed one. Thus, rather than assume a constant discounting rate, I estimate quasi-hyperbolic discounting functions, which model the extent to which people are more patient in the long run than in the more immediate future, producing two different measures of participants' time preferences: their level of long-term discounting (δ—their shadow of the future), and their degree of present bias (β).[49]

A similar procedure was used to measure participants' risk preferences, using instrumentation from Wang, Rieger, and Hens.[50] Participants were presented with two hypothetical lottery questions in which they were given the option of winning a particular amount of money, and asked how much they would be willing to pay for a lottery ticket to play in the lottery. To measure risk aversion, participants were asked how much they would be willing to pay to buy a ticket in a lottery with (i) a 60% chance to win \$100 but otherwise nothing, and (ii) a 60% chance to win \$400 but otherwise nothing. Risk aversion (ρ) was measured by averaging over the relative risk premium for each question, calculated by subtracting the expected value of the lottery from the respondent's willingness to pay for a ticket, and dividing the difference by the expected value.[51]

---

48 I calculate discount rate R using the formula below, where F is the future value, P represents the present value, and t the time to be waited: $F = P(1 + R)^t$. Since $P = 100$ and $F = X$, we can rearrange to solve for R for both $t = 1$, and $t = 10$: $R_1 = \frac{X}{100} - 1$, and $R_{10} = (\frac{X}{100})^{0.1} - 1$.

49 If $u(x_0, x_1...x_T) = u(x_0) + \sum_{t=1}^{T} \beta \delta^t u(x_t)$, both δ and β can therefore be estimated using the values of X respondents provided in the two matching questions: $\delta = (\frac{X_1}{X_{10}})^{1/9}$, and $\beta = \frac{100}{\delta X_1}$.

50 Wang, Rieger, and Hens 2016.

51 $RRP_{100} = \frac{(0.6*100)-\lambda_{100}}{(0.6*100)}$, $RRP_{400} = \frac{(0.6*400)-\lambda_{400}}{(0.6*400)}$. An alternative measure of risk aversion was calculated using the Arrow-Pratt measure of absolute risk aversion (Hartog, Ferrer-i Carbonell, and Jonker, 2002), in which α is the probability of winning the lottery, Z the value of the prize, and λ the participant's willingness to pay, thus: $\rho = \frac{\alpha Z - \lambda}{\frac{\lambda^2}{2} + \frac{\alpha Z^2}{2} - \alpha \lambda Z}$.
Since only the scale of the denominator differs between the Arrow-Pratt measure and the relative risk premium, the results in the models that follow are substantially similar regardless of which measure is used.

Each of these measures paints a similar picture of the participants as being overwhelmingly risk-averse; of the 316 participants who completed the risk lottery questions, only one was truly risk-acceptant ($\rho < 0$), five were risk-neutral ($\rho = 0$), and the remaining 310 were risk-averse ($\rho > 0$). Prospect theory finds that individuals in the domain of gains are more risk-averse than in the domain of losses—for example, when given the choice between receiving $3,000 for sure or an 80% chance of winning $4,000, most people will choose the former, but when given the choice between losing $3,000 for sure or an 80% chance of losing $4,000, most people will choose the latter—so in this sense, the skewed distribution of risk preferences is sensible.[52] It is also reassuring given that prominent rationalist theories of war assume that actors are risk-averse or risk-neutral.[53] Because of the distribution of risk preferences among participants, the relationship between risk preferences and resolve in the analyses that follow is thus a matter of exploring relative levels of risk aversion, rather than examining the entire risk spectrum.

Honor orientations were measured using a four-item scale, where participants were asked the extent to which they agree or disagree with the statements "It's always important to be true to your word," "A man should be willing to defend himself if he's insulted in public," "I think many people don't care enough about their reputation, and "People will take advantage of you if you don't stand up for yourself."[54]

Finally, the dispositional questionnaire included the "urgency" and "perseverance" subscales of Whiteside and Lynam's trait self-control model.[55] Each subscale contains four items, with urgency measuring the extent to which participants agreed or disagreed with the statements "I have trouble controlling my impulses," "When I am upset I often act without thinking," "I have trouble resisting my cravings (for food, cigarettes, etc.)," and "It is hard for me to resist acting on my feelings." Perseverance measures the extent to which participants agreed or disagreed with the statements "I generally like to see things through to the end," "I tend to give up easily," "Unfinished tasks really bother me," and "Once I start a project, I almost always finish it."[56]

Table 3.3 shows the estimates of two event history models that control not just for the four situational treatments, but also for participants' time preferences (as measured both by participants' discount factor and present

---

52 Kahneman and Tversky 2000. See also the discussion of the "Asian disease" experiment in chapter 6.

53 Fearon 1995.

54 The honor measure has relatively low reliability ($\alpha = 0.511$), potentially suggesting that the construct has multiple dimensions, although principal axis factoring with oblimin rotation suggests the four-item measure has only one factor according to the Kaiser criterion.

55 Whiteside and Lynam 2001.

56 Both trait self-control subscales were reliable (urgency: $\alpha = 0.73$, perseverance: $\alpha = 0.71$).

TABLE 3.3. Dispositional and Situational Determinants of Resolve (1)

	ALL PARTICIPANTS		PRO-INTERVENTION PARTICIPANTS	
	B	HAZARD RATIO	B	HAZARD RATIO
Anticipated costs	−0.296	−25.6%	−0.409	−33.5%
	(0.135)	[−40.5%, −7.0%]	(0.167)	[−49.5%, −12.6%]
Reputation costs	−0.213	−19.2%	−0.174	−16.0%
	(0.135)	[−35.3%, 0.9%]	(0.172)	[−36.7%, 11.5%]
Casualties	0.250	28.3%	0.280	32.3%
	(0.135)	[2.8%, 60.3%]	(0.169)	[0.1%, 74.8%]
Order	−0.007	−0.7%	0.072	7.5%
	(0.133)	[−20.2%, 23.5%]	(0.169)	[−18.6%, 41.8%]
Discount factor (δ)	−1.072	−65.8%	−1.419	−75.8%
	(0.544)	[−86.0%, −16.3%]	(0.637)	[−91.5%, −31.0%]
Present bias (β)	−0.142	−13.2%	−0.331	−28.2%
	(0.171)	[−34.6%, 15.0%]	(0.217)	[−49.7%, 2.5%]

TABLE 3.3. (*continued*)

| | ALL PARTICIPANTS | | PRO-INTERVENTION PARTICIPANTS | |
	B	HAZARD RATIO	B	HAZARD RATIO
Honor orientations	−1.134	−67.8%	−0.842	−56.9%
	(0.633)	[−88.6%, −8.9%]	(0.790)	[−88.2%, 58.0%]
Risk aversion	2.556	*	2.404	*
	(1.426)	*	(1.685)	*
Risk aversion^2	−2.491	*	−2.554	*
	(1.146)	*	(1.389)	*
N	292		202	

Main entries are Cox model coefficients; SEs in parentheses; 90% CIs around hazard ratios in brackets. Positive coefficients indicate a greater likelihood of "cutting and running."

bias), risk aversion, and honor orientations.[57] The first model analyzes the impact of these dispositional factors on all subjects, regardless of their initial stance toward the intervention, while the second model only analyzes those subjects who initially wanted to intervene. In support of H3A, participants with more patient time preferences as measured by their long-term discounting factor (δ) displayed more resolve: an increase in δ from 0 to 1—corresponding with a change from completely discounting future costs, to treating future costs as equivalent to present costs—decreases the likelihood of withdrawal by 65.8%. The more participants value the future, the more likely they are to stick it out rather than cut and run. In line with H5A, honor orientations are also statistically significant, and produce a similar effect: moving from the lowest to highest level of honor orientations corresponds with a 67.8% decrease in the likelihood of cutting and running. Risk aversion displays a significant effect, but against H4A and in support of H4B, its impact on resolve is nonlinear: participants with a moderate degree of risk aversion ($\rho = 0.5$) are 92.5% more likely to withdraw than risk-neutral participants ($\rho = 0$), but past this point of risk aversion, participants actually become more resolute: a jump in risk aversion from ($\rho = 0.5$) to ($\rho = 1$) is associated with a 44.6% *decrease* in the likelihood of withdrawal, as illustrated by figure 3.6.[58] This bell-curve-like shape is consistent with the more formal discussion in appendix A.3 of what we would expect if participants in the sample see both fighting and backing down as risky, but the balance between these countervailing risk perceptions changes with levels of risk aversion. In particular, the concave shape of the quadratic effect—with relatively risk-averse and relatively risk-acceptant participants displaying more resolve than participants with moderate levels of risk aversion—is what we would expect if risk-averse participants were more likely to see backing down as risky than less risk-averse participants; sure enough, analyzing the manipulation check finds that perceived reputation costs increase with levels of risk aversion ($p < 0.01$), corroborating the interpretation above.

57 Importantly, none of the dispositional measures displayed significant interaction effects with the order manipulation, suggesting that we can think of these measures as reflecting stable dispositions rather than responses to the intervention scenario.

58 To test for nonlinearity without imposing a particular functional form, risk aversion was estimated with a penalized smoothing spline with the number of degrees of freedom determined by AIC scores; the resulting model appeared to be quadratic, and a series of likelihood ratio tests confirms that the spline fails to better fit the data than a simple quadratic ($\chi^2 = 0.198$, $p < 0.359$), and that the quadratic strongly outperforms a linear fit ($\chi^2 = 11.663$, $p < 0.001$). Penalized smoothing splines were also added to other predictors in the model to test for nonlinearity, but in all cases failed to improve model fit. As a robustness check, the results were also re-analyzed without the one risk-acceptant participant in the sample, but the quadratic shape of risk aversion remains.

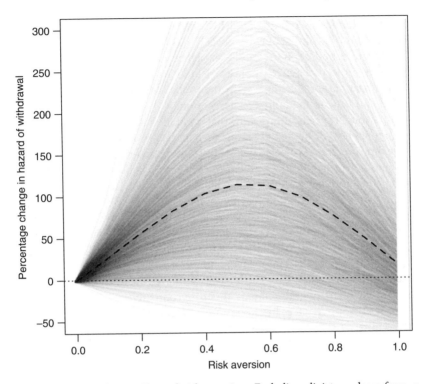

FIGURE 3.6. Quadratic effect of risk aversion. Each line dipicts a draw from a multivariate normal distribution (with N = 2500 simulations), given $\hat{\beta}$ and $\widehat{var}(x)$ from model 1 of table 3.3, such that darker lines indicate a more concentrated probability mass. The dashed black line represents the mean prediction. Note that the y-axis is scaled such that higher values indicate a greater probability of withdrawal (and thus, less resolve).

The second model replicates these analyses, but only for those subjects who initially advocated intervening. Reflecting the selection effect hypothesis suggested by the mediation analysis, reputation costs and honor orientations drop well out of the range of statistical significance, and as the right-hand panel of figure B.2 in appendix B.1 shows, the impact of risk aversion is much the same as in the full sample (participants with a moderate degree of risk aversion ($\rho = 0.5$) are 75.7% more likely to withdraw than those who are risk-neutral, and the extremely risk-averse ($\rho = 1$) are 51.0% less likely to withdraw than those with moderate risk aversion), but the impact of long-term discounting increases: a jump in δ from 0 to 1 decreases the likelihood of withdrawal by 75.8%. Similarly, present bias (β) acquires borderline statistical significance: an increase in β from 0 to 1—which is substantively equivalent to participants becoming more patient, as a quasi-hyperbolic discounting model is equivalent to an exponential discounting model when $\beta = 1$—is associated with a 28.2% decrease in the likelihood of withdrawal.

I therefore find support for the existence of dispositional determinants of resolve: time preferences, honor orientations, and risk attitudes all have substantively important impacts on the probability of participants choosing to "cut and run" in the military intervention, and in sensible directions. The multiple model specifications show that reputation and honor considerations weigh more heavily in the full sample than in the pro-intervention subsample, while time preferences display the opposite effect, increasing in both statistical and substantive significance in the pro-intervention subsample. One potential explanation for this pattern is that honor orientation, as the dispositional counterpart of the reputation cost manipulation, bolsters resolve as the reputation cost treatment does, by increasing initial support for the mission. Indeed, controlling for the situational manipulations and a host of demographic variables, participants high in honor orientation were 26.7% more likely to strongly support intervening than those low in honor orientation. Thus, it follows that when only those participants who initially supported the intervention are being studied, the effect of honor should dissipate compared to the full sample. In contrast, time preferences have no significant effect on the initial question of intervening, since the question of whether the United States should intervene lacks the clear temporal dynamics of the question of how long the United States should stay. The nonlinear impact of risk aversion is notable because political scientists often assume risk attitudes to display a more conventional linear effect.[59] When we refer to crisis bargaining as "competition in risk-taking," the tacit assumption is that resolve should be inversely related to risk aversion, presumably in a linear fashion.[60] However, just as war has many costs, it also has many risks: both withdrawing and persisting may be perceived as risky choices, and given the presence of these countervailing risk perceptions, we end up with the curvilinear relationship between risk and resolve illustrated in figure 3.6.

Although participants' scores on the urgency subscale had no significant relationship with the resolve they displayed in the intervention scenario, perseverance had an effect that is both statistically significant and substantively interesting. Table 3.4 replicates table 3.3, but controls for participants' perseverance scores rather than risk preferences—the extent to which participants reported being resolute in their daily lives, finishing tasks they start, seeing things through, tending not to give up, and so on.[61] As the coefficient plots illustrated in figure 3.7 show, although perseverance has no significant impact

59 E.g., Kam and Simas 2010; Eckles and Schaffner 2011.
60 Schelling 1966.
61 The model displays very similar results when both perseverance and risk preferences are included, although the statistical significance weakens.

TABLE 3.4. Dispositional and Situational Determinants of Resolve (2)

	ALL PARTICIPANTS		PRO-INTERVENTION PARTICIPANTS	
	B	HAZARD RATIO	B	HAZARD RATIO
Anticipated costs	−0.280	−24.4%	−0.407	−33.5%
	(0.133)	[−39.3%, −5.9%]	(0.165)	[−49.2%, −12.8%]
Reputation costs	−0.184	−16.8%	−0.170	−15.6%
	(0.133)	[−33.2%, 3.6%]	(0.168)	[−36.0%, 11.3%]
Casualties	0.269	30.9%	0.317	37.3%
	(0.132)	[5.4%, 62.7%]	(0.165)	[4.6%, 80.1%]
Order	−0.006	−0.6%	0.100	10.5%
	(0.132)	[−20.0%, 23.5%]	(0.167)	[−16.1%, 45.5%]
Discount factor (δ)	−0.822	−56.0%	−1.166	−68.8%
	(0.529)	[−81.6%, 5.0%]	(0.637)	[−89.1%, −11.2%]
Present bias (β)	−0.104	−9.9%	−0.324	−27.6%
	(0.168)	[−31.7%, 18.9%]	(0.215)	[−49.2%, 3.1%]
Honor orientations	−1.065	−65.5%	−0.523	−40.7%
	(0.634)	[−87.9%, −2.1%]	(0.782)	[−83.6%, 114.7%]
Perseverance	−0.501	−39.4%	−1.686	−81.5%
	(0.637)	[−78.7%, 72.7%]	(0.858)	[−95.5%, −24.1%]
N		292		202

Main entries are Cox model coefficients; SEs in parentheses; 90% CIs around hazard ratios in brackets. Positive coefficients indicate a greater likelihood of "cutting and running."

on the full sample, it has a highly significant effect among those participants who initially supported the intervention, associated with an 81.5% decrease in the probability of withdrawing at any given point in time. In other words, more persistent individuals also displayed greater persistence in the military intervention—but only if they approved of going in in the first place. The implications here are threefold. First, the fact that the perseverance measures were obtained in an apolitical domain means that we have evidence of resolve as a general phenomenon rather than a domain-specific one, similar to findings in social psychology.[62] Second, just as resolve was defined as a steadfastness of purpose, the results show that participants cannot be deemed to lack perseverance when they oppose US troops going in, and then are quick to recommend they withdraw. Instead, perseverance has an impact on the

62 E.g., Baumeister, Vohs, and Tice 2007.

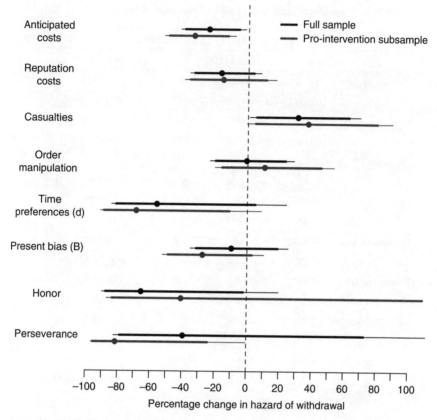

FIGURE 3.7. Coefficient plot of situational and dispositional correlates of resolve. Point estimates of percentage change in the hazard ratio incurred by moving from a 1-unit change in each variable, with 90% and 95% confidence intervals. Negative values indicate a decreased probability of withdrawal, and thus, greater resolve.

duration of the mission only among participants who supported going in in the first place. Third, the results suggest a qualification of H6, in that although trait self-control is positively related to resolve, resolve is related to one dimension of trait self-control in particular—perseverance—rather than the construct as a whole.

Finally, a number of supplementary analyses were conducted controlling for a range of demographic characteristics to probe the robustness of the findings; these results are reported in table B.2 in appendix B.1.

Interactionist Analyses

Thus far, the analyses have shown that resolve is both situational and dispositional: it is affected both by the human costs of war and the reputational costs of backing down, as well as time preferences, risk preferences, perseverance, and to a lesser extent, honor orientations. The question becomes whether, as hypothesized, these dispositional characteristics moderate the impact of situational features. The findings presented below offer support for some of the interactionist hypotheses, but not for others: in particular, against H5B, honor orientations have no significant interaction effects with the costs of backing down. However, in support of H3B and H4C, time preferences and risk aversion display a number of significant interaction effects with the situational manipulations.

Time Preferences

It was hypothesized in H3B that time preferences would moderate the impact of the costs of war on actors' resolve: since reputation costs are predominantly paid in the future while casualties are principally paid in the present, it was hypothesized that the longer participants' time preferences were—that is, the greater their long-term discounting (as measured by δ) and the lower their present bias (as measured by β), the more sensitive they would be to reputational costs, and the less sensitive they would be to casualties. Participants' long-term discounting, although highly statistically significant as main effects in all of the dispositional models estimated in tables 3.3 and 3.4, displayed no significant interaction effects with the situational manipulations. Long-term discounting, reputation costs, and the human costs of war thus appear to operate simultaneously, but in an additive rather than an interactive relationship.

In the dispositional analyses, present bias (β) only approached statistical significance in the pro-intervention subsample, suggesting that present bias may only affect resolve among the participants who wanted to intervene in the first place. However, it displays significant interaction effects with the casualty manipulation in both the full sample ($p < 0.08$) and pro-intervention subsample ($p < 0.09$), and in the direction predicted by the hypotheses: the more impatient participants are, the more the casualty manipulation makes them want to cut and run, while I fail to find evidence that relatively patient participants are significantly affected by the casualty manipulation. This interaction effect is illustrated in figure 3.8, which plots the combined coefficient of the treatment effect conditional on participants' degree of present bias, with 90% confidence intervals, and the dashed vertical line indicating the point on the x-axis at which we can no longer distinguish the effect of the casualty treatment from zero. Notably, present bias did not moderate the impact of the reputation cost manipulation in either the full or the pro-intervention subsample, suggesting that time preferences moderate the impact of the costs of fighting, but not the costs of backing down.

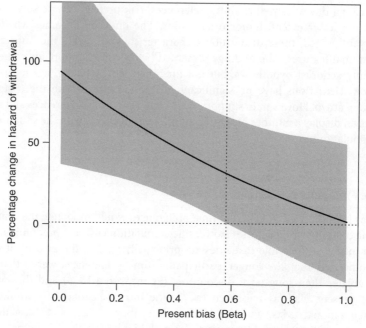

FIGURE 3.8. Impatience increases sensitivity to casualties. Individuals with high present bias (low β) are less resolute (more sensitive to casualties) than more patient individuals. The dark line indicates the point estimate of the combined coefficient for the conditional effect, while the shaded grey depicts 90% confidence bands calculated using draws from a multivariate normal.

Risk Preferences

As discussed above, the dispositional set of analyses showed that risk aversion was a highly significant predictor of participants' resolve, and that it displayed a quadratic effect, with resolve lowest among participants with moderate levels of risk aversion: as participants moved toward risk acceptance, they appeared to be more likely to want to stick things out, while as participants moved toward higher levels of risk aversion, they appeared to be more likely to maintain course. It was suggested that this curvilinear effect stemmed from the fact that both standing ground and cutting and running can be perceived as risky, and supplementary analysis suggested that we would see this particular curvilinear effect if participants who were relatively risk-averse were more likely to see backing down as risky than participants who were relatively risk-acceptant. As shown by figures 3.9 and 3.10, a series of interactions between risk aversion and the two main situational manipulations of

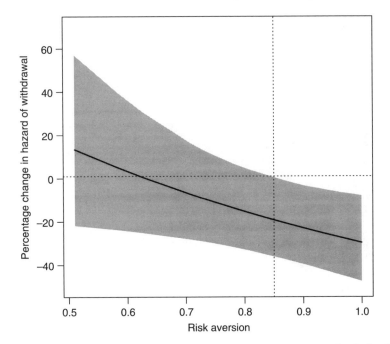

FIGURE 3.9. Risk aversion increases sensitivity to reputation costs. Individuals who are relatively risk-averse are more sensitive to reputation costs. The dark line indicates the point estimate of the combined coefficient for the conditional effect, while the shaded grey depicts 90% confidence bands calculated using draws from a multivariate normal.

interest—reputation costs, and casualties—offers support for this interpretation, and thus, support for H4C.

First, risk aversion has a statistically significant interaction with the reputation manipulation in both the full sample ($p < 0.08$) and the pro-intervention subsample ($p < 0.02$), illustrated in figure 3.9. The more risk-averse participants are, the more persuaded they are by the reputation cost manipulation to stay the course. In contrast, we fail to reject the null hypothesis that the reputation cost treatment does not affect resolve among those participants whose risk aversion scores are lower than $\rho = 0.84$, suggesting that as risk acceptance increases, so too does willingness to risk the reputational costs that arise from backing down in the face of aggression; indeed, as mentioned in the previous section, analyses on a manipulation check for perceived reputation costs finds a highly significant relationship ($p < 0.01$): risk-averse individuals are far more likely to view steep reputational costs for the United States withdrawing, and the effect (+0.56 on a scale of 1 to 5) is as large as that of party ID.

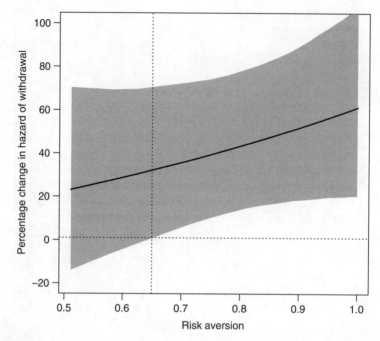

FIGURE 3.10. Risk aversion increases sensitivity to casualties. Individuals who are relatively risk-averse are more sensitive to casualties. The dark line indicates the point estimate of the combined coefficient for the conditional effect, while the shaded grey depicts 90% confidence bands calculated using draws from a multivariate normal.

Second, a similar interaction effect is evident with respect to casualties (although only in the pro-intervention subsample: $p < 0.04$) but in the opposite direction. As figure 3.10 shows, the more risk-averse participants are, the more sensitive they are to the casualty manipulation, while we fail to find that casualties significantly lower resolve for participants whose risk aversion scores are lower than $\rho = 0.66$. Thus, for both manipulations, risk aversion's moderating effect is associated with greater caution, but in opposite directions, reflecting the extent to which the casualty treatment pushes participants out of the intervention, while the reputation treatment pulls participants in.

CONCLUSION

In this chapter, I turned to experimental methods to test an interactionist theory of resolve in the context of public opinion about military interventions, pointing to specific dispositional characteristics to explain variations in sensitivity to particular situational features, and in so doing, seeking to disaggregate the cost of war.

The experimental results provide three main findings. First, although IR scholars have largely treated resolve as a situational feature, throughout the results the substantively largest effects are dispositional; the costs of war matter—when the costs of fighting decrease, or the reputational costs of backing down are rendered more salient, actors are more likely to stay the course—but not as much as characteristics of actors themselves. Actors who are relatively impatient, moderately risk-averse, low in honor orientations, and scoring low in the perseverance subscale of trait self-control are also more likely to be irresolute. Predicting when actors will be more or less resolved thus demands paying closer attention to actor-level attributes rather than just the environment they face. However, although the importance of these dispositional factors in predicting resolve is significant, it is also important not to make too much of the imbalance in the relative contribution of situational and dispositional factors in the experiment. As I note in chapters 4 and 5, it is possible that the situational treatments were relatively weak; after all, the situational factors in the experiments are hypothetical, while participants' dispositional characteristics are real. Second, and relatedly, although IR research on resolve has been largely disconnected from the growing body of research on willpower and self-control taking place outside political science, the major role played by the same sorts of dispositional factors that psychologists and behavioral economists routinely study when addressing similar questions in their own work suggests that resolve is not necessarily domain-specific, and that social scientists interested in resolve stand to gain by crossing disciplinary borders. Third, resolve is not only situational and dispositional, but also interactionist: impatient individuals are more sensitive to casualties than are their patient counterparts, while risk-averse individuals are more sensitive to both casualties and reputational costs.

These results raise a number of methodological issues for political scientists. First, this is the first experimental study in IR I am aware of that models both the selection into, and duration of, military operations. Although the international security literature suggests that war initiation and duration are two parts of the same continuous process, the extant experimental literature studies each step in isolation, modeling either the initial decision to use force or the question of whether troops should be withdrawn from a mission that has already begun.[63] Since the question of whether a mission is worth continuing is unlikely to be independent of the question of whether it was worth fighting in the first place, modeling both phases in one experimental design captures a selection process that IR scholars frequently discuss but rarely get to directly observe.[64] Indeed, the results of the mediation analysis

---

63 Filson and Werner 2002; Herrmann, Tetlock, and Visser 1999; Boettcher and Cobb 2006; Gartner 2008b.
64 Gelpi, Feaver, and Reifler 2009; Reed 2000; Sartori 2005.

suggest that if one only analyzed the duration of an ongoing intervention, the importance of reputation costs could potentially go unnoticed. Second, the fact that the dispositional sources of resolve were measured in domains unrelated to that of the intervention scenario allows for greater confidence that the results are speaking to underlying dispositions, and in the case of risk-attitudes, sidesteps the problem of selecting a meaningful reference point from which to judge what counts as risk acceptant or risk-averse.[65] The literature on risk and war frequently infers that leaders were in a state of risk acceptance based on their propensity to engage in conflict or make rash decisions, implying that actors should be more belligerent the more risk-acceptant they become.[66] My results, however, show that when risk attitudes are measured independently of the behavior they are being used to explain, the relationship is highly nonlinear, and that moderately risk-averse participants are likely to display less resolve than either their risk-acceptant or highly risk-averse counterparts.

Third, it is important to note that although much of the discussion of dispositional and situational theories of resolve have tended to treat rational choice theories of resolve as falling into the latter camp, there is nothing inherent about rational choice that prevents scholars from emphasizing dispositional features. Indeed, both time and risk preferences—the two dispositional variables that display significant interaction effects with the situational manipulations—are integral parts of many rational choice theories of conflict.[67] Largely for analytic reasons, however, much of the focus has been on actors' payoff structures, such that the discipline has been able to use "the costs of war" as shorthand for an actor's resolve. The above results, then, should less be seen as challenging game theoretic models of war as reminding us that dispositional features merit at least as much attention as situational ones.

The findings also suggest a number of important implications for policy-makers. The conventional image of the American public is of an audience highly sensitive to the costs of war.[68] The results here not only support arguments that different segments of the public respond to casualties in rather different ways, but remind us that war has costs beyond casualties, and that at

---

65 O'Neill 2001.

66 The fact that much of the risk literature in IR derives its predictions from prospect theory complicates the comparison, since prospect theory treats risk attitudes as situational (a function of whether participants are in the domain of gains or the domain of losses) rather than as an actor's disposition (Kahneman and Tversky, 2000). I return to this point in chapter 6.

67 However, although repeated games model an actor's δ parameter, because they tend to assume exponential discounting functions, they do not incorporate a β parameter, when the results here suggest that β, rather than δ, displays the significant interaction effect with the cost of fighting.

68 E.g., Mueller 1971.

least in the intervention scenario studied here, participants were also sensitive to the reputational costs of backing down.[69] A White House interested in drumming up support for a military intervention it believes to be in the national interest may thus find widespread sympathy for reputational justifications for the intervention, although the results of the mediation analyses show that these arguments will be most effective in raising the *initial* level of support for the mission, rather than prolonging support once the intervention has already begun. The significant effect of the anticipated cost manipulation in rendering participants more patient with a prolonged intervention suggests that one of the Bush administration's mistakes in selling the war in Iraq to the American people was in underselling the amount of force the mission would require, as displayed by Vice President Cheney's infamous suggestion in March 2003 that the United States would "be greeted as liberators" by the Iraqi people. When President Bush posed with a "Mission Accomplished" banner on the deck of the USS *Abraham Lincoln* while announcing the end of major combat operations in Iraq in May 2003, he may have engendered a short-term boost in public support, but in the long run it made the turmoil that followed seem costlier in the public's eyes than it otherwise would have been. More generally, it points to an important intertemporal tradeoff policymakers face with regard to the domestic politics of foreign affairs: decision-makers have an incentive to downplay the costs of war in order to bring the public on board in the short term, but this can backfire in the long run.

The experiment also lays the groundwork for the empirical investigations that follow in subsequent chapters. Although the use of undergraduate student samples is useful in gaining leverage over psychological processes, it poses potential challenges when trying to generalize the findings to the population at large.[70] Thus, chapter 4 follows up with the results from an embedded survey experiment administered to a nationally representative sample of adult Americans. Chapter 5 then takes the book in a very different direction. Since the purpose of the experimental analyses is to investigate the origins of resolve among ordinary members of the public, the experiments deliberately sidestep the elites versus masses question that, as noted in chapter 2, would manifest itself for both the situational and dispositional variables if studied with observational data. Chapter 5 tackles this level of analysis question head-on.

69 Gelpi, Feaver, and Reifler 2009.
70 See the discussion in Druckman and Kam 2011.

CHAPTER 4.

Experimental Microfoundations

for Resolve: II

The previous chapter offered a valuable first look at the situational, dispositional, and interactionist determinants of resolve at the individual-level. Because of random assignment, the laboratory experiment offers *causal validity* for the situational variables.[1] Inasmuch as the panel experimental structure corresponds to my posited theory about how information about different types of costs of war is moderated by dispositional characteristics in shaping how much resolve actors display, offers *construct validity* as well, testing the phenomenon under investigation.[2] However, there are at least two reasons why one would want to supplement these findings. The first concerns representativeness. The lab experiment is based on a convenience sample, and if I am interested in resolve in the context of American public opinion about military interventions, one might wish to run the experiment on a sample more representative of the American population as a whole.[3] The student sample was younger, more educated, and disproportionately male compared with the national population; given changing societal expectations of war, and generational effects, for example, older respondents might respond to the casualty treatments in very different ways.[4] The second concerns replication. Oftentimes in survey research the conclusions we draw are influenced by the instrumentation we employ.[5] If I find similar results despite using slightly

---

1 As noted in chapter 3, the dispositional variables are not causally identified, since they are measured rather than manipulated.

2 Shadish, Cook, and Campbell 2002.

3 As Morton and Williams (2010, 265) argue, although political scientists frequently refer to representativeness as an *external validity* issue, external validity involves generalizing findings *beyond* the target population, such that one should think of the task here as addressing *internal validity* instead. See also McDermott 2011a. For limitations on the inferences one can draw from a student sample, see Mintz, Redd, and Vedlitz 2006; for a contrary view, see Druckman and Kam 2011. Of course, even a national representative American sample will not be representative of humanity as a whole—see Henrich, Heine, and Norenzayan 2010.

4 Smith 2005; Schuman 1992.

5 Presser and Schuman 1981.

different operationalizations of some of the key concepts, it offers greater faith in the findings, and further confidence in my understanding of the microfoundations of resolve. Thus, in the summer of 2012, an experiment was embedded in a national survey of American adults, further investigating individual-level determinants of resolve in the context of public opinion about military interventions.

Like the lab experiment in the previous chapter, the survey experiment manipulates situational features of a hypothetical military intervention, and measures a number of dispositional traits using instruments from elsewhere in the behavioral sciences. The experimental results in this modified setup suggest that the costs of fighting have relatively little effect on the amount of resolve participants display, while the reputational costs of backing down play a relatively significant one. Once again, however, the largest effects are dispositional: time and risk preferences are significantly associated with resolve, as is a behavioral measure of trait self-control. The results also show how dispositional traits can be used to disaggregate the costs of war: risk preferences moderate the impact of reputation costs, honor considerations magnify the effects of anticipated costs, and a behavioral trait self-control measure diminishes the impact of casualties. The discussion that follows first presents the study materials and experimental design, before presenting the experimental results and broader conclusions.

MATERIALS

In the summer of 2012, an online survey experiment was administered to a national probability sample of 1,078 adults, replicating parts of the lab experiment and modifying others, while also seeking to generalize the findings to the public writ large.[6] As a national probability sample, the survey participants look like the American public as a whole, and compared to the lab experiment, are older (on average, survey participants were 49.7 years old, compared to 21.3 in the lab experiment), less educated (38.2% received a high school education or less), and feature slightly lower proportions of whites (75.0% of survey respondents, compared to 77.4% of lab experiment participants), and males (49.6% of respondents identified as male in the survey experiment, compared to 60.1% in the lab experiment).

---

6 The study was fielded by GfK Custom Research (formerly known as Knowledge Networks), thanks to support from the National Science Foundation's Time Sharing Experiments for the Social Sciences initiative. 2,051 panelists were randomly drawn from the GfK panel; 1,263 responded to the invitation, 1,078 of whom qualified for the survey, producing a field stage completion rate of 61.5% and a qualification rate of 85.4%. The recruitment rate was 15.2% and the profile rate was 65.4%, for a cumulative response rate of 6.1%. The survey was administered online, and the median survey length was 7 minutes.

Intervention Scenario

Similar to the laboratory experiment, the survey consisted of three parts: a factorial experiment manipulating the human and reputational costs of a hypothetical military intervention; a dispositional questionnaire measuring time preferences, risk preferences, and honor orientations; and a concluding questionnaire measuring general demographic characteristics. As was the case with the lab experiment, participants randomly received either the dispositional questionnaire, or the intervention scenario, first, such that the experimental design is once again a 2 (ex ante human costs: low or high)× 2 (ex post human costs: low or high) × 2 (reputation costs: implicit or salient) × 2 (order manipulation: scenario 1st or 2nd) fully crossed factorial experimental design. The structure of the experiment is summarized in figure 4.1.

In the intervention scenario, as before, participants are presented with a hypothetical military intervention on behalf of an ally under siege, and asked whether they think the United States should send troops; regardless of participants' responses, the intervention proceeds, and participants are then asked about the possibility of withdrawing troops. The intervention scenario differs from its predecessor in two ways. First is in the measurement of the dependent variable. Whereas the laboratory experiment employed a panel structure, in which participants received information about the intervention once a "year" and were presented with the option of withdrawing after each briefing (for up to seven years), cost constraints mean that the survey experiment relies on a simple one-shot measurement technique, in which, after the first year, participants are simply asked how long they think troops should remain involved in the mission.

Second, compared to the lab experiment, the survey experiment features a higher dosage of reputation costs. In the lab experiment results, the reputation cost treatment raised resolve by around 18%, but the treatment effect was only significant at around the $p < 0.11$ level. Thus, in the survey experiment I raise the reputational costs of backing down by rendering them more salient. In the new formulation of the reputation cost treatment, an ally the participant cares a lot about publicly warns that if the United States does not stand up to aggression now, our allies will doubt our likelihood to stand firm in the future. The element of publicity is important here, since reputation costs require an audience capable of monitoring behavior, so the treatment should bolster the reputational consequences of backing down.[7] As before, participants are presented with a manipulation check asking about potential damage to the US reputation, but in the survey experiment, the manipulation check immediately follows the pre-intervention scenario, rather than after the intervention

---

7 Schelling 1960, 29–30; Fearon 1994.

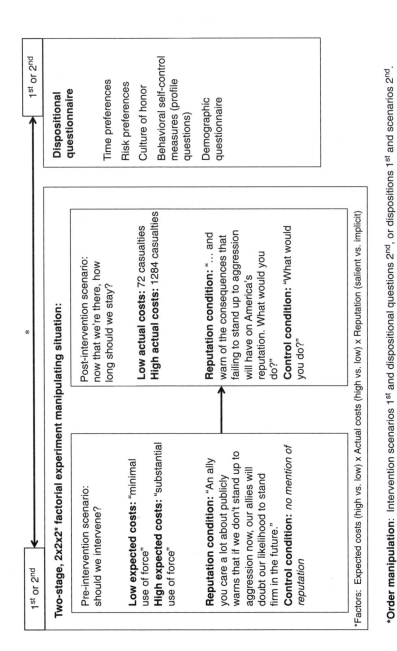

Two-stage, 2x2x2* factorial experiment manipulating situation:

1st or 2nd

Pre-intervention scenario: should we intervene?

Low expected costs: "minimal use of force"

High expected costs: "substantial use of force"

Reputation condition: "An ally you care a lot about publicly warns that if we don't stand up to aggression now, our allies will doubt our likelihood to stand firm in the future."

Control condition: *no mention of reputation*

Post-intervention scenario: now that we're there, how long should we stay?

Low actual costs: 72 casualties
High actual costs: 1284 casualties

Reputation condition: " … and warn of the consequences that failing to stand up to aggression will have on America's reputation. What would you do?"

Control condition: "What would you do?"

1st or 2nd

Dispositional questionnaire

Time preferences

Risk preferences

Culture of honor

Behavioral self-control measures (profile questions)

Demographic questionnaire

*Factors: Expected costs (high vs. low) x Actual costs (high vs. low) x Reputation (salient vs. implicit)

Order manipulation: Intervention scenarios 1st and dispositional questions 2nd, or dispositions 1st and scenarios 2nd.

FIGURE 4.1. Survey experiment structure.

has concluded, and thus refers to the reputational consequences of the United States *not intervening,* rather than the reputational consequences of the United States withdrawing from the intervention.[8]

Dispositional Questionnaire

The dispositional questionnaire of the survey experiment measures a number of individual characteristics, which partially overlap with those featured in the lab experiment, but also include a number of revisions and extensions. Time preferences are once again measured by participants' long-term discounting (δ) parameter, which corresponds to how much the participant values the future relative to the present.[9]

Risk attitudes are measured in three different ways. First, as in the lab experiment, lottery tasks are used to estimate participants' degree of risk aversion (as measured by ρ, the relative risk premium); higher values of ρ indicate higher degrees of risk aversion. As before, ρ is estimated by averaging across the risk premia calculated from the responses participants provide to the two lottery questions.[10] However, prospect theory notes that risk attitudes vary depending on whether individuals are in a domain of gains or losses.[11] Whereas the previous lottery questions measured risk aversion, or risk attitudes in the domain of gains, a second set of lottery questions was used to measure loss aversion, or risk attitudes in the domain of losses. Participants were presented with two lottery questions in which they had a (i) 50% chance to lose $25 but a 50% chance to win $X, or (ii) a 50% chance to lose $100 but a 50% chance to win $X, and asked how much X would have to be to make them want to buy a ticket. Loss aversion (θ) parameters were estimated for each question by dividing each $X by 2, and then averaging across the two θs to produce an average measure of loss aversion.[12]

Relatedly, in the psychological literature, risk attitudes are frequently studied as a general dispositional orientation measured with self-report items.[13]

---

8 Of course, as Berinsky, Margolis, and Sances (2014, 744) note, researchers face considerable tradeoffs with the use and positioning of manipulation checks: administering the manipulation check after the measure of the dependent variable, as in the previous chapter, may affect responses to the manipulation check, while administering the manipulation check before the measure of the dependent variable, as in this chapter, can effectively treat participants twice and thus affect responses to the dependent variable. The approach I adopt here is to use both methods, and triangulate across multiple studies.

9 As in the lab experiment, δ is estimated using the values respondents provide to the two matching questions (with a one-year and ten-year delay, respectively): $\delta = (\frac{X_1}{X_{10}})^{1/9}$.

10 Thus: $R_1 = \frac{X}{100} - 1$, $R_{10} = (\frac{X}{100})^{0.1} - 1$.

11 Kahneman and Tversky 2000; for applications to International Relations, see Boettcher 1995; Berejekian 1997; Levy 1997; McDermott 1998.

12 More formally, $\theta = \frac{\frac{X_1}{2} + \frac{X_2}{2}}{2}$. See Wang, Rieger, and Hens 2016.

13 E.g., MacCrimmon, Wehrung, and Stanbury 1986; Kowert and Hermann 1997; Kam and Simas 2010.

Accordingly, a dispositional measure of risk orientation ("In general, people often have to take risks when making financial, career, or other life decisions. Overall, how would you place yourself on the following scale?", with a seven-point scale with options ranging from "Extremely comfortable taking risks" to "Extremely uncomfortable taking risks") was borrowed from Ehrlich and Maestas, reverse-coded such that higher values indicate greater degrees of risk acceptance.[14]

Third are honor orientations. The survey experimentation measures honor orientation differently from the lab experiment, employing items from a scale developed in cross-cultural psychology by Osterman and Brown.[15] Although the honor measure in the lab experiment was indeed associated with higher levels of resolve, its reliability was relatively low, and failed to significantly moderate the impact of the costs of war. The new three-item scale ("A real man never leaves a score unsettled," "A real man is seen as tough in the eyes of his peers," and "A real man should be willing to defend himself if he's insulted in public") taps into similar constructs as the previous measure in its emphasis on standing up for oneself, reputations for toughness, and so on, but also has the advantage of being developed and validated outside the realm of this study.[16]

Fourth is trait self-control. The lab experiment included the perseverance and urgency subscales of Whiteside and Lynam's trait self-control scale—which measures trait self-control using cognitive self-report items (e.g., "Unfinished tasks bother me"), but social scientists often measure self-control using either behavioral tasks or behavioral report items.[17] Thus, I also include items measuring the frequency with which participants report exercising, "avoiding food high in fat and/or calories," and smoking—since self-control is understood to be associated with success in pursuing these first two activities, and successful avoidance of the latter.[18] Although these items are deliberately far removed from the world of international politics, if the predictors of political will are indeed related to the predictors of personal will, one might imagine that resolve will "spill over," in that participants who score high in the behavioral trait self-control measures will also display greater persistence in the military intervention scenario. A behavioral self-control score was thus

---

14 Ehrlich and Maestas 2010.

15 Osterman and Brown 2011.

16 The Osterman and Brown honor measure employs more gendered language than the honor scale in the previous chapter, but the reliability of the scale does not significantly vary based on the gender of the participant ($\alpha = 0.78$ for males, $\alpha = 0.75$ for females), and when interaction terms between honor and gender are added to table 4.2, they are never significant ($p < 0.405$ and $p < 0.303$, for models 1 and 2, respectively).

17 Whiteside and Lynam 2001; Baumeister, Vohs, and Tice 2007; Galliot and Baumeister 2007; Tittle, Ward, and Grasmick 2003.

18 Perri, Richards, and Schultheis 1977; Sniehotta, Scholz, and Schwarzer 2005; Papies, Stroebe, and Aarts 2008.

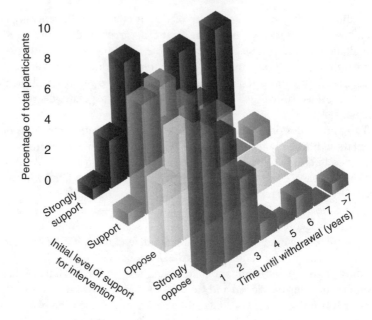

FIGURE 4.2. Initial attitudes toward the mission predict the duration of support.

created using factor scoring, with scores scaled to range from 0 to 1 for ease of interpretability.[19]

RESULTS

As in the previous chapter, the results are discussed in a number of phases, first examining the dependent variable of interest; second, analyzing the impact of the situational treatments; third, incorporating the dispositional characteristics into the analysis, and fourth, testing the interactionist hypotheses.

How Resolved Were the Participants?

Figure 4.2 shows that, as was the case in the lab experiment, there was considerable variation in how much resolve participants displayed. On the whole,

---

19 Principal axis factoring with oblimin rotation suggests the three items load onto a single factor; because inspection of the factor matrix suggests that smoking habits load less strongly than exercise and dietary habits, regression factor scoring was used to create a measure of behavioral self-control, rescaling the factor scores to range from 0 to 1 to facilitate a straightforward comparison with the other regression coefficients.

the national sample was less inclined to intervene than the lab experiment participants, as only 52% of survey respondents supported the United States sending troops, compared to nearly 70% support in the student sample. Given that the survey experiment featured a steeper reputation cost manipulation—which likely boosted participants' initial degree of support for intervening compared to the setup in the lab experiment—the fact that support for the intervention actually dropped by 18 percentage points shows just how much less interventionist the national sample was compared to the student sample. This intervention gap also likely reflects the drop in education of the sample as well; an analysis of 28 years of polling data from the American National Election Studies, for example, has found that highly educated Americans are around 17% less likely to endorse isolationism than their least educated counterparts.[20] These differences aside, however, the general pattern in the distribution of responses is the same. First, participants display a clear variation in resolve, with 16.4% of respondents wanting to pull out troops after the first year, and 17.8% of respondents calling for troops to remain six years or longer. Second, like in the lab experiment, the amount of time participants wanted troops to stay depended on whether they wanted them to be there in the first place ($\chi^2 = 331.834$, $p < 0.000$): 41% of respondents who strongly opposed the United States sending troops advocated for withdrawal after just one year, compared to only 2.5% of the respondents who strongly supported the intervention. Thus, as was the case in the lab experiment, I find little evidence of sunk cost logic driving attitudes toward the intervention, as participants who initially opposed intervening were unlikely to change their mind once troops were actually deployed; "sunk cost frames" may indeed mobilize support in traditional public opinion experiments, but the two-stage within-subject setup of the experimental designs employed here show little indication that participants who were initially opposed to the mission become more supportive once boots hit the ground.[21]

Situational treatments

Table 4.1 and figure 4.3 depict the treatment effects for the four treatments (anticipated costs, reputation costs, casualties, and the order manipulation).[22]

---

20 Kertzer 2013. An ordered probit regression model confirms that participants without a college education are less likely to want to intervene; there are no significant differences in desire to intervene with respect to age.

21 Boettcher and Cobb 2009.

22 Because the dependent variable was measured with an open-ended question, there are extreme outliers in the right tail of the distribution of the dependent variable; 90% of respondents advocate withdrawal after six years, but 2.5% of respondents were still willing to let the intervention persist after 11 years (and one respondent suggested 1,001 years). Following an inspection of the score residuals, I dropped these 27 outliers from the analysis, since residual-based tests of the proportional hazard assumption are sensitive to other forms of model misspecification (Keele, 2010).

TABLE 4.1. Treatment Effects Based on Initial Decision to Invade

	ALL PARTICIPANTS		GO IN		STAY OUT	
	β	HAZARD RATIO	β	HAZARD RATIO	β	HAZARD RATIO
Anticipated costs	−0.079	−7.6%	−0.130	−12.2%	−0.145	−13.5%
	(0.062)	[−16.6%, 2.3%]	(0.087)	[−23.9%, 1.2%]	(0.092)	[−25.6%, 0.6%]
Reputation costs	−0.130	−12.2%	−0.131	−12.3%	−0.224	−20.0%
	(0.062)	[−20.8%, −2.8%]	(0.086)	[−23.9%, 1.1%]	(0.091)	[−31.2%, −7.1%]
Casualties	−0.071	−6.8%	−0.090	−8.6%	−0.066	−6.4%
	(0.062)	[−15.9%, 3.2%]	(0.087)	[−20.8%, 5.4%]	(0.092)	[−19.5%, 8.8%]
Order	−0.069	−6.7%	−0.013	−1.3%	−0.205	−18.5%
	(0.062)	[−15.8%, 3.3%]	(0.087)	[−14.4%, 13.8%]	(0.091)	[−29.8%, −5.3%]
N		1039		540		498

Main entries are Cox model coefficients; SEs in parentheses; 90% CIs around hazard ratios in brackets. Positive coefficients indicate a greater likelihood of "cutting and running."

As was the case in the lab experiment results, the first model of the table depicts the treatment effects for the full sample; the second model looks at the treatment effects for those respondents who initially supported the intervention, while the final model displays the treatment effects solely among those respondents who never supported intervening in the first place.[23] These same effects are visually depicted in figure 4.3, which also plots the percentage change in the hazard of withdrawal from the full sample with population weights added.[24]

23 Thus, table 4.1 differs from its counterpart in the previous chapter in that the larger sample size allows us to compare the determinants of resolve between the pro- and anti-intervention subsamples, rather than just comparing the pro-intervention subsample with the full sample.

24 The population weights post-stratify on a variety of demographic characteristics to adjust for non-response and over- or under-sampling of particular groups, such that the data speak to the population of American adults as a whole. As Mutz (2011, ch. 7) notes, practices differ in the survey experiment literature as to the handling of population weights; scholars who approach survey experiments from a survey tradition tend to employ weights regularly because they enable the researcher to extrapolate to the population as a whole, whereas those who approach survey experiments from the experimental tradition tend to be less enamored with weights, since the estimates of the sample treatment effects are already unbiased without them. Here, I restrict the use of weights to one of the models presented in figure 4.3, showing how the treatment effects change when weights are added, but do not include weights in any of the dispositional analyses that follow, for two reasons. First, many of the dispositional variables are likely to be correlated with the demographic characteristics used to predict selection into the sample—and thus, weighting can cause us to underestimate the effect of the dispositional variables (Brehm, 1993, 119). Second, and relatedly, the subsequent analyses also control for many of the demographic characteristics

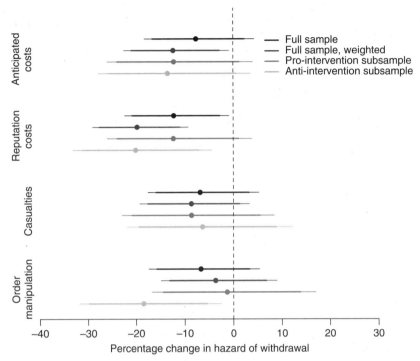

FIGURE 4.3. Coefficient plot of situational determinants of resolve. Point estimates of percentage change in the hazard ratio incurred by each of the four experimental manipulations, with 90% and 95% confidence intervals. Negative values indicate a decreased probability of withdrawal, and thus, greater resolve.

The treatment effects plotted in figure 4.3 suggest three important points. First, the reputation cost treatment displays the same resolve-bolstering effect as in the lab experiment, but at a higher degree of statistical significance: participants who received the reputation cost treatment were 12.2% less likely to withdraw at any given time (a rate that grows to 19.7% once the population weights are added, and 20.0% among the anti-intervention subsample). The only model where the reputation cost treatment failed to achieve statistical significance was among the pro-intervention subsample, although the non-parametric mediation analyses reported in figure 4.4 find that the impact of reputation costs is not mediated by the initial decision to intervene. In the lab experiment, the reputation cost treatment displayed a "selection effect," in that participants took reputation costs into account when deciding whether to intervene initially, which thereby had no effect once the intervention took

that are themselves being used to generate the weights. For more on the difficulties that arise with the use of survey weights in a multivariate context, see Winship and Radbill 1994; Gelman 2007.

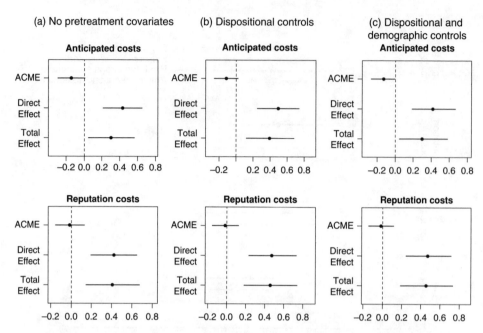

FIGURE 4.4. Nonparametric mediation effects: survey experiment. Mediation effects plotted using the mediation package from Tingley et al. (2014). All models are estimated using 1500 simulations with 90% quasi-Bayesian confidence intervals. Anticipated costs bolster resolve by making participants more patient after the intervention takes place, while reputation costs bolster resolve by making participants more likely to approve of the mission in the first place. Because the software cannot currently conduct sensitivity analyses on duration data, I run three iterations of the analyses: first, on a model with no pretreatment covariates; second, controlling for the dispositional factors of interest; and third, controlling for both the dispositional variables and demographic characteristics. I thus cannot eliminate the possibility that the results are an artifact of pretreatment confounders, but I can test how robust they are to the inclusion of a large number of pretreatment controls.

place. The shaming ally reputation cost treatment in the survey experiment, however, operates through a different causal pathway: the warnings from the ally did not affect the initial decision to intervene, but did make participants more likely to want to stay once the intervention took place.[25]

---

25 As was the case in the previous chapter, the nonparametric mediation analyses were conducted with mediation version 4.0 (Tingley et al., 2014), which estimates the survival model using parametric Weibull models rather than the semiparametric Cox models employed in the main analyses. The pattern of results is similar to those presented in table 4.1, although the casualty and anticipated cost treatments more closely approach statistical significance in a Weibull model than in a Cox model.

Second, while the costs of backing down play a larger role in the survey experiment results than in the lab experiment, the costs of fighting play a somewhat different one. Casualties appear to raise rather than lower participants' resolve, although the treatment fails to achieve statistical significance across all four models. In supplementary analyses in appendix B.2, I explore why the resolve participants displayed in the survey experiment was unaffected by casualties, showing that this pattern is not due to a failed manipulation, noncompliance, a higher dosage reputation treatment, or characteristics of the sample, but rather, is likely related to the one-shot design of the survey experiment compared to its lab counterpart, which increases participants' uncertainty about future trends.

Although the anticipated cost treatment is statistically significant once population weights are added (participants warned in advance of high expected costs of fighting were 12.3% less likely to withdraw at any given point in time), it otherwise fails to achieve statistical significance. Many of these rejections of the null hypothesis are relatively narrow, but it is notable that the uncertainty around the treatment effect would be greater in the survey experiment than its lab experiment counterpart, given that the sample size is three times bigger in the former than the latter. Results from nonparametric mediation analyses depicted in figure 4.4 offer one potential explanation for the weak effect of the anticipated cost treatment: in this modified scenario, higher expected costs of fighting make participants both *less* likely to want to intervene and *more* patient once the intervention takes place, an "inconsistent mediation effect" in which the average causal mediation effect (ACME) and direct effect point in opposite directions, thereby suppressing the magnitude of the total effect.[26] This two-pronged pattern of results—in which higher costs of fighting make Americans both less likely to want to intervene and more patient when they do—is also of theoretical interest because it offers micro-level evidence consistent with two prominent strands of the sprawling literature on democracies in war: institutional variants of democratic peace theory that suggest that the large size of winning coalitions in democratic regimes means that democracies are sensitive to the costs of fighting and thus should be less likely to initiate costly conflict, and a parallel literature that finds democracies are more likely to win the wars they do fight.[27] These experimental results cannot adjudicate debates about "democratic distinctiveness" because of the absence of a non-democratic reference category, but given the extent to which much of the democracy in war literature developed without the use of micro-level evidence, this corroboration is noteworthy.

Finally, although the order manipulation achieves statistical significance within the anti-intervention subsample (in which participants who completed

---

26 MacKinnon, Krull, and Lockwood 2000.
27 Bueno de Mesquita et al. 1999; Lake 1992; Reiter and Stam 2002.

the dispositional questionnaire prior to the intervention scenario were 18.5% less likely to withdraw at any given point in time), the manipulation on the whole remains nonsignificant, suggesting that completing the dispositional questionnaire does not significantly affect participants' responses to the intervention scenario, increasing my confidence in the results.[28]

Dispositional and Demographic Results

Thus far, I have shown that participants respond similarly to the costs of backing down across the two experiments, but not the costs of fighting, likely due to the divergent setups of the experiments, rather than characteristics of the samples. What about the dispositional characteristics?

One of the striking results from the lab experiment was that the substantive magnitude of the dispositional variables was larger than those of the situational ones; although it is possible that this asymmetry in effect size was due to the lab experiment employing better dispositional measures than situational manipulations, the results nonetheless suggested that strictly situational accounts of resolve that focus solely on the nature of the environment that actors face miss an important part of the story. Given the greater uncertainty present in the survey experiment, one might imagine that the dispositional variables should play an even greater role here.[29]

The first model in table 4.2 presents the results of the experimental treatments alongside time preferences, risk aversion, loss aversion, honor orientations, and behavioral self-control. The second model adds a series of demographic controls (party identification, gender, race, education, and income). The substantive effects are also presented with 90% and 95% confidence intervals in figure 4.5.

The treatment effects in model (1) are largely similar to those estimated in table 4.1—reputation costs are the only significant treatment effect, bolstering participants' resolve by 14.4%, while anticipated costs narrowly escape statistical significance, raising resolve by 9.9%. More interesting, though, are the dispositional effects. A change in time preferences from $\delta = 0$ to $\delta = 1$ is associated with a 40.9% increase in resolve; participants with longer shadows of the future in general thus also display more resolve in the intervention scenario. As in the lab experiment, risk aversion has a significant quadratic effect,

---

28 Similarly, a series of Wilcoxon rank-sum tests suggest that responses to the dispositional questionnaire are not significantly affected by the intervention scenario. Of the items in the dispositional battery, only the responses to the lottery measures of risk aversion significantly change as a result of the order manipulation ($W = 144027.5$, $p < 0.033$), and the difference is both substantively small (the medians of each category differ by only 0.008), and disappears when the results are analyzed using a t-test rather than a rank-sum test ($t = -0.1095$, $p < 0.9128$).

29 Kertzer and McGraw 2012.

TABLE 4.2. Dispositional and Situational Determinants of Resolve

	(1)		(2)	
	β	HAZARD RATIO	β	HAZARD RATIO
Anticipated costs	−0.104	−9.9%	−0.090	−8.6%
	(0.065)	[−19.1%, 0.3%]	(0.066)	[−18.0%, 1.8%]
Reputation costs	−0.155	−14.4%	−0.155	−14.4%
	(0.064)	[−23.0%, −4.8%]	(0.065)	[−23.0%, −4.7%]
Casualties	−0.083	−8.0%	−0.057	−5.5%
	(0.065)	[−17.2%, 2.3%]	(0.065)	[−15.1%, 5.1%]
Order	−0.050	−4.8%	−0.035	−3.4%
	(0.064)	[−14.4%, 5.8%]	(0.065)	[−13.2%, 7.4%]
Discount factor (δ)	−0.525	−40.9%	−0.564	−43.1%
	(0.201)	[−57.5%, −17.7%]	(0.201)	[−59.1%, −20.8%]
Risk aversion	−0.474	*	−0.507	*
	(0.327)	*	(0.312)	*
Risk aversion^2	0.549	*	0.591	*
	(0.300)	*	(0.296)	*
Honor orientations	0.020	2.0%	−0.008	−0.8%
	(0.139)	[−18.8%, 28.1%]	(0.141)	[−21.4%, 25.2%]
Loss aversion (logged)	−0.011	−1.1%	−0.013	−1.3%
	(0.007)	[−2.2%, 0.1%]	(0.007)	[−2.5%, −0.2%]
Behavioral self-control	−0.251	−22.2%	−0.227	−20.3%
	(0.147)	[−39.0%, −0.9%]	(0.152)	[−38.0%, 2.3%]
Party ID			−0.479	−38.1%
			(0.096)	[−47.1%, −27.5%]
Male			−0.169	−15.6%
			(0.066)	[−24.3%, −5.8%]
White			−0.002	−0.2%
			(0.081)	[−12.6%, 14.0%]

TABLE 4.2. (*Continued*)

	(1)		(2)	
	β	HAZARD RATIO	β	HAZARD RATIO
Education			−0.086	−8.3%
			(0.110)	[−23.5%, 10.60%]
Income			0.262	30.0%
			(0.150)	[1.5%, 66.4%]
Age			−0.003	−0.3%
			(0.002)	[−0.7%, 0.0%]
N	973		973	

Main entries are Cox model coefficients; SEs in parentheses, 90% CIs around hazard ratios in brackets. Positive coefficients indicate a greater likelihood of "cutting and running."

plotted in figure 4.6.[30] In the lab experiment, where participants were moved both by the costs of fighting and by the costs of backing down, I found that both highly risk-averse participants and relatively risk-acceptant participants displayed a greater level of resolve. Consistent with the relatively modest role of the cost of fighting in the survey experiment, I find participants are swayed primarily by the risks of backing down: highly risk-averse participants are more likely to stay in than relatively risk-acceptant ones, who are more willing to cut and run. I once again find a curvilinear relationship between risk and resolve, but with a different shape. The impact of loss aversion, although narrowly escaping statistical significance until demographic factors are controlled for in model 2, is suggestive: an increase from the minimum to the maximum level of loss aversion is associated with a 25.9% increase in resolve. Thus, for both risk attitudes in the domain of gains, and risk attitudes in the domain of losses, I find evidence that increased acceptance of risk and loss is associated with an increased willingness to cut and run. In this sense, I once again find no support for the idea that resolve simply increases with risk acceptance, offering further evidence that both pressing on in a quagmire and backing down in the face of reputational consequences can be perceived as risky by different observers.

The behavioral self-control score also offers some provocative findings: moving from the minimum to the maximum score is associated with a 22.2% increase in participants' resolve in the military intervention scenario:

30 Likelihood ratio tests indicate the quadratic fits better than a linear one ($p < 0.02$), and fails to find evidence that it is outperformed by a nonparametric smoothing spline ($p < 0.24$).

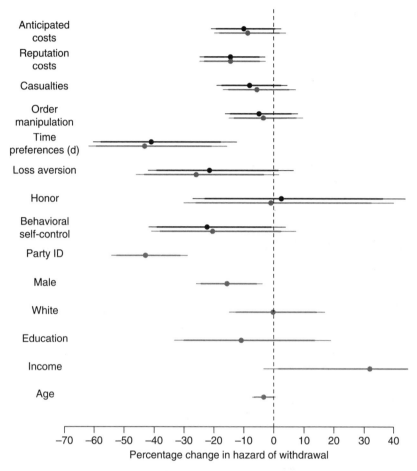

FIGURE 4.5. Coefficient plot of situational and dispositional correlates of resolve (1). Point estimates of percentage change in the hazard ratio (with 90% and 95% confidence intervals) incurred by moving from a 1-unit change in each variable—which corresponds to a change from the minimum to the maximum value, except for δ, for which a one-unit change from 0 to 1 is substantively meaningful, and age, where the hazard ratio depicts a 10-year increase. Negative values indicate a decreased probability of withdrawal, and thus, greater resolve. Darker estimates from model 1 in table 4.2; lighter estimates from model 2.

those participants who display self-control in their daily lives as measured by their dietary, exercise, and smoking habits also displayed more resolve in the military intervention. Since these habits are also likely to correlate with socioeconomic characteristics, it is important to note that the effect of behavioral self-control largely persists even when demographic characteristics

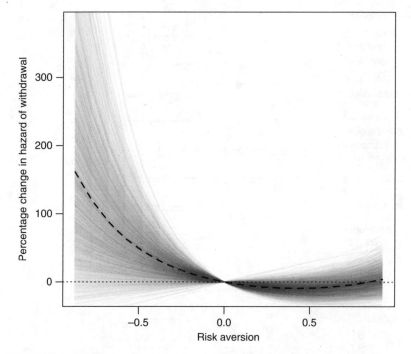

FIGURE 4.6. Quadratic effect of risk aversion. Each line depicts a draw from a multivariate normal distribution (with N=2500 simulations), given $\widehat{\beta}$ and $\widehat{var}(x)$ from model 1 of table 4.2, such that darker lines indicate a more concentrated probability mass. The dashed black line represents the mean prediction. Note that the y-axis is scaled such that higher values indicate a greater probability of withdrawal, and thus, less resolve.

like education, income, gender, and race are controlled for, thus offering further evidence that personal and political will are related to one another. These findings are also consistent with other psychological research on the extent to which behavioral or somatic characteristics are associated with political judgments more generally: for example, men with greater upper body strength are not just more likely to fight in interpersonal conflicts, but are also more likely to advocate the use of force in international conflicts—a pattern of results that would be puzzling from a classic rational choice approach, but that is highly sensible from an evolutionary psychological one.[31]

Just as important as the factors that achieve statistical significance are those that fail to do so. In the lab experiment in chapter 3, honor orientation

31 Sell, Tooby, and Cosmides 2009. They are also more likely to favor redistributive policies consistent with their economic interests—see Petersen et al. 2013.

was positively associated with participants' resolve, but with the alternative measure of honor used in the survey experiment, I find that honor almost uniformly lacks statistical significance.[32] As figure 4.7 illustrates, honor orientation appears to affect resolve conditionally: among those participants who were initially opposed to the intervention, honor boosts resolve by 34.0%— these respondents perhaps subscribing to what Gelpi, Feaver, and Reifler call the "Pottery Barn" rule of military interventions ("you broke it, you fix it")— while it has no significant relationship in the pro-intervention subsample.[33] Given the modest nature of these results, however, one should be less confident about honor's role in the experimental findings than those of time and risk preferences.[34] Similarly, although the general risk orientation measure is borderline significant as a predictor of resolve in a simple model with just the four treatment variables, it quickly loses significance once other predictors are added, and is omitted from the models presented in table 4.2.

Finally, the second model in table 4.2 includes a series of demographic controls, whose inclusion substantively changes neither the treatment effects nor those of the dispositional variables, but which are nonetheless interesting in their own right. Party identification powerfully predicts resolve: strong Republicans are 38.1% less likely to withdraw at any point in time than strong Democrats, even when controlling for a host of dispositional factors. Men display 15.6% more resolve than women, and older participants are more resolved than younger ones: a ten-year increase in age is associated with a 3.4% decrease in the probability of withdrawal. Interestingly, income has the only statistically significant positive coefficient: moving from the lowest to the highest income grouping in the sample is associated with a 30.0% decrease in resolve. This effect is notable because of its substantively large magnitude and also because previous research has found that higher income is positively associated with support for more active or extroverted foreign policies, whereas I find the opposite here.[35] Since the effect's statistical significance weakens when party ID is not also being controlled for, however, one should be wary of drawing too many conclusions from it.

32 Supplementary analyses indicate that, unlike its lab experiment counterpart, the measure of honor employed here is uncorrelated with party identification ($r = -0.01$) and liberal-conservative political ideology ($r = 0.001$), suggesting it is tapping into a somewhat different construct, though interestingly, the correlation between honor and conservative ideology is stronger and negative ($r = -0.133$) among participants in the American South than in other regions of the country ($r = 0.077$).

33 Gelpi, Feaver, and Reifler 2009.

34 In contrast, the coefficient estimate in the pro-intervention subsample is positive, but not statistically significant ($p < 0.22$).

35 Wittkopf 1990, 39; Kertzer 2013. To be sure, an active or extroverted foreign policy is not completely identical to a resolved one, but if one thinks about resolve in the context of Klingberg's (1952) mood theory, the idea of "losing heart" in a military intervention is conceptually similar to a descent toward foreign policy introversion.

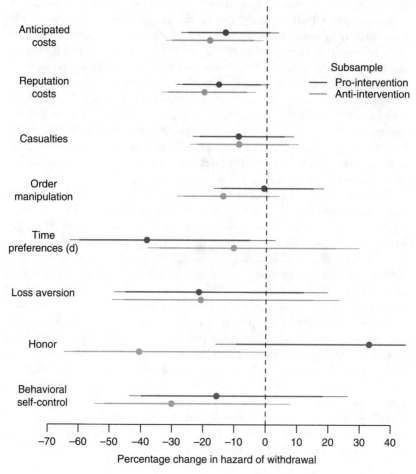

FIGURE 4.7. Coefficient plot of situational and dispositional correlates of resolve (2). Point estimates of percentage change in the hazard ratio incurred by moving from a one-unit change in each variable (with 90% and 95% confidence intervals)— which corresponds to a change from the minimum to the maximum value, except for δ, for which a one-unit change from 0 to 1 is substantively meaningful. Negative values indicate a decreased probability of withdrawal, and thus, greater resolve. Darker estimates are from a model estimated on those participants who initially supported the intervention; lighter estimates are from a model estimated on those participants who initially opposed the United States going in.

Interactionist Results

Lastly, I find a number of theoretically meaningful interaction effects, one of which reproduces a pattern present in the lab experiment, and two of which take advantage of the additional instrumentation in the survey experiment to illustrate new dynamics. In the lab experiment, time preferences were found to moderate the human costs of fighting, and risk preferences moderated both the human costs of fighting and the reputational costs of backing down. Given that the casualty treatment lacked significant effects due to the one-shot format of the survey experiment, it should not be surprising that the interaction effects with casualties in the lab experiment do not materialize in the survey experiment. However, I once again find a significant risk x reputation cost interaction, ($p < 0.06$) this time using the measure of dispositional risk orientation. As the combined coefficient and 95% confidence bands in figure 4.8 illustrate, participants who self-described as relatively risk-averse were more sensitive to the reputational costs of backing down: it is only for those participants who rate themselves at the midpoint of the risk orientation scale or below that I can be 95% confident that the reputation cost manipulation boosts resolve, offering further evidence that backing down in the face of reputational consequences can be seen as risky.

Just as in the lab experiment, honor orientation fails to moderate the impact of reputation costs; in the survey experiment, however, I find that honor moderates the impact of the anticipated cost treatment ($p < 0.01$). As shown in figure 4.9, the higher participants scored in honor orientation, the more being warned in advance that the expected costs of fighting would be high bolstered resolve; among those participants with honor scores lower than 0.4, I fail to find evidence with 95% certainty that the anticipated cost treatment bolsters their resolve whatsoever.

Finally, the behavioral self-control factor scores did not significantly moderate any of the treatments in theoretically meaningful ways,[36] but one of the items used to generate the behavioral self-control score—participants' smoking habits—displays a significant interaction effect with the casualty manipulation ($p < 0.01$). As illustrated in figure 4.10, those participants who reported smoking every day displayed far less resolve in response to the casualty treatment than those participants who display the self-control to either limit their smoking or avoid smoking altogether. The fact that the interaction is produced with smoking behavior but not the behavioral self-control score means that the findings should be treated as tentative. Yet, given the relative absence of treatment heterogeneity with the casualty treatment in

---

36 A significant interaction effect exists between behavioral self-control and the anticipated cost treatment, but the sign of the interaction term is unexpectedly positive.

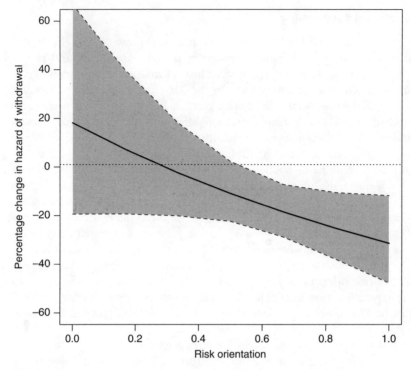

FIGURE 4.8. Risk orientation increases sensitivity to casualties. Participants who self-described as relatively risk-averse (higher values on the x-axis) were more sensitive to the reputational costs of backing down, similar to the risk aversion × reputation interaction effect detected in the lab experiment. The dark line indicates the point estimate of the combined coefficient for the conditional effect, while the shaded grey depicts 95% confidence bands calculated using draws from a multivariate normal.

the supplementary analyses in appendix B.2, the effect shown here is striking, particularly because it grows rather than shrinks in statistical significance once socioeconomic demographic controls are present.

CONCLUSION

In this chapter, I took another look at individual-level microfoundations for resolve, presenting the results from an online survey experiment that, like the lab experiment presented in the previous chapter, manipulated situational features of a hypothetical military intervention and measured a series of dispositional characteristics borrowed from social psychology and behavioral economics. The survey experiment borrowed much of its instrumentation

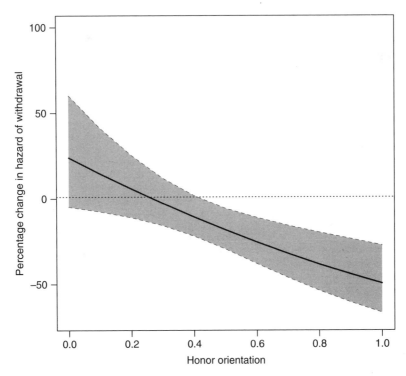

FIGURE 4.9. Honor orientation increases the impact of anticipated costs. Participants high in honor orientation became more stalwart in response to the expected costs of fighting. The dark line indicates the point estimate of the combined coefficient for the conditional effect, while the shaded grey depicts 95% confidence bands calculated using draws from a multivariate normal.

from its lab experiment predecessor, but also included a number of modifications, including a slightly different reputation cost treatment, a dispositional risk orientation measure, a different honor orientation measure, a behavioral self-control measure, and a different measure of the dependent variable. In this sense, the survey experiment offers a chance to explore two different types of generalizability: examining whether effects hold up among a less homogenous sample, and observing how relationships among the variables change when one employs slightly different measures of the key concepts.

Because the two studies differ in multiple ways, a direct pairwise comparison is somewhat complicated, but table 4.3 highlights the key results. First, the human costs of fighting play a smaller role in the survey experiment than the lab experiment—likely due to the former's one-shot structure, whereas the reputational costs of backing down play a larger role in the survey experiment, stemming in part from the public shaming reputation treatment. These findings make clear that participants are swayed by both the costs of fighting

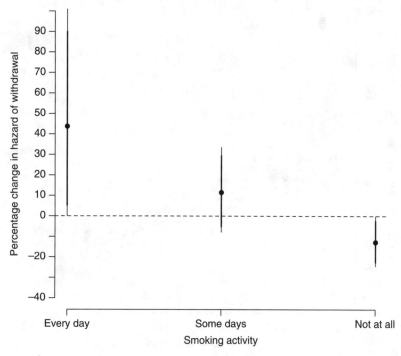

FIGURE 4.10. Sensitivity to casualties increases with smoking behavior. Even when controlling for a range of demographic characteristics, participants who smoke every day were far more sensitive to the casualty manipulation than those who smoked some days, or not at all. Effects depicted with 90% and 95% confidence intervals calculated using draws from a multivariate normal.

and the costs of backing down, although how much participants respond to each treatment is partially a function of how the particular manipulations are designed. In this sense, the findings should make us wary of attempts to draw inferences about the relative importance of different types of costs of war from experimental studies, since so much depends on the dosage of the experimental treatments. That said, given how central casualties are to our theories of public opinion about the use of force, the fact that it plays a weak role in the survey experiment—its treatment effect is about such half the size of the reputation cost treatment—is notable, which I return to in the discussion in Chapter 6.[37] The relative weakness of the effects of the costs of fighting in the experiment is also noteworthy because one concern sometimes expressed about laboratory and survey experiments is that, although these research designs are good at

37 Mueller 1971; Gartner 1997.

TABLE 4.3. Comparison of Results across Experimental Formats

	EFFECT ON RESOLVE DISPLAYED	
VARIABLE	LAB EXPERIMENT	SURVEY EXPERIMENT
Situational variables		
Anticipated costs	**+18.3%**	+7.6%
Reputation costs	+17.5%	**+12.2%**
Casualties	**−31.9%**	+ 6.8%
Dispositional variables		
Discount rate (δ)	**+65.8%**	**+40.9%**
Risk aversion (ρ)	**Quadratic**	**Quadratic**
Honor orientation	**+67.8%**	−2.5%
Trait / behavioral self-control	**+81.5%***	**+22.2%**
Interaction effects		
Time preferences × casualties	✓	
Risk preferences × casualties	✓	
Risk preferences × reputation costs	✓	✓
Honor × anticipated costs		✓
Smoking habits × casualties		✓

Effects significant at $\alpha = 0.1$ bolded. Situational effects in the lab experiment from table 3.1, dispositional effects from tables 3.3 and 3.4. Situational effects in the survey experiment from table 4.1, and dispositional effects from table 4.2. *Conditional on support for the mission.

capturing the effects of stimuli, individuals in a more naturalistic setting may never be exposed to the treatment in the first place, either because they are relatively inattentive to politics, or, in the context of this experiment, because of the latitude that leaders have in "diluting" the costs—whether through reframing the situation, or by reallocating the costs through the use of private military contractors, whose casualties tend to receive less public attention.[38] If we are uncertain about the effects of the costs of fighting on resolve in a clean experimental context, one might imagine that in a public opinion context in daily life, these effects are likely to be smaller, rather than larger.

38 Gaines, Kuklinski, and Quirk 2007; Barabas and Jerit 2010; Levendusky and Horowitz 2012; Avant and Sigelman 2010.

Second, compared to the situational treatments, I find more consistently significant results with the dispositional variables. In both the lab and survey experiments, participants with longer shadows of the future displayed more resolve in the intervention scenario; similarly, I find across both experiments that risk has a quadratic relationship with resolve, although the shapes of the curves vary across the two studies. In the lab experiment, where participants seem concerned about both the costs of fighting and the costs of backing down, I find that relatively risk-acceptant and highly risk-averse participants are more likely to display resolve; in the survey experiment, on the other hand, where participants seem to be concerned mostly about the reputational costs of backing down, I see that highly risk-acceptant participants are far less resolved than highly risk-averse ones. In modeling both risk aversion and loss aversion, the survey experiment also shows us that risk attitudes predict resolve in both the domain of gains and the domain of losses. Honor's effects are weaker in the survey experiment than the lab experiment, and self-control plays a large role in both, albeit in slightly different ways. In the lab experiment, where perseverance is used as a measure of trait self-control, self-control has a significant conditional effect upon resolve, in that perseverance strongly predicts how much resolve participants displayed among those participants who initially approved of the intervention. In the survey experiment, where self-control was measured through behavioral report items, I find that self-control has a significant unconditional effect on resolve.

Third, only one of the interaction effects from the lab experiment manifests itself in the survey experiment—risk attitudes moderating the effects of reputation costs—and even then, the interaction in the survey experiment holds with the dispositional measure of risk attitudes rather than the lottery measure used in the lab. In this sense, the survey experiment offers further evidence of dispositional characteristics moderating the impact of situational features, and finds evidence for some theoretically meaningful interaction effects not detected in the lab, but also shows the extent to which our findings are often shaped by the instrumentation we employ—an important question worthy of future research, particularly given the diversity of measures employed in the behavioral decision-making literature.

More generally, these experiments suggest that I should think of resolve in military interventions as a function of both stakes and traits—situational variables and dispositional ones.[39] The advantage of the experimental methods employed in these two chapters is that they allow us to cleanly manipulate situational features of military interventions and directly measure dispositional characteristics of participants, while letting us study resolve as a *dependent variable* by observing how changes in these situational and dispositional

---

39 AIC scores confirm that despite the reduction in parsimony, the dispositional and demographic models presented in table 4.2 are superior to the purely situational model from table 4.1.

variables affect how much resolve participants display. If I were solely interested in explaining resolve in the context of public opinion about military interventions, I might end my investigation here, having found that political will is more than just a figure of speech, and that many of the same factors that behavioral economists and social psychologists use to predict willpower in our daily lives also moderate the impact of the cost of war, and explain variation in the public's resolve.

However, the experimental results presented over these past two chapters also present us with another possibility. As I argued in chapter 1, one of the chief reasons why political scientists have had such a hard time studying resolve is because we have often been forced to tautologically infer it from the effects we try to use it to explain—the argument, for example, that the United States lost in Vietnam because Washington was less resolved than Hanoi, so to win in war, actors need to be more resolved. The reason both pundits and scholars have been so quick to reach for this tautology is because resolve in the real world is not directly observable, so we have been forced to grapple with resolve's effects by inferring resolve based on what we can observe. Thus, the next chapter alters the focus of the analyses. Having used the controlled experimental environment to study resolve's *causes*, I then build on these individual-level microfoundations to study resolve's *consequences*. Doing so allows me to move beyond the experiments' focus on resolve in the context of public opinion to look at resolve with respect to elite decision-makers, and also to test whether resolve has the effects on victory we often claim it does—using measures of resolve derived independently of the outcomes I am using it to explain.

CHAPTER 5.

Resolve in Great Power Military Interventions, 1946–2003

The previous two chapters employed lab and survey experiments to study resolve as a *dependent variable*: by manipulating situational features of military interventions and measuring dispositional characteristics of participants in a controlled experimental setting, I am able to make fairly fine-grained distinctions about the associations between dispositional traits and resolve, and draw causal inferences about the relationship between different types of costs of war and resolve. In this chapter, I shift the focus of the analysis, turning to a different question: can resolve explain conflict outcomes? Many of our theories of international politics assume that resolve matters, but have struggled with the question of how to test its effects. In this chapter, I propose a new way of studying resolve, treating the experimental results as theoretical microfoundations for a Boolean statistical model of great power military interventions in the post–World War II era. Having already established evidence for situational and dispositional determinants of resolve with experimental data at the individual-level, I operationalize these same variables with observational data at the country- and leader-levels to construct composite situational and dispositional measures of the resolve of the great powers in military interventions from 1946 to 2003. The results of my analyses suggest that the situational and dispositional determinants of resolve also positively predict the probability of victory, but at different levels of analysis: conflict outcomes appear to be a function of situational determinants of resolve at the country-level, but dispositional determinants of resolve at the leader-level. In this sense, the large-N analyses both support and enrich the results from the preceding two chapters.

Since the type of analysis I perform here is somewhat unusual, I begin with a discussion of the importance of microfoundations in IR theory, before suggesting that in treating resolve as the function of two latent pathways, Boolean statistics offers a potential solution for a problem that has bedeviled international security scholars for some time: how to test the effects of resolve on conflict outcomes without resorting to inferring resolve from the same outcomes it is being used to explain. I then discuss the construction of the dataset and present results from a series of conjunctural Boolean statistical models in which resolve is modeled as a latent variable, a function of both situational *and* dispositional sources. The major results are fourfold. First, I find relatively weak support for the costs of fighting, but more support for the costs of backing down, in terms of both intrinsic stakes and extrinsic reputation costs. Second, I find fairly strong support for leader-level dispositional variables, reinforcing the importance of incorporating attributes of decision-makers into our models of international politics. Third, I find different patterns of results for the situational variables than I do for the dispositional ones: the situational variables that seem to exert the greatest impact are at the country-level, whereas the dispositional variables that demonstrate the most important effects are at the leader-level. Interestingly, evaluating the results as a whole, the most statistically and substantively significant effects are always dispositional, repeating a pattern from the previous two chapters. Finally, the results that suggest that resolve matters: when situational and dispositional sources of resolve are relatively high, so too is the probability of victory.

MICROFOUNDATIONS AND LATENT VARIABLES

Especially once we move away from grand theories toward the "middle-range theories" that dominate the study of international security, a significant proportion of our accounts of international politics rely on *microfoundations—* individual-level "cogs and wheels" posited to act as mechanisms linking cause and effect.[1] There has been a considerable push for microfoundations in the social sciences in the past several decades, especially by "strong" methodological individualists, for whom theories that fail to specify individual-level mechanisms are "lazy and frictionless."[2] Although macro-theorists warn that the search for microfoundations can sometimes be problematic—some causal mechanisms exist only at the macro-level (e.g., supply and demand in economics), while multiple realizability means that many macro-level outcomes

1 Merton 1968; Elster 1989, 3. The term "microfoundation" tends to be used in a wide variety of ways. Achen (2002, 437), for example, uses microfoundations to refer to "a formal model of the behavior of the political actors under study" to guide our use of particular statistical estimators, a definition that need not imply that the mechanism connecting the *explanans* and *explanandum* exists at a particular level of analysis. Instead, I use microfoundations here to refer to an analytic strategy where one explains outcomes at the aggregate level via dynamics at the individual level, consistent with how it is used in economics ("to refer to schemes which can be broadly regarded as attempting to reduce macroeconomics to microeconomics") (Nelson, 1984, 575), and sociology, which justifies the search for microfoundations by suggesting that "social phenomena...are in principle explicable in ways that only involve individuals—their properties, their goals, their beliefs, and their actions" (Elster, 1985, 5). Since the key logic behind the search for microfoundations is to identify the micro-level processes that explain how the phenomena of interest occur, microfoundations are often associated with causal mechanisms, but as Gerring (2007) points out, not all causal mechanisms implicate microfoundations.

2 Elster 1982, 453. On methodological individualism more generally, see Udehn 2001.

cannot simply be reduced to micro-level causes—it is worth noting that even structural and institutionalist theories frequently rely on micro-level assumptions.[3] Rational choice theory, for example, is often used to showcase the power of institutions, but also relies upon assumptions about the content and shape of actors' utility functions.[4] Realist theories of international politics are often viewed as structural theories par excellence, but also rely on particular sets of assumptions about the behavioral consequences of uncertainty and fear, for example, which are only felt by individuals.[5] In this respect, one need not be a strong methodological individualist to argue that microfoundations matter: complexity theory, for example, is built upon the premise that one cannot explain systems solely by reference to the behavior of each of its components—and thus, the rejection of methodological individualism—yet complexity scholars in IR frequently use agent-based modeling to show how the emergent properties of systems depend on the parameters of agents' preferences and behaviors.[6]

An equivalent problem exists with the study of international security, then, is not that our theories lack microfoundations, but rather, that (i) we often fail to specify what these microfoundations are—democratic peace theory, for example, is "an empirical regularity in search of a theory," and (ii) we rarely test them.[7] Our theories of the effects of coercive bombing on military outcomes, for example, rely on a set of widely held micro-level assumptions about how individual civilians respond to coercion, but whose validity is seldom directly tested; the same could be said of audience cost theory and its vision of a monolithic public responding in unison like the chorus in a Greek tragedy.[8]

An equivalent problem exists with the study of resolve. As I suggested in chapter 1, although resolve is one of our central explanatory variables in the study of international security, we have very little sense of where resolve itself actually comes from: we lack microfoundations. This absence of microfoundations is problematic because of theoretical underspecification, and empirical misspecification: we not only use the concept inconsistently, but we also have difficulty measuring it with observational data, such that we either tend to relegate our favorite independent variable to the error term, or

3 Schelling 1978, 13; Wendt 1999, 150–157. For applications of multiple realizability to IR, see Most and Starr 1984; Thompson 2003. The study of power laws and scale invariance (Richardson, 1948; Cederman, 2003) offers another good example of multiple realizability, and theories reliant on macro- rather than microfoundations.

4 Simon 1985.

5 Waltz 1979; Kertzer and McGraw 2012. On collective emotions in IR, see Hall 2015.

6 Udehn 2001, 336; Hedström and Ylikoski 2010, 59-60; Miller and Page 2007, 3; Axelrod 1997; Cederman 1997.

7 Hopf 1998, 191.

8 Pape 1996; Lyall, Blair, and Imai 2013; Kertzer and Brutger 2015.

infer it tautologically from the outcomes we are using it to explain, thereby turning it into a catchall residual category used ex post to explain otherwise unexplainable conflict outcomes. "They succeeded because they were resilient" is only a compelling causal explanation if resilience is not simply being measured by success.

The chief difficulty political scientists have faced in studying resolve with observational data is that resolve in the real world is not directly observable: it is a *latent variable*.[9] I am not the first person to think of resolve in this manner;[10] if resolve was directly observable, actors would not need to go through the trouble of signaling their resolve, and there would be no incentives for actors to misrepresent it in the first place.[11] In this sense, it is precisely because resolve cannot be directly observed that it plays such an important role in rationalist theories of war. Yet the very unobservable quality that gives resolve such explanatory power in our theories also renders us powerless when we try to test them empirically. Although political scientists regularly study latent variables—personality orientations, regime type, ideal point models of state preferences, and so on, the idea being that when a construct is not directly observable, we can model it based on its observable implications—resolve is different in that establishing its implications is our goal in the first place.[12] When it comes to regime type, we cannot directly measure how democratic a state is, so instead we measure how free and fair its elections are and treat that as an indirect measure of democracy, since the competitiveness of the executive recruitment process is logically constitutive of what democracy means. The relationship between resolve and military victory, on the other hand, is precisely the empirical question we are trying to explore.[13]

This challenge means that there are at least seven different empirical strategies one can adopt facing the prospect of studying resolve with observational data, based on how one answers five different questions, all of which are depicted by the decision tree in figure 5.1. First, one can simply decide to avoid studying resolve altogether (option A in figure 5.1). Merom takes this route, eschewing "motivational theories" of asymmetric conflict outcomes for being too tautological.[14] Rummel similarly notes that for many scholars "will

9 Bollen 1989; Wansbeek and Meijer 2000.

10 For related arguments, see Clark and Regan 2003, who use a split population model to study opportunity (although not willingness) as an unobserved latent process (see also Xiang 2010) and Renshon and Spirling 2015, who model "effectiveness" as a latent variable using Bradley-Terry models. Each of these works shows that the study of unobservable factors poses important implications for how we test our theories, although both opportunity and effectiveness are closer to capabilities than resolve, per se. For a rather different take on latents in international security, see Rummel 1975a, ch. 9–10.

11 Fearon 1995.

12 Mondak 2010; Treier and Jackman 2008; Voeten 2000.

13 Rosen 1972; Maoz 1983.

14 Merom 2003.

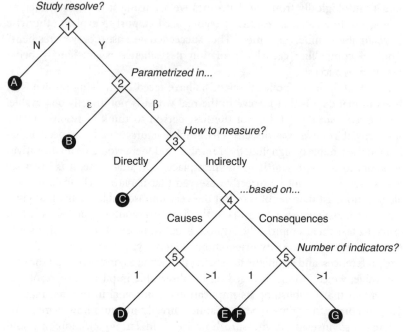

FIGURE 5.1. Seven ways to study resolve with observational data.

is a metaphysical concept, not quite respectable for 'scientific' interest."[15] If one decides to study resolve despite these challenges, the second question becomes how to parameterize it. Noting that resolve is "notoriously difficult to measure," Sartori pursues option B in figure 5.1, treating resolve as part of the correlated error terms in a unified model of conflict onset and escalation.[16] Although a clever way to handle selection effects in a theoretically informed manner, relegating resolve to the error term is less helpful in testing its effects, per se—unless we are comfortable assuming that the correlation in the disturbances is due specifically to resolve rather than other omitted variables, hence why Reed is careful to note that resolve is one of a number of potential culprits.[17]

Thus, rather than treating resolve as the error term, a number of works in IR choose to study resolve as a variable in its own right. The third question is therefore whether to measure resolve directly (option C in figure 5.1) or indirectly (options D–G). If resolve is indeed a latent variable, however, then it cannot directly be observed, precluding the possibility of option C. Thus, most

15 Rummel 1975b, 275–276.
16 Sartori 2005, 91.
17 Reed 2000, 90.

of the existing empirical studies of war adopt option F, inferring resolve based on one of its posited consequences: Rosen and Mueller infer resolve based on the number of casualties each side is willing to suffer, Maoz proxies resolve by the highest level of severity of the dispute, Langlois and Langlois infer resolve based on the percentage of the country's population in the military, Cline measures resolve via military expenditures, while Sullivan treats the magnitude of ground troop deployments as an indicator of "commitment."[18] Lewin's study of resilience in war is illustrative in this regard: his six cases of a lack of "national resilience" are military defeats, while his three cases of national resilience are military victories: resilience might indeed lead to victory, but we would not be able to tell.[19]

Inferring resolve based on its consequences raises three potential concerns. First, as argued above, some of these measures of resolve veer dangerously close to tautology and assume axiomatically what should be proven empirically (is it the case that more resolved states suffer more casualties?). Second, as Gelpi and Griesdorf note, there is an important distinction "between demonstrations of resolve and the underlying preferences that may give rise to such demonstrations": escalatory policies may indeed signal resolve, but the resolve these demonstrations are intended to signal may not be sincere—hence why states with low levels of resolve can often prevail in crisis bargaining through successful bluffing.[20] If I want to study the effects of resolve—rather than the effects of signals of resolve—I need to adopt an empirical strategy that avoids conflating the two. Third, if resolve is indeed a latent variable—the motivation for measuring it indirectly in the first place—a single indicator will do a poor job of characterizing the underlying construct.

METHODS

Thus, I employ option E from figure 5.1: rather than inferring resolve based on its consequences, I study it based on its causes, using the results from the lab and survey experiments as individual-level microfoundations for resolve, which I then gather measures of at the country- and leader-levels with observational data. The advantage of this approach is threefold: by focusing on resolve's causes rather than consequences I steer clear of tautology; by turning to microfoundations I offer a more satisfying theoretical explanation, and by employing more than just a single indicator, I can increase my confidence in the results. As was the case in the experiments, I focus on resolve in the domain of military interventions, this time focusing on factors shaping the great powers' resolve in their military interventions in the postwar

---

18 Rosen 1972; Mueller 1980; Maoz 1983; Langlois and Langlois 2009; Cline 1975; Sullivan 2007.
19 Lewin 2012.
20 Gelpi and Griesdorf 2001, 638; Powell 1987.

era. I focus on resolve in this realm for both theoretical and substantive reasons. First, it parallels the micro-level analyses, which also focus on military interventions; whereas the experiments use hypothetical interventions to study the determinants of resolve at the individual level, the large-N analyses employ real interventions and examine multiple levels of analysis. Second, if resolve is defined as akin to persistence or sticktoitiveness—a steadfastness of purpose that maintains a policy over time despite contrary inclinations or temptations to back down—international interventions are a perfect forum in which to explore resolve at work, as leaders and their publics frequently intervene only to seek an exit option as the pressure mounts.[21]

The theory I am interested in testing is an interactionist one: that resolve is a function of both situational stakes, *and* dispositional traits, such that actor-level variables moderate the impact of situational ones. Accordingly, for the analyses that follow, I employ a Boolean logit model, in which the situational determinants of resolve are grouped into one path, and the dispositional determinants of resolve into another. In this setup, resolve is represented by two sets of fitted values: a situational resolve score, and a dispositional resolve score.[22] I can thus interpret the results in two stages: first, examining the individual effects of each variable on conflict outcomes to see if the situational and dispositional factors that predict resolve in the experimental analyses also predict the probability of victory in great power military interventions, and then analyzing the product of these two sets of factors to model resolve in an interactionist fashion.

The attraction of this Boolean approach is that it allows me to tractably employ an empirical model that corresponds to my interactionist theory.[23] If the situational and dispositional factors that predict resolve in the experimental analyses similarly predict the probability of victory in great power military interventions, and the product of these two sets of logit-transformed fitted values shows that the probability of victory increases with both situational and dispositional sources of resolve, I can increase my confidence that resolve actually predicts conflict outcomes, using measures of resolve derived independently of the outcomes I am using them to explain.

---

21 Sullivan 2008; Polsky 2010; Koch and Sullivan 2010.

22 More formally, I employ a conjunctural Boolean logit model (Braumoeller, 2003), in which λ refers to the inverse logit function $\frac{1}{1+e^{-x}}$, the situational determinants of resolve are grouped into one "path" (represented by the vector B_S) and the dispositional determinants of resolve into another (depicted by B_D), with $P_{i,t}$ as the probability that the great power achieves its objectives (and thus, declares victory) at time t: $Pr(y_{i,t} = 1|\alpha, \beta, x_{i,t}) = \lambda(\alpha_1 + B_S x_{i,t}) * \lambda(\alpha_2 + B_D x_{i,t})$. Resolve is thus represented by two sets of fitted values: a situational resolve score ($\alpha_1 + B_S x_{i,t}$), and a dispositional resolve score ($\alpha_2 + B_D x_{i,t}$).

23 As Braumoeller and Carson 2011 show, although it is possible to represent the Boolean logit functional form as a single logit with multiplicative interaction terms, doing so would require a sufficient number of interaction terms so as to render the model extremely difficult to interpret.

Before discussing the data, I should note four methodological considerations. First, although IR scholars have been incorporating experimental methods into their research designs with increasing frequency over the past decade, the role they play here represents a departure from the manner in which experiments are often used in the field, even when employed as part of other multi-method frameworks.[24] Experiments in IR are traditionally used for *assumption validation*, in which scholars have a theory that relies on particular assumptions and they turn to experiments to test their assumptions validity. In some cases, the assumptions being tested directly concern the mass public, while in others the reference units are at the state-level, and experimenters "scale up" the results.[25] In my case, the experiments serve a different purpose: *theory-building*. In addition to providing valuable information about the dynamics of resolve in public opinion, the experiments also establish empirical regularities to generate new theories which can be tested in a large-N context, at different levels of analysis.[26]

As a result, although my empirical strategy is a "two-stage" strategy in the sense that I first employ experiments and then build on their insights with observational data, it is not a formal two-stage structural model where estimates from one stage are directly plugged into a second.[27] Thus, I do not weight the impact of different sources of resolve based on the experimental results, for example. I avoid this strategy because, as I noted in chapter 4, a simple comparison between the lab and survey experiment results shows that operationalizing treatments differently produces effects of different magnitude: treatments with stronger "dosages" produce stronger effects. Although the experimental results show that the dispositional variables explained more of the variance in resolve than the situational ones, this could simply be a function of better dispositional measures and weaker treatments. I therefore bypass the question of weighting altogether.

Second, although we often think of resolve in a dyadic fashion such that we can speak of the "balance of resolve," in the analyses that follow I focus solely on *the resolve of the intervening power*, rather than also looking at the resolve of the target state, or how the resolve of the latter affects the resolve of the former.[28] This is partially due to data limitations, but also for statistical reasons: given that my composite measures of resolve are (a) likely to have a high degree of measurement error, and (b) driven by the interactions between multiple actor characteristics and the situations actors are facing, conceptualizing resolve in a dyadic fashion risks overprocessing the data. In

24 McDermott 2011b; Hyde 2015.
25 For examples of the former, see, e.g., Tomz 2007a; for the latter, see Tingley and Walter 2011.
26 On experiments for theory-building, see Kagel and Roth 1995; McDermott 2002.
27 E.g., Flores and Nooruddin 2009.
28 Maoz 1983; Powell 1987.

chapter 6, I suggest a number of ways one might examine resolve dyadically with observational data in future work and some of the interesting theoretical questions this raises.

Third, although the rationalist bargaining literature in particular frequently models resolve as affecting not just the outcome of an intervention but also whether a party gets involved in the first place, I am not employing a selection model.[29] Not only do statistical solutions for selection bias tend to be quite brittle and plausible instruments hard to come by, but I already have experimental analyses explicitly designed to model this selection process, which find that inasmuch as not controlling for selection bias affects the results, it actually produces a more conservative test, biasing coefficient estimates downward, since variables that increase the probability of intervention appear to have a weaker relationship with resolve once the intervention takes place. Thus, if I still find factors like reputation costs have a significant impact, it will increase my confidence in their importance. More conceptually, the work in IR that carves out the largest role for resolve as causing actors to select into conflicts also tends to conflate resolve with an actor's preference or intention. If, as I've argued here, resolve is a second-order phenomenon, reflecting not the content of an actor's desire, but the sticktoitiveness with which it is being pursued, the resolve-shapes-selection story becomes more theoretically murky—a proposition to which I return in chapter 6.

Finally, in a more traditional latent variable model of resolve (e.g., option G in figure 5.1), I would want to test whether the multiple indicators of resolve are intercorrelated to ensure the reliability of the composite measure, or employ factor analysis to see whether the indicators load onto a single factor. Although this rule holds in classical test theory (in which indicators $x_{i...j}$ are understood to be effects of the latent variable ξ), the theoretical relationship being tested by option E is akin to what the measurement literature calls a formative indicator model, in that the indicators of resolve are not its effects, but its causes.[30] Whereas one expects the *consequences* of a phenomenon to be correlated with one another (e.g., if stable borders affect both the likelihood of conflict and the likelihood of democracy, democracy and the probability of conflict should be intercorrelated), this is not necessarily the case with the *causes* of a phenomenon: for example, although security scholars believe that both the offense-defense balance and democratization cause war, the two phenomena

---

29 E.g., Fearon 2002.

30 Edwards and Bagozzi 2000; Diamantopoulos and Winklhofer 2001. Interestingly, then, political scientists who estimate traditional ("effect indicator") structural equation models or factor analyses in situations where our measures are causes rather than consequences of our unobserved constructs are technically estimating the wrong model. The analyses that follow do not employ a structural equation modeling setup, and thus do not formally employ formative indicator models, but because of the considerations discussed below, the analogy holds.

need not be correlated with one another.[31] Thus, this approach would be inappropriate in this context.

DATA AND VARIABLES

The backbone of the analyses that follow is the Military Interventions by Powerful States (MIPS) dataset, which includes all of the military interventions conducted from 1946 to 2003 by the five permanent members of the UN Security Council (the United States, the United Kingdom, France, Russia, and China).[32] Military interventions are defined broadly to refer to the use of armed forces (involving an official deployment of at least 500 military personnel) in pursuit of political objectives against a foreign adversary (whether a state or non-state actor). Thus, the interventions under investigation here range in severity, from simple displays of force—the United States sending troops to the Dominican Republic to stabilize the country following the assassination of Rafael Trujillo in 1961—to full-on ground combat, such as the Soviet invasion of Afghanistan in 1979. Because I am interested in leader-level variables that can change over time, the unit of analysis is the conflict-month. The dependent variable is whether the great power has achieved victory at time t, based on the ATTAIN variable from the MIPS data, which measures whether the mission's objective was achieved and maintained for at least 30 days. Because of the conflict-month unit of analysis, the variable is recoded such that monthly observations for ongoing interventions are coded 0, as are the final observations for interventions terminated short of victory. To make the results easier to interpret, all variables are rescaled from 0 to 1.

Situational Variables

The Costs of Fighting

Although the lab and survey experiments use casualties as the chief measure of the costs of fighting, two considerations caution against their use here. First are data availability concerns: accurate monthly casualty estimates are more easily accessible for some interventions than for others. Second, casualties are the ex post costs of fighting; although total casualty figures suffered over the course of the intervention are available, treating the number of casualties sustained at the end of the conflict at time $t+1$ as a predictor of the intervening power's behavior at time t suffers from obvious endogeneity concerns. Instead,

---

31 Gibler 2007; Hopf 1991a; Mansfield and Snyder 1995.

32 Sullivan and Koch 2009. The dataset contains 126 interventions in all, listed in appendix B.2; because of missing data for some of the covariates of interest, the analyses below focus on 109 interventions.

I measure the costs of fighting by looking at the level of force employed by the intervening power using the force type variable from the MIPS data.[33] An ordinal variable, it ranges from a simple display of force to actual ground combat. In this sense, force type is similar to the anticipated cost manipulation from the lab and survey experiments, which told participants the intervention would require either "minimal" or "substantial use of force." The one respect in which it differs is that since force type here is coded to reflect the amount of force used at the height of the conflict, it is not an entirely ex ante measure, but is nonetheless a better indicator than measures like casualties or the highest number of intervening troops, since intervening powers that have pledged troop deployments are more likely to know in advance whether an intervention will consist of a limited use of force or not, rather than accurately anticipate the precise number of casualties.[34]

The Costs of Backing Down

In the previous chapters, I argued that just as pressing on in a conflict is costly, so too is backing down, such that one can think of three different types of costs that actors pay when they back down: the stakes of the conflict (the intrinsic interests for which we were fighting in the first place), reputation costs (the extrinsic interests), and domestic audience costs, which in a broad sense are a kind of reputational cost paid by leaders to their domestic constituencies. For reasons of tractability, the experiments manipulated reputation costs but kept the stakes fixed, but the use of observational data allows us to examine the impact of multiple types of costs of backing down, at both the country-level and leader-level.

The first measure of the cost of backing down is the distance between the intervening power and the target of the intervention; this serves as a useful measure of intrinsic interests since "proximity magnifies the stakes involved and distance attenuates them."[35] To calculate distances, I employ the cshapes package in R, drawing on GIS data to calculate the minimum distance between the intervening state and target at the time of the intervention, thereby accounting for changes in countries' borders over time.[36]

Second, I examine whether the intervention is taking place in a current or former colony or possession of the intervening power, operationalized based on whether the intervening state had at any point been the central governing

---

33 Sullivan and Koch 2009.

34 There is of course a strategic element here, in that larger sized deployments, although more expensive in financial terms, could be deployed because of higher sensitivity to the human costs of war, out of the assumption that employing overwhelming force reduces the likelihood of casualties. On the tradeoff between human and financial costs of war, see Gartzke 2001; Caverley 2009/10.

35 Braumoeller and Carson 2011, 297.

36 Weidmann, Kuse, and Gleditsch 2010.

authority of the territory. The Soviet Union had more of its reputation at stake in its interventions in Poland in 1956 than it did in its intervention in the Sudanese Civil War in 1971; interventions taking place in current or former colonies will be more likely to implicate reputational costs than those occuring further afield, and speak to higher intrinsic interests at stake as well. Here I recode the COLONY variable from the MIPS data, collapsing current and former colonies into one category to produce a dichotomous variable indicating the presence or absence of colonial ties.

Third, the costs of backing down are likely to be higher if there are major economic interests at stake: if the great power is intervening to prop up a regime in a friendly trading partner, it is likely to pay heavy consequences if the friendly regime falls. As a measure of economic interests, I calculate the great power's trade flows with the location of the intervention at its onset, using version 4.1 of Gleditsch's 2002 Expanded GDP and Trade data.[37] I calculate dyadic trade flows with respect to the location of the intervention rather than the target of the intervention, since the relevant trade flows in the Gulf War, for example, are between the United States and Kuwait, rather than the United States and Iraq.

Fourth, the costs of backing down in interventions carried out in allied states are likely to be higher: not only are the reputational costs of backing down greater, but so too are the inherent stakes of the intervention. I employ the Alliance Treaty Obligations and Provisions (ATOP) data, coding whether an alliance exists between the great power and the location where the intervention is taking place at the time of the intervention—since, to continue the Gulf War example from before, I am more interested in whether the United States has an alliance with Kuwait rather than with Iraq.[38]

Finally, whereas the above measures of the cost of backing down focus on the stakes and reputational costs inherent in the intervention at the country-level, one can also think about stakes and reputation costs existing for the leaders themselves. I follow Croco in modeling audience costs as a function of leader culpability: leaders are more likely to pay audience costs if they back down in an intervention that they themselves (or a fellow member of their political party) were responsible for getting the country into, whereas leaders who inherit an intervention from a political opponent are often praised rather than punished when they terminate it, because they are seen as extricating a country from a quagmire rather than having gotten the country into it in the first place.[39] I use the Archigos data, cross-referenced with Lentz, to

---

37 Gleditsch 2002. Trade flows are logged because of the skewed distribution. To minimize missing data, I employ the "nearest neighbor" method if there is a non-missing observation within a five-year period of the intervention.

38 Leeds et al. 2002.

39 Croco 2011.

record the leader in power for each month of the intervention; if a leadership transition occurs within a particular conflict-month, I record the identity of the replacement leader rather than his or her predecessor.[40] I then use Lentz to note whether, for any given conflict month, the leader in power is either the leader under whose tenure the intervention began, or is a member of the same political party.[41]

As alternative operationalizations for supplementary analyses, I also simply note whether the leader in power is the leader on whose watch the intervention began, and sum the number of previous interventions carried out by the leader, under the assumption that leaders who intervene frequently will be more concerned with the reputational consequences of withdrawing short of victory. This measure follows the logic of Walter's study of why governments choose to fight some secessionist movements and not others: leaders that frequently engage in international interventions bear larger reputational costs of withdrawal short of victory, since it is likely to undermine their credibility in interventions in the future.[42]

Dispositional Variables

In the lab and survey experiments, I focus on four dispositional sources of resolve: time preferences, risk preferences, honor orientations, and to a lesser extent, trait self-control. There is an interesting levels-of-analysis question here with regard to dispositional measures (are these the dispositions of individual leaders or the public at large?), such that I investigate some of these dispositions both for publics in general and at the leader-level, as part of growing interest in the study of individual leaders in international politics, especially by political psychologists.[43]

Time Preferences

In an ideal world, I would measure leaders' time preferences by presenting leaders with the delayed choice tasks used in the lab and survey experiment, to obtain precise estimates of leaders' δ and β parameters. Since resurrection is beyond the scope of this project, I adopt a less direct approach, employing two situationally induced measures of leaders' time horizons. First, I calculate the average number of leadership transitions during the previous 20 years, since leaders in countries with higher turnover rates have shorter time horizons,

40 Goemans, Gleditsch, and Chiozza 2009; Lentz 1994.

41 Lentz 1994.

42 Walter 2006.

43 Bueno de Mesquita and Siverson 1995; Stanley 2009; Chiozza and Goemans 2011; Saunders 2011; Jervis 2013; Hermann et al. 2001; Dyson 2007; Renshon 2009.

leaving them more sensitive to short-term costs of war than leaders who can expect to remain in power for decades. Given work on the survival of leaders who take their countries to war, regime type is an alternative way of looking at leaders' time horizons, but given the sample of countries considered here (the US, UK, France, China, and Russia), leadership tenure is a better and more direct measure.[44] Second, I also operationalize leaders' time horizons by generating predicted values of leaders' survival rates from Chiozza and Goemans's leader survival model.[45] The logic here is the same: leaders whose expected probability of remaining in office at any given time is low will have shorter time horizons than leaders who can expect to remain in power for some time.[46]

Risk Preferences

I measure risk orientations using a similarly indirect approach. At the leader level, I follow Horowitz and Stam, whose work on individual leader characteristics studies risk acceptance by turning to leaders' military experience—the logic being that time in the military molds attitudes toward the risks of war.[47] Biographies of military leaders frequently make similar claims: for example, the notion that Sir Winston Churchill's famous "love of risk" (claiming "it is never possible to guarantee success; it is only possible to deserve it") was tied to his experiences as a soldier: "charging at Omdurman, escaping from a prisoner-of-war-camp and having the plume snipped from his hat by a Boer bullet at Spion Kop left [Churchill] with an abiding sense of destiny" that deeply shaped his orientation toward the world around him.[48] Thus, cross-referencing Lentz and Horowitz and Stam, I generate a dichotomous variable indicating whether each leader had previous military experience before assuming power.[49] There are two caveats about this measure. First, scholars of civil-military relations are divided as to whether military experience indeed fosters greater acceptance of the risks of war.[50] Second, the previous chapters demonstrated that both fighting and backing down can be perceived as risky; if we think of the relationship between military experience and risk as an instance of a more general phenomenon of risk orientations being shaped by formative experiences, one might imagine that

---

44 Bueno de Mesquita and Siverson 1995; Chiozza and Goemans 2004.

45 Chiozza and Goemans 2004.

46 Although the two measures of time horizons tap into the same construct, they are not highly collinear ($r = 0.12$).

47 Horowitz and Stam 2014. This argument leads to a similar conclusion—albeit through a different causal mechanism—as Sechser 2004.

48 Pearson 1991, 81; Hayward 1997, 81; Holmes 2005, 8.

49 Lentz 1994; Horowitz and Stam 2014.

50 See, e.g., Huntington 1957; Feaver and Gelpi 2005.

the effect of military service is going to be contingent on the nature of these experiences.[51]

For risk preferences at the societal level, I take advantage of data from the World Values Survey, which has two self-report items measuring respondents' risk orientations.[52] The first item asks participants to choose between endorsing "One should be cautious about major changes in life" vs. "One should act boldly to achieve"; the second borrows an item from the Schwartz Portrait Value Questionnaire (PVQ), which presents respondents with descriptions of hypothetical individuals and asks participants to indicate how much they resemble the individuals described. To measure risk orientation, I use responses to the World Values Survey item: "It is important to this person: being adventurous and taking risks."[53] Since the central premise of much of cross-cultural psychology is that these basic values are relatively stable in societies across time, I average across each country's score for each item to produce a risk orientation score I use for the entire 1945–2003 time period, a maneuver that therefore treats societal risk attitudes as equivalent to a country-level fixed effect—albeit stemming from a theoretical variable.[54] Similarly, in their study comparing risk attitudes in China and the United States, Hsee and Weber suggest that risk acceptance increases with collectivism: societies with close social networks have higher levels of risk acceptance out of the belief that your social network will cushion you if you fall.[55] There is no obvious analogue to this cushion in a foreign policy context (we call the international system a self-help system for a reason), but if risk orientations are general dispositions rather than highly context specific, it is worth including a measure of collectivism as well. In the World Values Survey, collectivism is typically measured with a series of "Important child qualities" questions, in which participants are presented with "a list of qualities that children can be encouraged to learn at home," and asked to provide up to five that are especially important. I therefore calculate collectivism scores based on

---

51 See, e.g., Callen et al. 2014; Bernile, Bhagwat, and Rau Forthcoming. Horowitz and Stam (2014) gain further traction by distinguishing between military experience and actual combat experience; due to the relatively small number of leaders I am investigating (N=53), this distinction is not feasible here, such that I simply record whether leaders had any military experience, whether as part of guerrilla warfare (e.g., Andropov) or as a high-level military commander (e.g., De Gaulle, see Lentz 1994; Horowitz and Stam 2014). Although distinguishing between combat and non-combat is helpful and important, future work can take the distinction further by looking at the valence and outcome of the experience.

52 World Values Survey Association 2009.

53 WVS questions E045 and A195. E045 was administered in China in 1990 and 1995, the US in 1990 and 1995, France in 1990, Great Britain in 1990, and Russia in 1990, 1995 and 1999. A195 was administered in China in 2007; the US in 2006, France in 2006, Great Britain in 2006, and Russia in 2006.

54 Green, Kim, and Yoon 2001.

55 Hsee and Weber 1999.

responses to the qualities "tolerance and respect for other people," "religious faith," "unselfishness," and "obedience."[56] As before, I average across each country's responses to produce a country-level collectivism score I use for the entire time period under investigation.[57]

Cultures of Honor

Honor culture is historically associated with conservative political ideology, and in the lab experiment results, conservatives score much higher in honor orientation than liberals. Thus, at the leader-level, I study honor culture indirectly by proxying it with political ideology, using a dummy variable indicating whether a leader is a member of a right-wing political party or not. To code ideology, I rely on Castles and Mair, Lentz, and Döring and Manow, deriving the ideology score from the political party the leader is a member of, rather than via the leader herself.[58] The meaning of left- and right-wing varies cross-culturally—particularly in the cases of China and Russia—so to avoid subjective coding decisions with regard to the ideological background of individual leaders, I simply code the Soviet and Chinese communist party leaders as being on the left; as a robustness check, I also drop all of the Chinese and Russian interventions and replicate the analyses on just the democratic countries in the sample.

Trait Self-Control

Finally, I measure trait self-control at the societal level using two "important child qualities" items from the World Values Survey, which evaluate the degree to which respondents emphasize "self-control" and "determination and perseverance" as especially important qualities for children to have.[59] As with

---

56 WVS questions A035, A040, A041, and A042. A035 was asked in China in 1990, 1995, 2001; France in 1981, 1990, 1999; Great Britain in 1981, 1990, 1998, 1999; Russia in 1990, 1995, 1999; the US in 1982, 1990, 1995, 1999. A040 was asked in China in 1990, 1995; France in 1981, 1990, 1999; Great Britain in 1981, 1990, 1998, 1999; Russia in 1990, 1995, 1999; the US in 1982, 1990, 1995, 1999. A041 was asked in China in 1990, 1995, 2001; France in 1981, 1990, 1999; Great Britain: 1981, 1990, 1999; Russia in 1990, 1995, 1999; the USA in 1990, 1995, 1999. A042 was asked in China in 1990, 1995, 2001; France in 1981, 1990, 1999; Great Britain in 1981, 1990, 1998, 1999; Russia in 1990, 1995, 1999; the US in 1982, 1990, 1995, 1999.

57 Whereas the experimental results pointed to nonlinear measures of risk attitudes, both of the operationalizations here are linear by necessity: the proxy for leader risk-attitudes is dichotomous, whereas the societal-level risk measures are constant for each great power through time, so there are too few observations here to meaningfully detect nonlinear effects.

58 Castles and Mair 1984; Lentz 1994; D'oring and Manow 2012. For a similar approach using political party as a proxy for individual decision-makers' dispositional characteristics, see Kertzer and Rathbun (2015).

59 WVS questions A037 and A039. A037 was administered in France in 1981, Great Britain in 1981, and the US in 1982. A039 was administered in China in 1990, 1995, 2001, and 2006; in

the other WVS data, I average across each country's responses to produce a country-level score I use for the entire time period.

RESULTS

Resolve: Situational and Dispositional

I begin the analyses by estimating a series of Boolean logistical regression models that treat resolve as a function of both situational and dispositional variables, at both the country-level and the leader-level.[60]

The results for these four models are presented in table 5.1. The first model in table 5.1 estimates the impact of country-level situational variables and leader-level dispositional ones; the second and fourth models add leader-level situational variables, while the third and fourth models add country-level dispositional variables.[61] Rather than discussing the results of each of the four models separately, I group them together, to better explore the robustness of the results and illuminate the relative contribution of leader- and country-level determinants of resolve to conflict outcomes. In lieu of using a knife-edge threshold for statistical significance, I present the bootstrapped p-value directly beside each effect estimate in table 5.1, so that readers can directly evaluate the magnitude of uncertainty around the estimates.

Beginning with the situational sources of resolve, I find no support for the conventional wisdom that resolve is shaped by the costs of fighting: although higher levels of costs of fighting are negatively associated with victory in models 1 and 2, the sign flips in models 3 and 4, and is always far from statistical significance. I find stronger evidence in support of the costs of backing down. Until I control for country-level dispositional characteristics in models 3 and 4, minimum distance from the homeland—a measure of the gravity of the issues at stake—is significantly negatively associated with

---

France in 1981, 1990, 1999, and 2006; in Great Britain in 1981, 1990, 1998, 1999, and 2006; in the US in 1982, 1990, 1995, 1999, and 2006; and in Russia in 1990, 1995, 1999, and 2006.

60 To settle on the appropriate model specification, the statistical models presented in table 5.1 were estimated a number of different ways, modeling duration dependence using either a logarithmic or quadratic functional form, leaving unit heterogeneity either unmodeled, or modeled using country-fixed effects; BIC scores were then used to adjudicate goodness-of-fit. To guard against the occasional instability of Boolean models, the models were estimated with a local nonlinear minimization optimizer (nlminb), a Broyden-Fletcher-Goldfarb Shanno (BFGS) optimizer, a genetic optimization algorithm (genoud) (Mebane and Sekhon, 2011), and a simulated annealing optimizer (SANN), finding the results hold. In the analysis that follows, I report the results from a BFGS optimizer with box constraints (L-BFGS-B) set to $\pm 3\sigma$, with $N = 5000$ cluster bootstraps (Field and Welsh, 2007).

61 The distribution of bootstrapped coefficient estimates, depicted in figure 5.2, shows that normal-theory p-values would be inappropriate here, so I calculate the p-values shown in table 5.1 simply by estimating the percentage of bootstrapped estimates crossing zero (denoted by the grey shading in the distribution plots).

TABLE 5.1. Boolean Model Estimates: Situation × Disposition

	(1)		(2)		(3)		(4)	
	β*	p*	β*	p*	β*	p*	β*	p*
Situational								
Intercept	0.328	0.461	0.296	0.494	0.485	0.428	0.363	0.466
	(1.355)		(1.635)		(1.520)		(1.789)	
Force type	−0.109	0.393	−0.093	0.405	0.226	0.469	0.21	0.469
	(0.863)		(0.902)		(0.993)		(0.994)	
Minimum distance	−1.378	0.047	−1.435	0.051	−1.024	0.183	−1.009	0.193
	(0.872)		(0.892)		(1.103)		(1.124)	
Trade	−0.054	0.291	−0.052	0.308	−0.048	0.334	−0.037	0.368
	(0.107)		(0.115)		(0.125)		(0.132)	
Colony	0.481	0.201	0.496	0.205	0.953	0.109	0.964	0.129
	(0.564)		(0.597)		(0.744)		(0.771)	
Alliance	0.601	0.12	0.631	0.128	0.616	0.162	0.662	0.16
	(0.546)		(0.570)		(0.612)		(0.634)	
Leader culpable			0.043	0.471			0.152	0.413
							(0.709)	

TABLE 5.1. (continued)

	(1)		(2)		(3)		(4)	
	$\beta*$	$p*$	$\beta*$	$p*$	$\beta*$	$p*$	$\beta*$	$p*$
Situational								
Duration (months)	−0.553	0.000	−0.468	0.380	−0.743	0.000	−0.697	0.088
	(0.457)		(0.523)		(0.437)		(0.483)	
Dispositional								
Intercept	−2.637	0.043	−2.564	0.044	−0.314	0.389	−0.257	0.387
	(1.552)		(1.521)		(5.722)		(5.865)	
Survival probability	3.007	0.002	2.893	0.003	3.089	0.003	3.068	0.005
	(1.441)		(1.396)		(1.519)		(1.545)	
Military service	−0.913	0.082	−0.902	0.079	−1.138	0.065	−1.155	0.063
	(0.679)		(0.671)		(0.796)		(0.812)	
Conservative	0.814	0.060	0.802	0.053	0.967	0.046	0.961	0.048
	(0.582)		(0.571)		(0.654)		(0.666)	
Leadership turnover	−2.867	0.005	−2.757	0.005	−3.429	0.006	−3.334	0.008
	(1.295)		(1.254)		(1.522)		(1.547)	

TABLE 5.1. (*continued*)

	(1)		(2)		(3)		(4)	
	$\beta*$	$p*$	$\beta*$	$p*$	$\beta*$	$p*$	$\beta*$	$p*$
Risk (WVS)					-8.898	0.181	-8.626	0.185
					(11.011)		(11.224)	
Self-control (WVS)					5.451	0.241	4.949	0.252
					(8.808)		(8.756)	
Duration (months)	-0.093	0.422	-0.176	0.382	0.043	0.508	0.01	0.545
	(0.587)		(0.584)		(0.492)		(0.499)	
Conflict months	2710		2710		2710		2710	
Interventions	109		109		109		109	
AIC	635.09		635.61		636.09		638.01	
BIC	824.64		833.89		841.79		849.73	

denotes leader-level variables. Main entries are coefficient estimates; standard errors in parentheses estimated using 5,000 cluster bootstraps. See figure 5.2 for illustrations of the bootstrapped p-values.

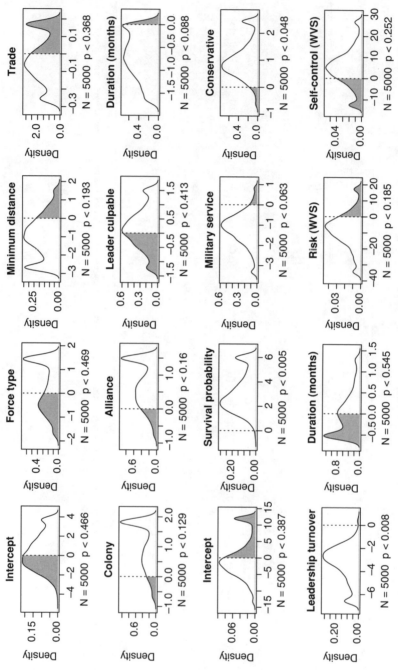

FIGURE 5.2. Bootstrapped Boolean Coefficient Estimates: Model 4 from table 5.1

the probability of victory; the closer to home the intervention is, the greater the probability of victory ($p < 0.047$ and $p < 0.051$ in models 1 and 2, respectively). I thus find some evidence in accordance with Braumoeller and Carson's finding that "proximity magnifies the stakes involved and distance attenuates them," though the substantive effect is small: all else equal, an intervention conducted next door has only a 0.9% higher probability of victory in any given month than an intervention conducted around 4,200 kilometers away.[62] Although I find no evidence that stakes as operationalized by trade flows affect military outcomes, I do find that stakes as operationalized by current or former colonial ties are positively associated with victory (a 1.3% increase in the probability of victory in models 3 and 4, with associated p-values ranging from $p < 0.109$ to $p < 0.129$). I find a similar effect with respect to interventions that take place in an ally: since great powers who are seen as abandoning an ally pay steeper reputational costs, interventions in allied states are associated with a 1.0–1.3% higher probability of victory at any given point in time ($p < 0.12$ to $p < 0.16$, depending on the model specification).

In this sense, higher costs of backing down—both in terms of intrinsic issues at stake (such as distance from the homeland) and reputation costs (such as the specter of abandoning an ally)—appear to increase the odds of victory, though many of the substantive effects are relatively small, and uncertainty about them relatively large. However, the measure of leader-level reputation costs—whether the leader or a fellow member of the leader's party began the intervention—never achieves anything close to statistical significance. Thus, unlike Croco, I fail to find evidence that culpable leaders are more likely to achieve better war outcomes.[63] The situational analyses suggest that different types of costs of war indeed positively predict victory in military interventions, but the most relevant costs of war appear to be at the country-level rather than the leader-level; I probe the robustness of the result in alternative model specifications in the next section.

Turning to the dispositional analyses, both measures of leaders' time horizons—the average number of leaders in power over the past twenty years (since leaders whose predecessors remained in office for relatively short periods of time should have shorter time horizons), and leaders' own probability of remaining in office—are significantly associated with the probability of victory. All else equal, an increase from the lowest to the highest rate of leadership turnover is associated with a 2.7–4.3% decrease in the probability of victory ($p < 0.005$ to $p < 0.008$). Meanwhile, moving from the lowest to the highest survival probability is associated with a 2.8–4.0% increase in the probability of victory ($p < 0.002$ to $p < 0.005$). Therefore, for both measures, longer leader time horizons predict a greater likelihood of victory. I find both substantively

---

62 The average distance from the homeland for all of the interventions in the data. Braumoeller and Carson 2011, 297.

63 Croco 2011.

and statistically weaker results for risk preferences, and in an unanticipated direction: leaders with histories of military service are 1.9–4.0% *less* likely to achieve victory at any given point in time, raising questions about the use of military experience as a proxy for risk attitudes given the complex nature of the relationship between risk and the costs of fighting.[64] However, I find significant results with the measure of honor culture: leaders from conservative political parties are 1.7% to 3.1% more likely to achieve victory at any given month than leaders from liberal parties ($p < 0.046$ to $p < 0.060$)— an effect that also holds when I drop the non-democratic great powers from the sample, as discussed below. Given recent work indicating a positive association between conservative ideology and self-control, the results are thus striking.[65] Importantly, neither of the societal-level dispositional variables—risk attitudes and trait-self-control—significantly predict the probability of victory.

Thus, the dispositional sources of resolve display the opposite dynamic as the situational measures: whereas military outcomes appear to be shaped by country-level situational variables but not leader-level ones, they also appear to be shaped by leader-level dispositional variables, but not country-level ones. Indeed, AIC and BIC scores suggest that the best fitting of the four models presented in table 5.1 is model 1, which restricts itself to country-level situational predictors and leader-level dispositional predictors. This pattern of results is instructive in suggesting that we should understand dispositional characteristics in IR as being fluid rather than fixed. Importantly, although one should exercise caution in generalizing to intervention behavior by countries beyond the five great powers examined here—for example, it is possible that the lack of significant societal-level dispositional characteristics is due to the relatively small sample of countries under consideration—it remains telling that the behavior of the five great powers that have dominated much of the international agenda in the post–World War II era is better explained by attributes pertaining to their leaders than of the countries as a whole.

Zooming out from the individual coefficients to the overall model dynamics, figure 5.3 plots the fitted values for the dispositional and situational measures of resolve against the probability of victory, calculating the fitted values based on the coefficient estimates for model 1 of table 5.1. The wireframe plot illustrates the joint impact of situational and dispositional sources of resolve. As the situational resolve scores (on the x-axis) increase, so too does the predicted probability of victory; as the dispositional resolve scores (on

---

64 Importantly, Horowitz and Stam (2014) focus specifically on combat experience rather than military experience more specifically, suggesting one potential explanation for the divergent results found here. Future work on the effects of combat experience may similarly benefit by employing more fine-grained measures: Lyndon Johnson, for example, was awarded a Silver Star for his experience as an observer on a single combat flight, a B-26 bombing run over Papua New Guinea, which is substantially different from the kind of combat experience experienced by Eisenhower or de Gaulle. See Caro 1990.

65 Clarkson et al. 2015.

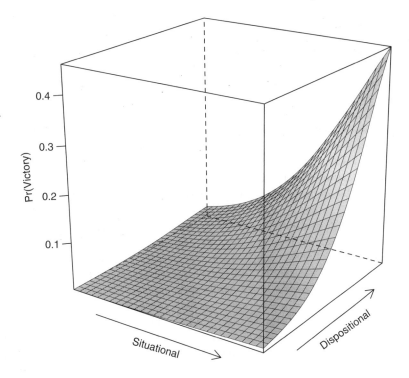

FIGURE 5.3. The probability of victory increases with situational and dispositional sources of resolve. The fitted values of the dispositional and situational resolve scores show that resolve indeed boosts the probability of victory: as actors' dispositional resolve increases, so too does their likelihood of attaining their primary mission objective; the same can be said for increases in their situational resolve scores. Since victory here is modeled as a function of both situational and dispositional resolve, the probability of victory is highest when both situational and dispositional resolve scores are high (the back-right vertex of the plot), and lowest when both situational and dispositional resolve scores are low (the front-left vertex). The fitted value scores here are derived from model 1 in table 5.1 and are clipped at the 2nd and 98th percentiles to drop outliers.

the z-axis) increase, the predicted probability of victory increases as well. The curvature of the plot's surface shows the extent to which dispositional aspects of resolve moderate the impact of situational features: the probability of victory is highest when both situational and dispositional sources of resolve are high; when dispositional sources of resolve are high but situational sources of resolve are low (the back-left vertex in figure 5.3), the probability of victory is relatively low, as is the case when situational sources of resolve are high but dispositional sources of resolve are low (the front-right vertex).

Alternative Model Specifications

To probe the robustness of the results, model 1 in table 5.2 replicates model 2 from table 5.1, but only for those military interventions carried out by the United States, France, and the United Kingdom, the three democratic great powers in the data. The basic pattern of results remains similar, although the role of the costs of backing down is somewhat smaller, with only alliances approaching conventional levels of statistical significance. Dispositional characteristics, however, retain their important role, with longer time horizons associated with a higher probability of victory, as is the conservativism proxy for honor culture. As before, I fail to find evidence that risk preferences as measured by military service is positively associated with a probability of victory.

The next two models in table 5.2 focus on alternative ways of operationalizing leader-level reputation costs. Model 2 in table 5.2 replicates model 4 from table 5.1, but using whether the leader in power also began the intervention as a measure of leader-level costs of backing down. Interestingly, I find that leaders who initiate conflicts themselves—and thus are likely to pay steeper reputational costs if they back down short of victory—are in fact 2.2% more likely to prevail ($p < 0.066$). Thus, whereas Croco finds that leader culpability is a better measure than leader initiation as a measure of leaders' stakes in conflict in general, this does not appear to be the case when it comes to great power military interventions in the postwar era in particular.[66]

Model 4 in table 5.2 replicates model 3 from table 5.1, but using the previous number of military interventions the leader has initiated as a measure of leader-level reputation costs, the logic being that reputational considerations should matter more for leaders who intervene more frequently. Instead, I find that the effect of the number of previous interventions is not statistically significant.[67] This null finding offers further support to the findings

---

66 Croco 2011.

67 One potential explanation for this null effect is that leaders with previous military interventions under their belt may actually bear lower reputational costs for backing down, already having established their reputations for resolve. Indeed, Wolford (2007) presents a formal model in which successors are more likely to be subject to (and initiate) military challenges than incumbents, whose reputations for resolve are already cemented. The empirical record is similarly mixed on this point: Gelpi and Grieco (2001) find that leaders are less likely to be targeted for military crises the longer they spend in office, but Bak and Palmer (2010) find that the effect of leadership tenure on the probability of military challenges is conditional on leaders' age—young leaders are actually *less* likely to be subjected to a challenge early on in their term, contrary to the leader-level reputation arguments (although they do not test whether leaders early on in their tenure are more likely to initiate military challenges themselves). Similarly, Horowitz, McDermott, and Stam (2005) find that older leaders are *more* likely to initiate military disputes.

TABLE 5.2. Alternative Model Specifications

	(1)		(2)		(3)		(4)	
	β*	p*	β*	p*	β*	p*	β*	p*
Situational								
Intercept	4.129 (−10.478)	0.452	−3.079 (−3.359)	0.164	0.387 (−2.903)	0.448	0.558 (−1.759)	0.418
Force type	1.715 (−4.768)	0.452	−0.127 (−1.719)	0.423	−0.15 (−1.738)	0.437	0.109 (−0.987)	0.51
Minimum distance	−2.035 (−7.153)	0.286	−0.574 (−1.807)	0.342	−1.795 (−1.326)	0.08	−1.237 (−1.163)	0.14
Trade	1.925 (−4.907)	0.568	−0.019 (−0.244)	0.41	0.003 (−0.253)	0.59	−0.055 (−0.124)	0.31
Colony	2.959 (−6.649)	0.252	2.347 (−2.196)	0.098	0.773 (−1.353)	0.251	0.677 (−0.699)	0.189
Alliance	5.735 (−7.122)	0.086	1.109 (−1.151)	0.134	1.041 (−1.016)	0.142	0.65 (−0.653)	0.174
Leader culpable	0.217 (−2.265)	0.471					0.064 (−0.721)	0.469

TABLE 5.2. (continued)

	(1) β*	(1) p*	(2) β*	(2) p*	(3) β*	(3) p*	(4) β*	(4) p*
Leader initiate			3.014 (−2.857)	0.066				
Prev. leader int.					0.465 (−2.119)	0.434	−0.658 (−0.516)	0.17
Duration (months)	−0.046 (−1.175)	0.408	0.181 (−0.954)	0.528	0.115 (−1.091)	0.496		
Dispositional								
Intercept	−4.732 (−2.276)	0.000	−0.232 (−4.057)	0.434	−2.299 (−0.881)	0.012	−2.915 (−3.974)	0.182
Survival probability	5.095 (−2.454)	0.006	2.677 (−1.140)	0.007	2.002 (−0.515)	0.003	3.155 (−1.550)	0.005
Military service	−1.182 (−0.713)	0.041	−1.305 (−0.659)	0.032	−0.728 (−0.451)	0.074	−1.027 (−0.744)	0.071
Conservative	0.844 (−0.475)	0.036	0.878 (−0.494)	0.032	0.565 (−0.333)	0.058	0.91 (−0.634)	0.052

TABLE 5.2. (*continued*)

	(1)		(2)		(3)		(4)	
	β*	p*	β*	p*	β*	p*	β*	p*
🦁 Leadership turnover	-2.098	0.017	-2.657	0.007	-1.981	0.004	-2.967	0.008
	(-0.918)		(-1.122)		(-0.613)		(-1.410)	
Risk (WVS)			-8.543	0.154				
			(-8.107)					
Self-control (WVS)			5.609	0.201			2.16	0.352
			(-6.331)				(-7.360)	
Collectivism (WVS)							-2.026	0.346
							(-5.078)	
Duration (months)	-0.437	0.000	-0.24	0.287	-0.436	0.176	-0.041	0.444
	(-0.285)		(-0.397)		(-0.410)		(-0.522)	
Conflict-months	2149		2710		2720		2720	
Interventions	77		109		109		109	
Democracies only?	Yes		No		No		No	
AIC	473.55		631.12		613.12		637.15	
BIC	552.97		725.65		695.83		731.69	

🦁 denotes leader-level variables. Main entries are coefficient estimates; standard errors in parentheses, estimated using 2000 cluster bootstraps. Bootstrapped p-values are one-sided.

from table 5.1 that leader-level costs of backing down seem to play less of a role than the country-level costs of backing down. Model 5 replicates model 4 from table 5.1, but using the World Value Survey collectivism scores as an alternative measure for societal risk attitudes. Once again, the measure is far from statistically significant, showing the weakness of time-invariant societal measures in predicting military outcomes. Finally, supplementary analyses in appendix B.3 replicate the analyses from table 5.1 using a more traditional logistic regression model, finding the results hold.

CONCLUSION

One of the chief impediments to studying resolve with observational data has been a lack of understanding about its microfoundations. This micro-level neglect has been one reason why our treatment of resolve in International Relations has been dissatisfying: not only are our theories of resolve underspecified, but our empirical tests are frequently misspecified, because we do not know how to measure resolve with observational data, forcing us to either to drop resolve from our empirical models, or infer it from one of its posited consequences. Indeed, it is striking how much of the literature that invokes resolve either laments how hard it is to measure—Organski, like Sartori, claims it is "extremely difficult to measure objectively," Rummel calls it "the most elusive and ambiguous of psychological variables," and Cline notes that the study of resolve is "a region where numbers can only be notations of highly subjective judgments, nothing more" —or complains that too many of the measures are derived ex post.[68] Rather than study resolve based on its consequences, I do so based on its causes, gathering measures of the same constructs tested in the lab and survey experiments, and using them to build composite dispositional and situational measures of resolve in the context of great power military interventions from 1946 to 2003.

I therefore turn to Boolean statistics as a new way to answer an old question. The analyses suggest a number of findings. First, and most importantly, resolve and victory are indeed positively related: the situational and dispositional predictors of resolve in the experimental results also predict the probability that the great powers achieved their objectives in their military interventions from 1946 to 2003. This effect is important for three reasons. First, and most obviously, because the measures of resolve are derived from resolve's causes rather than its consequences, I am able to test resolve's effects without lapsing into tautology. Second, I am focusing solely on great power military interventions, which raises some interesting case selection implications. If great powers

---

68 Organski (1968, 208); Sartori (2005, 91); Rummel 1975b, 318; Cline 1994, 98; March 1966, 61; Baldwin 1979; Jervis 1979, 316; Ray and Vural 1986; Morrow 1989; Merom 2003; Sullivan 2007.

tend to display more resolve than other states—perhaps because their resolve is what prompts them to become great powers in the first place, or perhaps because they tend to select more resolute leaders because of the frequency with which great powers tend to be involved in international crises—I am likely to be studying the impact of resolve in relatively high-resolve cases, thereby rendering my tests of resolve's effects relatively conservative.[69] The fact that I still find that resolve makes a difference *despite* this ceiling effect suggests that resolve's impacts on conflict outcomes have the potential to be even larger than what I find here. Third, and relatedly, the situational determinants of resolve I study here are observable ex ante—when deciding whether to intervene, decision-makers are aware of how far away the intervention would be, whether it involves an ally, and so on—and thus likely to factor into the initial decision of whether to intervene in the first place. Since I am not explicitly modeling this selection process, this ex ante observability raises the possibility that my estimates of the overall impact of resolve are biased. As I noted earlier in the chapter, however, the downward direction of this bias would make the impact of resolve *harder* to detect, thereby rendering my tests more conservative, and the significant relationship between resolve and conflict outcomes all the more noteworthy.

Second, of the situational variables, I find some evidence for the importance of the costs of backing down—both the intrinsic interests at stake, and reputation costs—but less support for the importance of the costs of fighting. This null finding could be due either to better measures of the former than the latter, or to selection effects, in that the cost of fighting may be taken into account when deciding whether to intervene in the first place, and thus have little impact on the probability of actually achieving military outcomes—similar to the effect found in the mediation analysis of anticipated costs in the survey experiment. The importance of reputation costs shows that even if decision-makers worry more about their national reputation than they should, these concerns do seem to guide their behavior: when the reputational consequences of walking away short of victory are higher, actors are more likely to emerge victorious.[70]

Third, with respect to the dispositional variables, I find fairly strong evidence that the probability of victory increases with leaders' time preferences and honor orientation, but no evidence in favor of societal-level risk-attitudes, or trait self-control. The relationship between leader-level risk preferences and military outcomes appears to be negative, encouraging further research investigating the microprocesses through which previous experiences shape

---

69 See chapter 6 for a discussion of the effects of selection mechanisms on distributions of dispositional characteristics.

70 Mercer 1996; Press 2005.

orientations toward risk. Just as in the survey experiments, it is possible that the relatively important role played by dispositional variables compared to situational ones is simply due to better measures of the former than the latter, but it is striking that as in the previous two chapters, dispositional variables appear to be doing more of the work.

The novel contribution of these analyses comes not from the individual variables themselves—few of which are particularly exotic in the study of war and peace—but from the overarching situational and dispositional framework in which they are incorporated. Thus, I find different patterns of effects for the situational and dispositional sources of resolve: when it comes to situational variables, the most relevant level of analysis for resolve seems to be that of the country as a whole, but for dispositional variables, the most relevant level of analysis appears to be the leader-level. Finally, I modeled resolve using a conjunctural Boolean model in which military outcomes are a function of both situational *and* dispositional sources of resolve, letting it explicitly model the notion that actor-level characteristics moderate the impact of the cost of war.

Several points should be noted here. First, the divergent findings between leader-level and country-level dispositional characteristics could simply stem from the former being time-varying while the latter are not. However, in emphasizing that our dispositional characteristics of interest are variables rather than constants, this pattern of findings nonetheless has implications for how we think about dispositions in IR: not as fixed and enduring national characteristics similar to early discussions in IR about "national character" or "national style," but as dynamic, evolving entities.[71] Thus, although country-level fixed effects might capture unit heterogeneity, they would do a poor job of capturing dispositional characteristics. Meanwhile, the importance of leader-level characteristics in the findings speaks to a growing body of research showing the importance of studying phenomena at the leader-level rather than simply the country-level as a whole.[72] The evolving nature of leader-level dispositional variables also suggests that leader dispositions are better modeled theoretically rather than controlled away using something like leader-level fixed effects.

Finally, many of the substantive effects reported here may seem small—for example, honor orientation's substantively largest effect in table 5.1 is only a 3.1% increase in the probability of victory. However, these small changes in predicted probability reflect the relatively low baseline probability of victory

---

71 Charlesworth 1967; Hoebel 1967; Gray 1981. Of course, it is also possible that time-invariant societal measures do have a role to play in theories of resolve, just not the particular measures employed in this study.

72 Hermann et al. 2001; Chiozza and Goemans 2011; Jervis 2013.

at any given point in time, as is common in quantitative studies of war.[73] Indeed, if these substantive effects are expressed in terms of odds ratios rather than predicted probabilities, their substantive magnitude appears far greater: at any given month of a military intervention, leaders from conservative political parties (and thus, with greater honor orientations) are 2.3 times likelier to prevail than those without. In the following chapter, I suggest ways to extend the analyses in future studies.

73 E.g., King and Zeng 2001.

CHAPTER 6.

Conclusion: Taking Resolve Seriously

In *War and Peace*, Leo Tolstoy analyzes the mechanics of war by using an analogy to physics, noting that "in warfare the force of armies is the product of the mass multiplied by something else, an unknown x."[1] The unknown x, he later explains, is resolve, a variable subjected to no less scrutiny by twenty-first-century political scientists and policymakers than nineteenth-century Russian novelists. Given the extent to which political science scholarship in general—and IR scholarship in particular—is often divided by both methodological and substantive sects, resolve's predominance presents something of a paradox.[2] On the one hand, it is a central protagonist in all quadrants of the field, looming large in everything from classical qualitative accounts of "national will" as a component of power, to seminal game theoretic models of crisis bargaining and battlefield outcomes, to influential quantitative studies examining whether democratic publics are really as irresolute or cost-sensitive as policymakers have often feared.[3] On the other hand, I argued here that despite its ubiquity in the discipline, resolve very much remains an "unknown x": conceptually, we do not know what it is, and tend to use it in a variety of inconsistent ways, often conflating it with capabilities and intentions. Empirically, we do not know how to measure it, and tend to either relegate it to the error term, or infer it tautologically from the outcomes we are using it to explain. Theoretically, we do not know where resolve comes from, and why some actors are more resolved than others. Yet for resolve to be a theoretically useful construct, it cannot simply be a magic variable we turn to after the fact. The motivating challenge for the book was to try to strip resolve of this magical quality, and determine if it remains analytically useful when we do.

Following Waltz, who noted that there is no "self-denying ordinance against the use of materials and techniques of other social scientists,"[4] I sought to

---

1 Part XIV, chapter II, cited in Morgenthau 1985, 151.
2 Lake 2011.
3 Wright 1964; Organski 1968; Morgenthau 1985; Snyder and Diesing 1977; Fearon 1995; Powell 2004; Mueller 1971; Reiter and Stam 2002; Gelpi, Feaver, and Reifler 2009.
4 Waltz 1959, 11.

TABLE 6.1. Comparison of Results: Experimental and Observational Data

	DEPENDENT VARIABLE		
	RESOLVE		MILITARY OUTCOMES
	LAB	SURVEY	BOOLEAN ANALYSES
Situational variables			
Cost of fighting			
Ex ante	✓	✗	✗
Ex post	✓	✗	
Cost of backing down			
Intrinsic (stakes)			∗
Extrinsic (reputation)	∗	✓	∗
Dispositional variables			
Time preferences	✓	✓	✓
Risk preferences	✓	✓	∗
Honor culture	✓	✗	✓
Trait / behavioral self-control	✓	✓	✗
Interactionist dynamics	✓	∗	✓

Evidence in favor: ✓: strong ∗: weak ✗: none
For a more detailed comparison of the lab and survey experiment results, see table 4.3.

provide microfoundations for resolve in IR by connecting IR scholarship with a burgeoning body of research on willpower and self-control in other disciplines, showing that some of the same dispositional characteristics that social psychologists and behavioral economists use to predict willpower in our daily lives also moderate the impact of the costs of war, and thus can be used to explain resolve in military interventions. I tested the theory with multiple methods, at multiple levels of analysis: first, using lab and survey experiments to study the determinants of resolve at the individual-level in the context of public opinion about military interventions, and subsequently using the experimental results as individual-level microfoundations for a series of country- and leader-level Boolean analyses of the probability of victory in great power military interventions.

On the whole, the results, summarized in table 6.1, offer relatively consistent evidence in favor of the importance of the costs of backing down, but less so with the costs of fighting. As shown in table 6.1, the evidence for the impact of the cost of fighting is mixed: both anticipated costs and casualties significantly shape resolve in the lab experiment, but not the survey experiment or the large-N analyses. The evidence for the impact of the cost of backing down is greater, for both reputation costs (tested in both the experiments and the large-N analyses) and the interests at stake (tested solely in the large-N analyses). Thus, although there is relatively weak evidence supporting the hypothesis that the costs of fighting lowers the amount of resolve displayed (and thus, decreases the probability of victory), there is more consistent evidence in favor of the contention that the costs of backing down increases the amount of resolve displayed (and thus, increases the probability of victory).

This pattern of results has implications for three different literatures. First, in showing that resolve should not simply be treated as the inverse of an actor's costs of fighting, the findings challenge one of the major working assumptions of the rationalist IR literature, which has tended to use the "costs of war" as a shorthand for resolve; across the empirical chapters, the cost of fighting appears to be neither the only nor even the predominant source of resolve. Second, the results also speak to the public opinion literature on the use of force, especially the "cost-benefit" model of public opinion, in that the benefits appear to offer higher explanatory power than the costs, strongly countering the prevailing wisdom among policymakers.[5] In this respect, although the public opinion literature has tended to focus quite heavily on casualties as a major determinant of public opinion about the use of force, they play much less of a role here.[6] One potential explanation for this discrepancy is that much of the experimental work that studies casualties tends to focus on it in isolation, producing rich and detailed portraits of the different ways in which casualties affect attitudes toward conflict, but giving little sense of the substantive importance of casualties relative to other factors.[7] Meanwhile, although analyses of attitudes toward the use of force using longitudinal observational data have tended to avoid this pitfall, the fact that casualties always accumulate as interventions proceed means that casualties are one of many factors correlated with time, making its relative effect difficult to disentangle.[8] Third, these dynamics also speak to a well-established literature evaluating the public's prudence, rationality, and consistency.[9] One of the striking points about the lab and survey experiments is that they consistently fail to find evidence in favor of "sunk cost" logic driving participants' attitudes toward military interventions. Since sunk cost effects are usually understood to be irrational, these results paint a relatively positive picture of the public.[10]

---

5 Larson 2000; Klarevas 2002; Gelpi, Feaver, and Reifler 2009.
6 E.g., Mueller 1971; Gartner 2008a.
7 Boettcher and Cobb 2006, Gartner 2008a, 2008b.
8 Smith 2005; Althaus and Coe 2011, 74.
9 Jentleson 1992; Page and Shapiro 1992; Almond 1950; Converse 1964.
10 Arkes and Blumer 1985, 124.

The results for the dispositional variables show that war is not just something that takes place on the battlefield, but also takes place "in between the ears." Indeed, one of the striking patterns across all three empirical chapters is that the effects of the dispositional variables are substantively larger than those of the situational ones. Longer time preferences are consistently associated with greater resolve in both the lab and survey experiments, and longer leader time horizons bolster the probability of victory in the large-N analyses. Honor orientations are associated with greater resolve in the lab experiment and higher probabilities of victory at the leader-level in the large-N chapter. Although the functional form of risk attitudes changes, it displays a significant nonlinear association with resolve in the experimental data, and a significant negative relationship with the probability of victory at the leader-level in the large-N analyses. Trait or behavioral self-control has a somewhat mixed fate, producing significant effects in the experimental data, but not the observational data. Given that the experiments employ more direct measures of trait self-control than the large-N analyses, it is possible that trait self-control indeed bolsters the probability of victory, but I am unable to find support for this hypothesis with the existing data. Since dispositional variables implicate an interesting level-of-analysis question, it is worthwhile to note that in the large-N analyses, the dynamic leader-level dispositional measures consistently perform better than static country-level ones, suggesting we should think of dispositions in IR as evolving rather than fixed entities, and focus more on individual leaders as the relevant unit of analysis rather than countries as a whole. These results should thereby lend some skepticism about IR theories that rely on national cultural generalizations rather than invoking more contingent or fine-grained accounts of dispositional tendencies.[11]

At a broader level, I also find evidence in favor of an interactionist theory of resolve—tested in the lab and survey experiments using a series of interactions between situational treatments and dispositional features, and in the large-N analyses by a Boolean statistical model, in which the probability of victory is modeled as the product of situational *and* dispositional features—thus taking the very functional form that Tolstoy predicts when he envisions material (situational) features being multiplied by x in *War and Peace*. Indeed, as noted in chapter 5, the novel contribution of the project comes not from the individual variables in the analyses, but from the ends to which they are applied and the overarching framework in which they are incorporated.

More important, though, is the following. Political scientists have long lamented our failure to subject theories of resolve to serious empirical scrutiny. As Ray and Vural complained, "If there were a dependable, widely accepted way to measure the "will to win," silly arguments and their advocates could not

---

11 E.g., Huntington 1993, as opposed to Hopf 2002.

escape detection so easily, and perhaps not at all."[12] The tests in chapters 3–5 suggest that the argument that resolve boosts the likelihood of victory is not so silly after all. That said, the dispositional side of resolve to which Ray and Vural are referring here is not as all-powerful as some of its boosters have claimed. Napoleon's famous dictum that in war, moral factors outweigh material factors by a ratio of three to one, for example, is not borne out by the data. If one thinks of dispositional sources of resolve as moral factors, and situational sources of resolve as material factors, the slopes of the two axes in figure 5.3 show that both factors are important, but the slope of the fitted values along the dispositional axis is not three times steeper than along the situational one.

By highlighting the importance of causal complexity in thinking about social phenomena and avoiding what Morgenthau called "the fallacy of the single factor," the results will likely disappoint scholars accustomed to understanding social phenomena as the function of a single treatment and a host of substantively uninteresting control variables.[13] The findings will also be troubling for policymakers looking for a monocausal explanation for resolve. Indeed, the results suggest there is no "magic bullet" for resolve: no single variable that political scientists and policymakers need to pay attention to in order to predict when some actors will display more resolve than others.

Rather than rehashing the main points outlined in the previous pages, I turn instead to a number of extensions, qualifications, and areas for future research. First, I speculate about the theory's applicability to other domains. I then discuss how the findings raise questions about two common assumptions in IR theory—the extent to which resolve is "private information" that decision-makers can access but foreign rivals cannot, and the dichotomy between capabilities and resolve in classical theories of war. I then suggest a number of ways resolve could be studied in a dyadic rather than a monadic fashion, and raise a normative question regarding the ethics of resolve. I subsequently revisit the situational versus dispositional distinction, push back against the notion that leaders are homogenous, and note how the use of text as data can offer a more direct way of measuring leaders' dispositional features. I conclude by responding to a potential objection from strong dispositionalists, and suggest a number of additional causes of resolve that could be incorporated into future studies.

RESOLVE IN OTHER DOMAINS

Although the theory of resolve advanced here is deliberately general, all of the empirical tests focus explicitly on the context of resolve in foreign

12 Ray and Vural 1986, 321.
13 Braumoeller 2003; Morgenthau 1985, 174.

military interventions. In this sense, although the results from chapters 3–5 are not intended to evaluate claims about the dynamics of resolve in other contexts (for example, Krauthammer's assertion that sufficient resolve can reverse the decline of American unipolarity), the overarching framework itself easily applies and lends itself to future tests.[14] For example, in the study of International Political Economy (IPE), "political will" is often used to explain phenomena like participation in IMF programs and the implementation of cooperative international agreements like TRIPS.[15] Although the costs of participation and the costs of backing down are different in an IPE context than an international security one, the basic framework still holds, as does the importance of dispositional variables like time and risk preferences.

Importantly, however, the nature of the relationships between these dispositional variables and resolve is likely to differ across issues or domains. For example, the positive association between time preferences and resolve discussed in the previous chapters follows in cases where the costs and benefits of a policy are temporally arranged in a particular manner, with the costs paid in the present and the benefits received in the future. Many policy issues reflect this temporal configuration: fighting climate change and global warming, for example, involves paying costs upfront to avoid greater costs in the future. Painful economic reforms like structural adjustment programs also involve experiencing an immediate economic burden in order to achieve longer-term economic benefits. However, there are other issues where costs and benefits display the opposite temporal configuration, whereupon one would expect longer shadows of the future to be associated with decreased resolve. One such example concerns surprise attacks. Jervis suggests that surprise attacks like the Japanese bombing of Pearl Harbor or Egyptian war of attrition are often surprising precisely because they are implausible, and are implausible precisely because although they offer benefits in the short term, they offer costs in the long run.[16] In these contexts, then, patience should be associated with decreased rather than increased resolve. Similarly, as discussed more formally in appendix A.3, the relationship between risk preferences and resolve varies with risk perceptions; the nonlinear effects found in the experimental chapters stem from military interventions being a domain where all policy choices can be seen as carrying their own risks. In issues or domains characterized by ill-structured decision environments, or where we lack objective measurable probabilities, the potential presence of countervailing risk perceptions means there are likely to be nonlinear relationships between risk and resolve.[17] In other issue areas, where there is relative intersubjective agreement about which

14 Krauthammer 2009.
15 Przeworski and Vreeland 2000; Levy 1999.
16 Jervis 1985b, 27.
17 Steinbruner 1974.

courses of action are seen as risky—either because of inherent characteristics of the issue, or because of a one-sided information environment—we should see a cleaner, linear relationship.

HOW PRIVATE IS PRIVATE INFORMATION?

One key implication of the above findings is that if resolve is indeed a function of both situational stakes and dispositional traits, it may be worth revisiting our standard understanding of resolve in rationalist IR as private information that (i) decision-makers can access but (ii) foreign rivals cannot.[18] My results challenge these assumptions from two different angles.

On the one hand, if resolve is indeed a state rather than a trait, one could argue that it is unclear why decision-makers should know their *own* country's resolve ex ante, since it is a second-order phenomenon, and a function of both situational and dispositional causes existing at multiple levels of analysis.[19] In this understanding, conflict and crisis bargaining are not merely about finding out your opponent's level of resolve, but about discovering your own resolve as well.[20] This finding comports with insights on willpower in social psychology and economics; in their study of willpower and personal rules, Bénabou and Tirole base their model on the assumption that "people have limited knowledge of their strength or weakness of will," consistent with a bevy of findings about self-serving and inaccurate assessments of one's own dispositions, and the tenets of self-perception theory, which argues that we are forced to make inferences about our own traits by observing our behavior just like external observers are.[21] If this is the case, war (and bargaining more generally) does not just involve learning about your opponent's reservation point, but learning about your own as well.[22]

The possibility of actors being uncertain about their own resolve raises two further implications for the study of conflict. First, if actors are less likely to know their own resolve ex ante, then resolve's role in shaping which conflicts actors choose to enter may be lower than many treatments in IR often claim. The body of research that has advanced this selection story most forcefully has been the bargaining literature, but it tends to both assume that actors know their own resolve and conflate resolve with the content of an actor's desire. If neither of these assumptions are correct, this story becomes less persuasive.

---

18 E.g., Goemans 2000.

19 This possibility is also raised by Morgan (1990, 280), as well as Walt (1999, 34, fn 85) in his critique of audience cost models.

20 Van Evera 1999, 27–28.

21 Bénabou and Tirole 2004, 159; Klein and Kunda 1993; Epley and Dunning 2000; Dunning, Heath, and Suls 2004; Bem 1967.

22 To be sure, psychologists argue we know more about ourselves than we do about others (Chambers et al., 2008), but this is a relatively low baseline.

Second, although a large and diverse IR literature exists on the various devices actors employ to signal their resolve to others, we have less of a sense of what heuristics actors use to infer their own resolve.[23] Because resolve is socially desirable (as discussed in detail below), one might imagine that actors tend to inflate their estimates of their own resolve, similar to the "Lake Wobegon" effect in psychology, where, for example, 94% of college teachers think they are better than average.[24] The affective forecasting literature in psychology similarly casts doubts on our ability to reliably predict our future mental states: if sports fans (whose teams play once a week) cannot accurately predict how their favorite sports team losing will make them feel, how can leaders accurately predict how much resolve their country will display in a dispute, particularly when war remains a rare event?[25] Alternately, decision-makers may employ rules-of-thumb governed by other dispositional beliefs: decision-makers who are "democratic defeatists," for example, may see the public as mercurial and unable to stomach mounting costs of fighting.[26] Indeed, one of the striking elements of American military interventions in the 1990s was the extent of the White House's skepticism about the public's level of commitment: NATO commanders instructed pilots to fly bombers at at high altitude not because the public told them to, but because the White House assumed the public was casualty-averse. Similarly, the White House withdrew from Somalia not because public opinion *had* turned after Mogadishu, but because they assumed it *would* turn, polling data revealing that Americans were far more willing to stick with the mission than either the White House or other Americans assumed.[27] In this sense, actors in world politics can also underestimate their resolve. Ultimately, though, if actors are uncertain about their own resolve, as well as uncertain about their rival's resolve—and presumably, uncertain about their rival's uncertainty about both their own resolve and their rival's resolve, and so on—the complex nature of the decision-making environment actors face stretches far beyond the limits of human cognition.[28] Future research should thus take up the challenge of studying the heuristics actors use to assess their own resolve, and whether they use different heuristics to assess their own resolve than the ones they use to assess those of others.

On the other hand, even if resolve itself is not directly observable, the premise for the large-N analyses in chapter 5 is that resolve has observable causes. Certainly, many of the proxies employed in the previous chapter—rates of leadership turnover, leaders' previous military experience, alliance

23 E.g., Fearon 1997; Huth 1997.
24 Alicke et al. 1995.
25 Wilson and Gilbert 2003.
26 Desch 2008.
27 Dauber 2001.
28 Mercer 2012.

commitments, and so on—are observable not just by analysts, but by decision-makers themselves, not just ex post, but ex ante. Yet if information about these factors is available ex ante, then this private information is in fact public information, and uncertainty about resolve can no longer explain why rational actors would fight in the first place. One potential explanation is that not all of these indicators are always public: alliances through the nineteenth and early twentieth centuries were often secret, for example—as reflected in the first of Woodrow Wilson's Fourteen Points, which called for "open covenants openly arrived at." Yet this caveat does not apply to the military interventions investigated in the previous chapter, and from a rationalist perspective, the fact that these conflicts took place suggests that the interventions' targets and initiators failed to accurately gauge each others' resolve. A more plausible explanation is that these measures are relatively rough and do not perfectly predict resolve, such that there is still substantial room for error. Another is that although this information might be observable ex ante, leaders might not avail themselves of it, or might aggregate it in idiosyncratic or biased ways, as suggested in the above discussion of heuristics. Indeed, as Morgan points out, this is a broader concern for game theoretic approaches, in that "if the players know the situation and the theory, they can predict with certainty the outcome and should not waste their time 'bargaining.'"[29] I may calculate fitted values from Boolean logistic regressions on situational and dispositional indicators of actors' resolve, but it is likely unrealistic to presume decision-makers do the same, rather than engaging in satisficing or motivated reasoning.[30] Indeed, as argued above, to simplify these difficult decision-making tasks, actors often turn to schema and heuristics to infer others' dispositional characteristics, such that rather than understanding conflict as a consequence of uncertainty, we can see it as the product of misplaced certainty instead, freeing us from the paradox Gartzke describes of viewing uncertainty as a necessary condition for war without seeing war itself as stochastic.[31]

RESOLVE AND CAPABILITIES

These findings also question some of the classical understandings about the relationship between capabilities and resolve. In the interactionist framework advanced here, capabilities are a situational source of resolve, inasmuch as increases in capabilities reduce the cost of fighting. If this framework is correct, although capabilities and resolve are distinct phenomena, it becomes conceptually difficult to treat them as competing explanations for military outcomes; accounts that attempt to do so are really contrasting the explanatory

29 Morgan 1990, 280.
30 Simon 1957; Kunda 1990.
31 Mitzen and Schweller 2011; Gartzke 1999.

power of a particular situational source of resolve versus a dispositional source, such that the real dichotomy is not between capabilities and resolve, per se, but between situational and dispositional features.[32]

Similarly, the classical realists who argued that "national morale" was a source of power have the causal arrow reversed: rather than resolve bolstering power, power increases resolve.[33] Claims about national morale or national will as a source of power show that the power literature suffers from many of the same tautologies that the resolve literature does: if power is defined via the outcomes it is used to explain, as in Dahl's seminal definition of power as "*A* has power over *B* to the extent that he can get *B* to do something that *B* would not otherwise do," it becomes impossible to empirically test the relationship between power and outcomes (since, by definition, *A* must prevail over *B* if the former is more powerful than the latter).[34] The "paradox of unrealized power" is only a paradox if we take this tautology at face value.[35]

In a sense, the move to studying power via material capabilities— exemplified by the Correlates of War project's focus on military expenditures and personnel, energy consumption, iron and steel production, and population as measures of national capability—represents a similar move to the one I employ here with respect to resolve in chapter 5: power is a latent variable, so rather than study it based on its consequences, we do so based on its causes.[36] Indeed, many of the most important variables in International Relations are also the hardest to measure: legitimacy, leadership, order, status, prestige, and so on. Like resolve, many of these variables tend to be studied based on their posited consequences in a manner that flirts with tautology. The two-stage measurement strategy I adopt here can be appropriated to study other such constructs as well.

A scholar from the "Peace Science" tradition might wonder whether the type of two-stage framework I employ here could be used to generate situational and dispositional resolve scores similar to the material capabilities (CINC) scores in the Correlates of War, which could then be exported to other contexts for for easy use in other studies.[37] Although this approach would be appropriate for dispositional resolve scores, it is less practical for situational resolve scores, since situational causes of resolve are relational to the costs and stakes inherent in a particular intervention, rather than monadic: for example, situational features shaping Chinese resolve during the Korean

32 E.g., Maoz 1983; Ray and Vural 1986.

33 Wright 1964; Morgenthau 1985.

34 Dahl 1957.

35 Baldwin 1979, 163. Note that this is different from the distinction between "latent capabilities" and actual capabilities (e.g., Walt, 1985), which refers instead to countries that have large-scale industrial production but have not converted it into military assets.

36 Singer, Bremer, and Stuckey 1972.

37 Kelman 1981; Bennett and Stam 2000.

War were fundamentally different than those shaping its resolve during its intervention in Burma on behalf of Chinese nationalists, even though the two military operations took place at the same time.

ON THE DYADIC NATURE OF RESOLVE

The relational nature of the situational resolve measures raises the question of the dyadic element of resolve. As noted in chapter 5, we often understand resolve dyadically, in terms of a "balance of resolve," but for reasons of tractability, neither the analyses with experimental data in chapters 3 and 4 nor the analyses with observational data in chapter 5 are fully dyadic. In the lab and survey experiments, rather than explicitly including information about the opponent's resolve in the experimental vignettes, participants must infer the resolve of the opponent through events on the battlefield.[38] If I sought to more explicitly study how these situational and dispositional predictors of resolve change in a dyadic experimental context, there are at least three ways I might do so, although two of them involve substantial tradeoffs, and the third ends up being similar to the experimental designs employed in chapters 3 and 4.

First, I could change the format of the experiment, from a vignette-based public opinion about foreign policy experiment to an economics-style bargaining game experiment where two players face off against one another.[39] I can manipulate situational determinants of resolve via the payoff structure, and as before, measure participants' dispositional traits using standard instruments from behavioral economics and social psychology. In abstracting to a bargaining game, though, I would lose the IR-specific content of the vignettes, the ability to make inferences about public opinion (since participants play as agents rather than principals), and the context of a military intervention more specifically: the players are simply challengers and defenders rather than an intervening power seeking to repel the invasion of its smaller ally by its larger neighbor; any contextual richness would be lost. Second, I could attempt to preserve the IR-specific content of the scenario through a crisis simulation game, where participants are leaders deciding whether to attack, and how long to persist.[40] Given potential divergences between non-elite participants and actual decision-makers—a point to which I return below—there is a tradeoff here as well.[41] Alternately, borrowing from attribution theory—in which the

38 Ramsay 2008.

39 E.g., Dickson 2009; Tingley and Walter 2011, Kertzer and Brutger 2016.

40 E.g., McDermott and Cowden 2001.

41 Mintz, Redd, and Vedlitz 2006; Hafner-Burton et al. 2014. This is especially the case given the extent to which the original experiments focus on public opinion in the context of American foreign policy, such that if one player is playing the United States, the other would be playing a less powerful rival. Herrmann et al. (1997) warn that the full range of images from Herrmann

resolve of another actor simply becomes part of your own situation—I could retain the original vignette-based public opinion-style experiment setup, but also manipulate the opponent's resolve. However, given that resolve is not directly observable, these manipulations of resolve essentially translate into manipulating signals sent or events on the battlefield, thus producing something strikingly similar to the experimental designs employed in chapters 3 and 4. More importantly, if the resolve of your opponent affects your resolve simply by affecting your costs of fighting, the more interesting question is not how your resolve is shaped by your opponent's resolve, but rather, how this balance of resolve affects actual conflict outcomes.

To extend the large-N analyses to capture more of this dyadic component, there are two different challenges to overcome, neither of which are insurmountable. The first involves calculating dispositional and situational resolve scores for the target of the intervention. This requires overcoming data availability issues, especially for the dispositional sources of resolve, as well as some conceptual considerations involving the relevant situational variables for the target. The second involves deciding the best way to operationalize the balance of resolve. One approach is to simply calculate the balance of resolve similar to how political scientists calculate the balance of capabilities—each actor's resolve score as a fraction of the total resolve of both actors.[42] However, whereas relative capabilities are measured using a single composite indicator for each side, in an interactionist framework there are two resolve scores for each side, which means calculating both a relative dispositional resolve score and a relative situational resolve score. A second approach, and more theoretically interesting, is to adopt a broader Boolean framework, in which the probability of victory is a function of situational and dispositional resolve for both the great power and the target.[43]

The computationally intensive nature of this setup—with four different paths, two for each actor—thus produces considerable data demands, but has the potential for some intriguing empirical tests. If balance of resolve models are correct, a simultaneous increase in each side's situational or dispositional resolve should have no corresponding increase on the probability of victory; it should only be when one side increases its resolve relative to the other that military outcomes should be affected. At the same time, there are interesting questions about logics of substitutability: *ceteris paribus*, if one

---

and Fischerkeller's (1995) image theory cannot be tested experimentally on an American sample because of an inability to imagine interacting with a more powerful other, suggesting the value of an experiment with a cross-national sample.

42 E.g., Reiter and Stam 1998b, 380.

43 In which λ once again refers to the inverse logit function $\frac{1}{1+e^{-x}}$, the revised Boolean framework would be $Pr(y_{i,t} = 1 | \alpha, B, x_{i,t}) = \lambda(\alpha_1 + B_{S_1} x_{i,t}) * \lambda(\alpha_2 + B_{D_1} x_{i,t}) * \lambda(\alpha_3 + B_{S_2} x_{i,t}) * \lambda(\alpha_4 + B_{D_2} x_{i,t})$.

side's situational resolve is higher, but the other side's dispositional resolve is higher, what impact does this have on conflict outcomes?

THE DARK SIDE OF RESOLVE

Left unmentioned in the previous chapters is a broader normative issue that is also worth reflecting on. Beneath the massive literature on willpower in the social sciences lies a normative agenda that is both tacit and pervasive: a sense that resolve is good. It might seem an overstatement for two prominent social psychologists to go so far as to suggest that willpower is the "master virtue," but cultural psychologists suggest that self-discipline is a universal value, and especially in Western political traditions, we look down upon the compulsive and weak-willed, caution against "taking the easy way out," laud those who overcome adversity, and treat bounded willpower as a deviation from classical rationality, an acknowledgment of the biases and frailties that characterize ordinary human decision-making.[44] The lionization of resolution reflects two motives. First are political ones, due to self-regulation's relationship with social order. Self-control, after all, is also a form of regulation: Elias's civilizing processes involve the rise of various norms and customs to regulate impulsive behavior, and Foucauldian analyses of governmentality focus on control of the body and the self, the word "government" referring to self-regulation in a medical or religious sense long before it adopted a legal or political connotation.[45] Second are instrumental ones: we reward motivation out of the belief that the motivated are themselves rewarded, since goals must be fought for in order to be achieved. Indeed, self-control is positively correlated with wealth, achievement, and well-being, and negatively correlated with crime and delinquency.[46] It is for this reason that the "libertarian paternalist" tradition in behavioral economics and public policy has begun reflecting on public policy solutions to "nudge" individuals to display more self-control, out of the assumption that willpower and welfare go hand in hand.[47] When we talk about resolve in IR, we tend to portray it in the same normative light: resolute states are posited to get more at the bargaining table and on the battlefield, while to suggest the public is more resolute than commonly thought is to paint a more favorable picture than that evoked by naysayers.[48]

Yet some of the decision-making literature suggests the potential for what one might call the "dark side of resolve." Evolutionary models suggest that

44 Baumeister and Exline 1999; Schwartz 1992; Jolls, Sunstein, and Thaler 1998; Ainslie 2001.
45 Elias 2000; Lemke 2001.
46 Offer 2006; Ameriks et al. 2007; Mischel, Shoda, and Rodriguez 1989; Magaletta and Oliver 1999; Gottfredson and Hirschi 1990.
47 Fennell 2009.
48 Morrow 1985; Powell 1987; Maoz 1983; Gelpi, Feaver, and Reifler 2009.

there are many contexts in which resolve may not be ecologically adaptive: the highly uncertain environments that characterized much of early human history, for example, rewarded impulsiveness rather than self-control, since hunter-gatherers who passed on an immediate reward might not encounter a larger later one.[49] Zeiler writes that "an animal that would forgo food now in the hope of getting a slightly larger quantity in the future would be the type of gambler welcome in Las Vegas."[50] Regardless of its cross-situational utility, if the will is a volitional faculty used to initiate action, then it can be employed for negative goals just like positive ones.[51] While myopic decision-making that neglects the future is one type of self-control problem, hyperopic decision-making that neglects the present is another.[52] Excessive self-control leads to "compulsions": excessive dieting can give rise to eating disorders, excessive attention to detail can border on obsessive behavior, and excessively future-oriented individuals can fall prey to martyr complexes and asceticism.[53]

A similar phenomenon can be understood in IR: some leaders are too indecisive and thus unable to "stay the course," while others are too dogmatic and unable to deviate from it, a "strategic rigidity" that is just as detrimental.[54] The sticktoitiveness that served Woodrow Wilson well in much of his political career also cost him Senate approval for the League of Nations, for example.[55] More generally, an argument could be made that many of the military interventions analyzed in chapter 5 were not in fact in the national interest of the intervening power; in one tranche of American political discourse, the chief lesson of the Vietnam War is not the importance of being resolved, but rather, the necessity of questioning whether a war is really worth fighting in the first place. Similarly, Gartzke, Li, and Boehmer note that there are some methods of signaling resolve that negatively impact your bargaining position, while Powell suggests that high levels of resolve can lead to perverse outcomes during crisis bargaining, since in order for states to screen out irresolute types, they have to escalate further, thereby rendering crises more likely.[56] The "bright line" rules actors make in order to bolster their commitment can then prove maladaptive.[57] In this sense, although this book may be a disquisition on resolve, it should not be mistaken for a veneration of it.[58]

49 Logue 1998.
50 Zeiler 1988, 696.
51 Kivetz and Simonson 2002; Fennell 2009.
52 Kivetz and Keinan 2006.
53 Ainslie 2001, 50–1; Posner 1997.
54 Polsky 2010.
55 Post 2015, 39.
56 Gartzke, Li, and Boehmer 2001; Powell 1987.
57 Schelling 1984; Ainslie 2001; Bénabou and Tirole 2004.
58 This is also setting aside the critical literature on resilience in military sociology, which suggests that the consistent emphasis on resilience in the armed forces produces detrimental

The notion that resolve is a second-order phenomenon, and thus neutral with respect to the content of the intentions underlying it, means that rather than thinking about resolve exclusively in terms of support for war, future research could also examine resolve not just in non-military domains, but also study resolve in terms of *staying out* of military misadventures. Indeed, although we tend to associate resolve with avoiding the temptation to withdraw—as in Henry Kissinger warning Richard Nixon that troop withdrawals are like "salted peanuts"—we can also understand resolve in terms of sailing against the predominant political winds and opposing intervention. It makes little sense to characterize political figures like Senator Wayne Morse of Oregon (a staunch opponent of the war in Vietnam) and Congressman Dennis Kucinich of Ohio (an outspoken critic of the invasion of Iraq) as irresolute because they steadfastly opposed military interventions they never supported in the first place. Similarly, George Washington's Farewell Address argued that as American power grows and foreign policy evolves, the country should avoid the temptation of entangling itself in European affairs—which suggests that one can be resolved about non-intervention just as one can be resolved about pursuing an intervention to victory.

ON THE DISTINCTION BETWEEN SITUATIONS AND DISPOSITIONS

One potential concern with the large-N analyses in chapter 5 is that some of the leader-level dispositional variables employed are not in fact measures of dispositions themselves, but rather, measures of the situational factors that produce them. Below, I suggest how the use of text provides one way to get cleaner measures of leader-level dispositional traits, but this question also raises a broader concern: namely, if situational variables can be used to proxy dispositional ones, how meaningful is it to distinguish between situational and dispositional variables anyway?

Although the situational-dispositional distinction has a long heritage in social psychology—and mirrors similar dichotomies like the agent-structure debate—it is worth noting that the situational-dispositional distinction can blur together in at least two ways that have interesting implications for the study of resolve, and for International Relations theory more generally.[59]

First, particularly from a thicker interactionist perspective, many factors we consider to be situational features are in fact dispositionally derived. "The stakes" inherent in a situation are laden with subjective (and intersubjective) meaning: protracted conflicts often persist over parcels of land not because

---

mental health consequences when military personnel attempt to reintegrate back into civilian life. See, e.g., McGarry, Walklate, and Mythen 2015.

59 Heider 1958; Ross 1977; Gilbert 1998; Wendt 1987; Dessler 1989; Carlsnaes 1992. See also Copeland 1997, who criticizes the situational-dispositional distinction in a different way.

of their innate physical characteristics, but because of the meaning with which they have been imbued.[60] Similarly, studies conducted before the recent Iranian nuclear deal suggested that some Iranians saw the pursuit of a nuclear program as a sacred value, such that abandoning the program in exchange for material incentives is perceived as taboo, thereby indicating that the stakes of the Iranian nuclear program are not simply a feature of the world, but vary systematically in the minds of Iranians.[61]

Just as some situational factors draw their meaning through dispositional characteristics, many dispositional traits are often assumed to have situational causes. There is some evidence that social and cultural factors shape time preferences, and that economic development is associated with longer discount rates.[62] The basic tenet of prospect theory is that risk attitudes depend on a situational feature—namely, whether the actor is in the domain of gains or losses.[63] Similarly, economists are increasingly interested in the extent to which formative experiences shape orientations toward risk: Americans' experience of stock market returns significantly shapes their subsequent attitudes toward financial risk, while Afghan civilians previously exposed to violence become significantly more risk-averse when primed to think of fearful experiences.[64] In their exploration of the December 1916 peace overtures during the First World War, Lanoszka and Hunzeker treat honor as situationally induced, deeming honor concerns as particularly likely to arise during preventive wars and territorial occupation.[65]

In a related vein, there is a long tradition of "geodeterminist" arguments that use environmental factors to explain the emergence of particular societal-level characteristics. In the history of political geography, Frederick Jackson Turner's famous frontier thesis, for example, argues that America's wide open spaces and expanding Western frontier were responsible for the individualistic nature of its political culture, while Sergey Solovyov, a nineteenth-century Russian historian, made similar arguments tracing Russia's unique national character to the flatness and vast expanses of its steppes.[66] Psychologists have found that climate extremity strongly predicts the distribution of collectivist orientations across Chinese provinces, and that disease prevalence predicts regional differences in personality traits.[67] Closer to home, Mead's argument about the Jacksonian tradition in America—a set of beliefs conceptually

---

60 Goddard 2006; Toft 2006; Hassner 2006/2007.
61 Dehghani et al. 2009, 2010.
62 Benjamin, Choi, and Strickland 2010; Wang, Rieger, and Hens 2016.
63 Kahneman and Tversky 2000.
64 Malmendier and Nagel 2011; Callen et al. 2014. Note in the former case that it is unclear whether it is risk preference or risk perceptions that changes.
65 Lanoszka and Hunzeker 2015.
66 Turner 1956; Bassin 1993.
67 Van de Vliert et al. 2013; Schaller and Murray 2008.

similar to an honor culture—draws from the work of the historian David Hackett Fischer in tracing Jacksonianism to the influence of the "borderers," immigrants from the Scottish-English and Northern Ireland border area, whose constant exposure to conflict inculcated a marked distrust of those outside of the "folk community."[68]

There are three speculative implications here that are of interest to theories of resolve like this one. First, if dispositional characteristics are indeed shaped over time by broader situational forces, distributions of dispositional characteristics should vary both within and across populations. Indeed, the premise of cross-cultural psychology is that distributions of dispositional characteristics vary across countries and regions, even if our perceptions of these "national characters" are often inaccurate.[69] The assumption that groups differ in characteristics like honor culture or orientation toward risk manifests itself frequently in political discourse. When the right-wing terrorist Anders Breivik was apprehended by Norwegian authorities in 2011 after detonating a bomb in Oslo and carrying out a mass shooting at a youth camp on Utoeya island, for example, he requested that he be examined by Japanese investigators, claiming that "the Japanese understand the concept of honor better than the Europeans."[70]

Regardless of the accuracy of our perceptions of them, if the distribution of dispositional characteristics varies across populations, and leaders are drawn from these populations, then one might imagine that leader-level dispositional characteristics should vary across countries as well, even if particular dispositional traits are correlated with the probability of becoming a leader in the first place (a question I return to below). Rather than leader-level dispositional characteristics "washing out," one would still expect different distributions to occur. Moreover, if institutions shape the process in which individual leaders are selected for office, institutional variation across countries should lead to greater dispositional variation across leaders, since different types of dispositional characteristics are likely to be beneficial in different types of institutional environments.[71]

Second, the relative contribution of dispositional sources of resolve on conflict outcomes should vary over time. If globalization is marked by diffusion processes and an increasing homogeneity among ruling elites, these dispositional differences should decrease over time, such that dispositional determinants of resolve would likely have had a greater impact on war outcomes 100 years ago than they will 100 years from now. Conversely, given the extent

68 Mead 2002; Fischer 1989; Haglund and Kertzer 2008.
69 McCrae and Terracciano 2005; Rentfrow, Gosling, and Potter 2008; Bartram 2013; Terracciano et al. 2005.
70 Post 2015, 8.
71 Rosen 2005.

to which "international society" in the seventeenth and eighteenth centuries consisted of what Morgenthau calls a "small, cohesive, and homogenous" aristocracy, who had received the same education, shared the same set of values, and were often part of the same family, one might imagine there were fewer dispositional differences among the European leaders 300 years ago than between present world leaders, such that the leader-level dispositional determinants of resolve should have had less of an impact on military outcomes then than today.[72]

Third, the proposition that familial ties among seventeenth-century European aristocracy can tell us anything about conflict behavior raises questions about genetic underpinnings for dispositional sources of resolve. The debate on genopolitics is vast and far beyond the scope of this book, but two points are especially pertinent.[73] First, many psychologists understand self-control to be a trait or individual difference, and since behavioral geneticists argue that many traits and individual differences are genetically determined, it should not be surprising that variations in self-control have been traced to heritable genetic influences as well, and that child levels of self-control are strongly predicted by parental levels of self-control.[74] Second, genetic arguments about willpower or self-control do not assume environmental factors are irrelevant. In the past two decades, a large body of work in epidemiology, behavioral genetics, and neuroscience has emerged emphasizing gene-environment interaction, in which the effect of environmental stimuli is conditioned by genetic makeup: rather than positing that genes cause psychiatric disorders, for example, there is growing evidence that pathogens in the environment are responsible for the disorders, but that susceptibility to the pathogens varies by genotype.[75] In the realm of willpower, scholars have found evidence of gene-environment interactions at work as well: individuals who suffer from childhood mistreatment are more likely to display chronic self-control problems as adults if their genetic makeup includes the low-activity version of the monoamine oxidase A (MAOA) gene, for example.[76] More broadly, though, if we think dispositions predict resolve, and we think of dispositional characteristics as being at least partly shaped by genetic makeup, there is nothing in the results presented in the previous chapters that precludes the possibility of genes playing a role here as well. Given the interplay of genetic and environmental factors, disentangling the

---

72 Morgenthau 1985, 236.

73 See Fowler and Dawes 2008; Hatemi and McDermott 2011; Charney and English 2012.

74 Muraven et al. 2005; Loehlin 1992; Bouchard 1994; Alford, Funk, and Hibbing 2005; Boutwell and Beaver 2010.

75 Caspi and Moffitt 2006.

76 Kim-Cohen et al. 2006; Beaver et al. 2010. This literature therefore offers us another reason why resolve should not simply be reduced to willingness to fight: the low-activity MAOA gene has also repeatedly been linked to propensity for aggression, in both observational and experimental studies. See Brunner et al. 1993; McDermott et al. 2009.

effects of genes from social forces is certainly challenging, but surely not more so than disentangling dispositional and situational factors more generally, as the preceding discussion makes clear. All three of these propositions are speculative and beyond the scope of the current study, but they each offer intriguing possibilities for further research.

ARE LEADERS HOMOGENOUS?

The potential relationship between institutional structures and dispositional variation raises a theoretically interesting counterargument to the prominent role of dispositions in the theoretical framework advanced here: although the experimental evidence in chapters 3 and 4 shows that ordinary citizens vary in dispositional characteristics like time preferences, risk orientations, honor cultures, and trait self-control, should there be a similar magnitude of variation in these characteristics across decision-makers? There are several versions of this argument. One variant embraces the realist romance of the "great statesman," simply positing that decision-makers are systematically different from the mass public, and particularly different from the kinds of participants taking part in psychology lab experiments.[77] One such permutation is given by Copeland, who suggests that "most leaders, given the obstacles that they must overcome to rise to the top of their nations, do not resemble the 'norm' of the population; that is, we would expect them to be much closer to the ideal-type Machiavellian rationalist than the average citizen."[78]

A related strand is less marinated in the mythos of Metternich, but em-phasizes the selection process inherent in the process of acquiring political power: if patience, a willingness to take risks, and a high level of self-control are helpful for acquiring a position of political leadership, one might imagine that the variation in these and other traits that make leaders more effective should be lower among decision-makers than in the public at large. Its corollary emphasizes a selection process of a different kind—not in terms of the traits that ease leaders into office, but those that get them kicked out: just as realists argue states will be selected out of the international system if they fail to emulate best practices, statesmen get selected out of office if they lack resolve (and thus, the dispositional characteristics associated with it), such that leaders, like states as a whole, should be "like units."[79]

---

77 See Beisner 1990.

78 Copeland 2001, 217.

79 Waltz 1979; Rousseau 2006, 98. Note that arguments about leader homogeneity are distinct from traditional Waltzian skepticism about the "first image." Waltz's (1959) argument is not that leaders are homogenous, but that the power of the situation trumps any effects that leader-level variation might have on international politics.

These counterarguments are important to consider, but suffer from a number of empirical and theoretical challenges. Diplomatic historians have long been skeptical of the notion that Castlereagh and Ceausescu are interchangeable, and political psychologists have shown that considerable variation exists across decision-makers: their temperaments, characteristics, operational codes, belief systems, and mental models.[80] Even for characteristics where elites do systematically differ from average citizens, the range across elites is vast. LeVeck et al., for example, conduct an innovative bargaining experiment on both a sample of undergraduate students and a group of elite decision-makers with an average of 21 years of experience in high-level negotiations.[81] Importantly for our purposes, they measure participants' time preferences using a similar instrument to the matching tasks employed in chapters 3 and 4, enabling us to directly compare the distributions of one of our dispositional characteristics of interest across samples of both elites and ordinary citizens. They find that on average, their elite sample is indeed more patient than their non-elite sample. However, comparing the distributions of time preferences between the two groups reveals that the group of elites demonstrate no less variation in their time preferences than their undergraduate counterparts. In fact, there is nearly six times as much variation *within* the groups as is there is between them.[82] Similarly, Loewen et al. administer the classic "Asian disease" experiment to members of parliament in Belgium, Canada, and Israel, finding that elite politicians display the same risk preferences (and also of interest, the same deviations from the classic "rational" decision-making models) as regular citizens.[83] Empirically, then, the differences between these groups are less stark than romantic visions of elite exceptionalism might suggest.

---

80 Axelrod 1973; Etheredge 1978; Murray 1996; Hermann et al. 2001; Saunders 2011; Rathbun 2014.

81 LeVeck et al. 2014.

82 More formally, when I estimate a one-way ANOVA on participants' level of patience, with a random effect on participants' elite status, the intraclass correlation is 0.148, showing that only 14.8% of the variation in patience is between groups.

83 Loewen et al. 2014. The "Asian disease" problem is a classic framing experiment from the prospect theory literature, in which the government is preparing for an outbreak of "an unusual Asian disease" expected to kill 600 people. All participants are presented with a choice between two programs to combat the outbreak. The two programs each have outcomes of equal expected value, but one of them is a certain choice (e.g., a program that will save 200 people), and the other is a risky one (e.g., a program in which there is a 1/3 probability that 600 people will be saved, but a 2/3 probability that no people will be saved). When participants are presented with this choice set in the domain of gains, most participants select the certain option. However, when participants are presented with an equivalent choice set in the domain of losses (e.g., a program in which 400 people will die, versus a program in which there is a 1/3 probability that no one will die, but a 2/3 probability that 600 people will die), most participants chose the risky option over the certain one. The results are typically used to show how people are more likely to make risky choices when in the domain of losses. See Kahneman and Tversky 2000.

There are similar concerns with a selection-based story. First, the precision of the processes through which decision-makers are systematically screened on their dispositional characteristics is an open empirical question.[84] Moreover, for selection to produce a homogeneous group of decision-makers, the selection process must be constant across environments, which either requires environmental features to be identical across political units, or for there to be a uniform selection process despite these environmental differences. Yet political scientists routinely argue that selection processes differ dramatically across states; Weeks, for example, argues that the nature of the selection process in different authoritarian regimes tends to produce leaders with dramatically different dispositions.[85] Hermann similarly notes that "some political leaders are elected, some are appointed, while others achieve office by revolution, assassination, or *coup d'etat*," concluding that "it seems unlikely that the same personal characteristics would depict such diverse people."[86] More generally, evolutionary theorists—whose field is defined by its focus on selection—emphasize the extent to which traits' ecological validity varies with the environment they face: by analogy, the kinds of characteristics that should ease leaders into office in certain milieus may obstruct them in others, as both the strength of selection pressures and the nature of the selection process vary.[87] The role of time preferences is illustrative in this regard. In some strategic contexts, good things come to those who wait; in others, fortune favors the bold. In this sense, any relationship between institutional structures and dispositional characteristics would actually facilitate dispositional diversity rather than dampen it. Future scholarship can therefore benefit from exploring this "first image reversed" approach further, empirically investigating—rather than just assuming—the relationship between selection mechanisms and distributions of traits, which offers a potentially fruitful way of thinking about the intersection between psychological and rational approaches more broadly.[88]

---

84 There is a certain irony in the extent to which critics of lab experiments on student samples in IR raise this selection story, given, as Tingley and Walter (2011, 363) note, that the students at elite universities that typically make up these subject pools are themselves the result of a competitive selection process on many of the same characteristics we ostensibly screen for when selecting our leaders. This is not to say that college freshmen and elite decision-makers are the same; only that the theoretically relevant ways in which they differ is a question that merits being the object of study, rather than a tenet of faith. For thoughtful experimental work on differences between elites and masses, see Renshon (2015).

85 Weeks 2014.

86 Hermann 1977, 15.

87 It is for this reason that leadership psychologists tend to reject the premise that good leaders possess a particular bundle of traits, noting that leader effectiveness is largely an interaction between characteristics of leaders and of the broader environment in which they are operating. See Fiedler 1965.

88 Gourevitch 1978; Mercer 2005; Rathbun, Kertzer, and Paradis 2014. One interesting potential example follows from Post's 2015 work on narcissism in politics. Post suggests that while political leaders tend on the whole to be more narcissistic than the general population, this is

TEXTUAL ANALYSIS OF LEADERS' SPEECHES

One theme woven through the previous chapters is the extent to which resolve has a discursive element, as rhetoric is used both to bolster and signal resolve.[89] Just as public health and social workers talk about "narratives" and "discourses" of resilience, both pundits and political scientists have noted the extent to which American foreign policy is often wrapped up in a rhetoric of resolve.[90] This rhetoric is reflected both in commonly invoked arguments about the need for America to maintain its reputation for resolve or else lose its credibility—the "cult of reputation"—and in the "Green Lantern" theories of politics referred to in chapter 1, in which the president of the United States simply has to "add resolve and stir" in order to achieve his or her foreign policy goals.[91] Indeed, resolve is rhetorically bandied about with such great frequency that Iyengar and Monten are able to construct a weekly time series of mentions of resolve by senior American officials in major media outlets during the Iraq War.[92] Similarly, when we think of famously resolute figures like Sir Winston Churchill, we think of the heresthetic component to resolve, in the role that his rhetoric played in rallying the British troops and people behind him.

The role of rhetoric also suggests a different way to study leader-level resolve than the one employed in chapter 5, which has the potential to circumvent concerns about the indirect nature of measures of leader-level dispositional sources of resolve. As noted in the previous chapter, there is increasing interest in the role of leaders in international politics, but extant quantitative studies of leaders in IR tend to predominantly focus on leader-level attributes, such as age, time in office, professional background, and education, rather than what leaders actually say.[93] Meanwhile, analysis of leaders' speeches figures prominently in the study of operational codes, but

---

especially true for autocratic leaders. Because narcissism is associated with a reduced capacity for empathy (Watson et al., 1984), one might imagine that dictators perform poorly in foreign policy crises not just because they surround themselves with yes-men, but because their low levels of empathy obstruct their ability to engage in the kind of perspective-taking necessary to correctly interpret the signals being sent by opponents—a fundamentally different informational mechanism than the institutional ones traditionally associated with the literature on regime type and crises (e.g., Schultz 1999).

89 Fearon 1994; Baum 2004; Trager 2011; McManus 2014. For this reason, it is interesting that resolve itself has historically played a larger role in the rationalist oeuvre than the constructivist canon, even though constructivists have historically been the ones to study communicative action and rhetorical contestation See Payne 2001; Müller 2004; Bially Mattern 2005; Krebs and Jackson 2007.

90 Ungar 2004; Lau and van Niekerk 2011.

91 Press 2005; Fettweis 2007; Tang 2005.

92 Iyengar and Monten 2008.

93 Horowitz, McDermott, and Stam 2005; Chiozza and Goemans 2004; Dreher et al. 2009; Besley and Reynal-Querol 2011.

has typically been idiographic rather than nomothetic, consisting of detailed case studies based on a small number of speeches.[94] Recent developments in automated content analysis and natural language processing offer an opportunity to bridge this gap.[95] The logic behind supervised learning variants of automated content analysis is to (i) build the corpus of relevant texts, (ii) hand-code a small subset of them based on particular categories of interest, and (iii) employ the subset as a training dataset based on which the remaining texts are coded. The key challenge is not coding leaders' time, risk preferences, and honor orientations, but rather, building the corpus, a systematic or otherwise representative repository of leader discourse. The advantage of this approach is not only that it would provide finer-grained measures of leader dispositional traits than the indirect measures obtained by measuring the dispositions' situational causes, but that these measures would be time-varying. In this sense, they avoid the challenge raised in chapter 5 of explaining conflict behavior via static measures of dispositional variables.[96]

AGAINST A PURE DISPOSITIONAL, AND A "GARBAGE CAN" MODEL OF RESOLVE

As noted in chapter 2, my theory of resolve relies on a particular ontological claim: that resolve is a *state* with both situational and dispositional causes. Pure dispositionalists, who conceptualize resolve as an inherent actor characteristic, may therefore object to these arguments: from their perspective, it is no more logically coherent to assert that environmental features make you more or less resolved than to assert that they make you more or less tall.[97] In this view, it is not that the costs of war affect your resolve, but rather, that actors respond to the costs of war, and resolved actors simply respond differently than irresolute ones.

Against the pure dispositionalists, I view resolve as a state rather than as a "type" or identity; in so doing, I borrow a maneuver from the person-situation debate in psychology, which faces a similar ontological conundrum about how to deal with phenomena that appear to have both situational and dispositional causes: "to be resolved," in this operation, is equivalent to "to display resolve," just as "to be angry" is equivalent to "to display anger." This conceptual move allows me to advance an interactionist theory of resolve, and understand the traditional dichotomy between moral and material factors in war as reflecting dispositional versus situational sources of resolve rather than

94 Leites 1951; George 1969; Walker, Schafer, and Young 1999; Renshon 2009.
95 See, e.g., Hopkins and King 2010; Spirling 2012; King, Pan, and Roberts 2013; Grimmer and Stewart 2013.
96 See also Bak and Palmer 2010, 259.
97 The effects of gravity on vertebral compression notwithstanding.

resolve versus capabilities, as I argued above. Indeed, I would suggest that despite its appeal on the surface, a pure dispositionalist theory of resolve leads to some theoretical conundrums.

For example, it seems plausible from a dispositionalist perspective to treat resolve and the costs of fighting as competing explanations, such that actors who persist in a conflict because the costs of fighting are low are not actually resolved—a claim that would likely strike many readers as sensible, in that the absence of situational resistance is not the same as the presence of personal persistence. However, as shown throughout the previous chapters, the costs of fighting are not the only costs of war, in that actors are also concerned with the costs of backing down. If we accept the premise that actors who persist in a conflict because the costs of fighting are low are not actually resolved, we should also find ourselves agreeing with the proposition that actors who persist in a conflict because the costs of backing down are high are not actually resolved, since again they are being extrinsically rather than intrinsically motivated. This move, of course, puts us in a strange position, in which actors who fight in order to maintain a reputation for resolve are actually deemed to *lack* resolve, since they are being motivated by instrumental situational forces rather than intrinsic dispositional ones—a conclusion that seems problematic. Ultimately, though, the question of whether resolve is a state or strictly a trait is an ontological claim, and thus beyond the realm of empirical verification or refutation. Further research should examine how our understanding of the dynamics of resolve changes when one begins from a different ontological premise.

Readers who accept my ontological claim that resolve is a state caused by both situational stakes and dispositional traits may nonetheless question the particular stakes and traits I have selected for study here. Indeed, there is perhaps an infinite number of potential dispositional and situational features that could merit study. To pick just a few, there is a large literature on the effect that optimism and overconfidence have on both willpower and military outcomes.[98] Similarly, classic studies of world politics often emphasized the roles of national identity and cultural homogeneity as important sources of national morale, a conclusion currently being extended at the micro-level by psychologists and anthropologists exploring the role of "identity fusion" on willingness to fight for a group.[99] Psychologists studying the "Big 5" personality traits would point to conscientiousness as a key predictor of resolve, while both IR and public opinion scholars emphasize the role that media and information

---

98 Magaletta and Oliver 1999; Watson, Chemers, and Preiser 2001; Bénabou and Tirole 2002; Blainey 1973; Johnson, Wrangham, and Rosen 2002; Johnson et al. 2006; Lewin 2012; but see Fey and Ramsay 2007.

99 Organski 1968, 186; Cline 1994; Swann Jr. et al. 2009; Atran, Sheikh, and Gomez 2014.

environments play in affecting how long the public stays on board.[100] The point, then, is not that reputation costs, the interests at stake, time and risk preferences, honor culture, and trait self-control are the *only* predictors of resolve. Rather, the motivation behind the framework is to use prior theoretical expectations to cull a finite number of variables out of a sea of possibilities, out of the belief that one of the valuable contributions of the social sciences is to draw sketches rather than just take photographs. In this sense, this project is designed not to be the last word on resolve, but an invitation for future conversation; I encourage scholars interested in other such variables to pick up where this work leaves off.

---

100 McCrae and Costa 1987; Roberts et al. 2005; Ameriks et al. 2007; Mondak 2010, 53; Johnson and Tierney 2006; Berinsky 2007.

APPENDIX A.

Supplementary Theoretical Materials

A.1. THE CENTRALITY OF RESOLVE IN RATIONALIST IR

One way of showcasing how central resolve is to our understanding of conflict is to show just how frequently we invoke it in our theoretical frameworks. Figure A.1 presents the results of a content analysis of three prominent articles by James Fearon; these works are chosen not because they are in any way a representative sample of IR scholarship on conflict as a whole, but because they are each widely cited pieces in an influential research tradition on bargaining models of conflict; as of October 2015, the three pieces have been cited more than 5,100 times according to Google Scholar. The results show that resolve and willingness are invoked nearly 170 times across the articles, making it the sixth-most popular term. As figure A.1 shows, Napoleon wasn't alone in deeming moral factors to outweigh material ones: across these three pieces, resolve is invoked nearly four and a half times more than capabilities, and five and a half times more than anarchy.

A.2. INTERACTIONISM IN ACTION: THE PERSON-SITUATION DEBATE

Personality psychology was constructed on the dispositional premise that individuals displayed stable traits or "individual differences"—the most prominent of which in the contemporary literature are the "Big 5" personality traits—that could be used to explain why people often behave strikingly differently from one another.[1] The central challenge for these approaches, however, was how stable traits could be used to explain the surprisingly high level of intra-individual variability evident when individual behavior is studied over time, particularly when the same individuals behaved remarkably differently across different situations.[2] The dynamics of the debate are less important for our purposes than the fact that it came to a conclusion "because both sides of the debate turned out to be right."[3] Rather than viewing traits as global and

1 McCrae and Costa 1987; Mondak 2010; Bauer 2011.
2 Mischel 1968.
3 Fleeson 2004, 83.

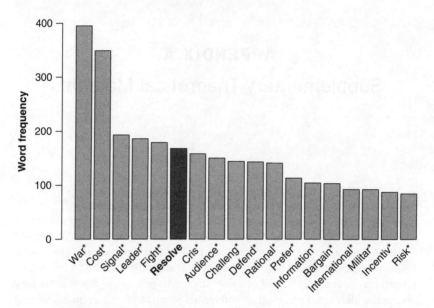

FIGURE A.1. What do we talk about when we talk about war? A content analysis of three classic pieces on bargaining theories of war by Fearon (1994, 1995, 1997) finds that resolve and willingness are used nearly 170 times across the three works, making them the sixth-most popular term. Resolve is invoked 1.63 times more than bargaining, 4.67 times more than capabilities, and 5.42 times more than anarchy. Analyses conducted using the tm package in R (Feinerer, Hornik, and Meyer, 2008).

situation-free, psychologists began to examine how these dispositional factors display conditional effects based on particular aspects of the environment, and a battery of increasingly sophisticated research designs revealed that although traits fare poorly at predicting single behaviors, they nonetheless do well at predicting overall tendencies.[4]

Figure A.2 is inspired by Fleeson's work, which seeks to reconcile the person-situation debate by viewing traits as "density distributions of states."[5] In this approach, an observer measures an actor's trait-relevant behavior (in our case, the extent to which an actor displays resolve, maintaining a policy despite contrary inclinations or temptations to back down) at repeated intervals. The multiple measures produce probability density functions (PDFs), whose moments (mean, variance, and so on) can be used to draw inferences about the different distributions of resolve that arise with different

4 Fleeson 2001; Mischel 2004.
5 Fleeson 2001.

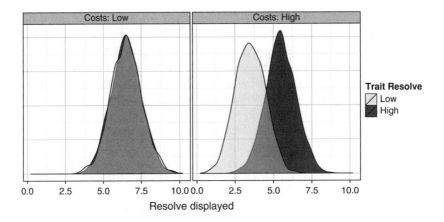

FIGURE A.2. Resolve as probability density functions.

types of actors in different types of settings. Thinking about resolve abstractly in this interactionist manner produces the stylized density distributions in figure A.2, in which each of the four probability density functions corresponds to the distribution of resolve manifested in a different dispositional-situational combination, with the x-axis measuring the level of resolve displayed at a given moment, and the y-axis depicting the density of each distribution. Moving horizontally between the two panels illustrates how resolve is affected by situational factors, with the left-hand panel depicting the amount of resolve displayed when costs are low, and the right-hand panel depicting the amount of resolve displayed when costs are high. Within each panel are two different distributions, each one mapping out the impact of a dispositional factor, which, borrowing from the psychological literature, I call "trait resolve," to refer to an actor's general tendency to maintain her policies despite contrary inclinations or temptations to back down.[6] Observations for an individual with low levels of trait resolve are depicted in light grey while the dark grey represents observations for an individual with high levels of trait resolve.

The key conclusion to be drawn from the figure is that when the costs of war are low (the left-hand side of the figure), a pooling equilibrium exists, as both resolute and irresolute "types" display the same level of resolve ($\bar{x} = 6.5$), such that the two distributions overlap completely. When the costs of war are high (the right-hand half), however, a separating equilibrium appears: resolute types will be less resolved than when they are facing lower costs of war ($\bar{x} = 5.5$), but nonetheless display more resolve than irresolute types, who wilt completely ($\bar{x} = 3.5$), such that the two distributions are now distinguishable from one

6 Tangney, Baumeister, and Boone 2004.

another. Notably, this pattern differs from those predicted by either the strict dispositional or the purely situational account specified by the endpoints of the dispositional-situational spectrum displayed in figure 1.1 in chapter 1. In a purely dispositional account, moving from the left-hand to the right-hand panel should not affect the distributions, while in a purely situational account, moving from the light grey distribution to the dark grey distribution should have a similarly nonsignificant effect.[7]

Figure A.2 is useful as a preliminary illustration of what testing an interactionist theory looks like, but has three major shortcomings, the first involving its dispositional traits, the second implicating its situational operationalization, and the third reflecting on the two-dimensional nature of the chart altogether. First, turning to the rows, we need to specify more precisely what the dispositional sources of resolve might be. Figure A.2 uses "trait resolve" as a placeholder, but since traits are defined as "intraindividual consistencies ... in propensities to behave," we run the risk of a tautology, attempting to explain variation in resolved behavior by simply positing that actors differ in their propensity to display resolve.[8] To produce a satisfactory causal theory—whether interactionist or dispositional—we need to specify which attributes of actors make them more likely to exhibit resolve in the first place, and thus more likely to display the patterns exhibited by the dark grey distribution rather than the light grey one. Second, turning to the columns, we need to further specify what counts as the costs of war. Since actors engaged in conflict must weigh a number of different types of costs (reputational costs, casualties, economic costs, opportunity costs, and so on), it is important to open up the black box of "costliness" and elaborate which types of costs count as costly. Moving from an abstract interactionist framework to an interactionist theory therefore requires us to more precisely stipulate what the dispositional and situational variables in the theory are—a task I attempt in chapter 2.

Third, although treating situational and dispositional factors as independent dimensions in a figure is a useful heuristic device, if we are interested in pursuing the thickest interactionist theorizing outlined in table 2.1, the structure of the plot is somewhat misleading, since it implies the existence of an objective situational reality apart from the observer, when dispositional factors may affect an actor's perception of the environment in the first place. Chapter 2 addresses these three questions, beginning by turning to the issue of costliness, which, once disaggregated, allows for situational features to be incorporated into actors' dispositions.

7 The plots are oversimplified in that the interactionist literature in psychology looks not just at the means of the distributions, but also at the variance. See Fleeson 2001; Mischel 2004.

8 Tett and Burnett 2003, 502.

A.3. CONCEPTUALIZING THE RELATIONSHIP BETWEEN RISK AND RESOLVE

As mentioned in chapter 2, IR scholars are used to thinking about risk preferences as having a *linear* relationship with resolve: that actors who are relatively risk-averse will display less resolve, and those who are relatively risk-acceptant will display more resolve. I suggested, on the other hand, that the relationship between risk and resolve is likely to be more complex, because the effect of general propensity for risk on specific policy preferences (such as pressing on in a military intervention) depends on actors' risk perceptions, and both fighting and backing down can be perceived as risky, particularly given the ill-structured decision environments that characterize international conflict. The coexistence of these potentially countervailing risk perceptions has important implications for the relationship between risk and resolve.

I express this relationship more formally as follows:

$$y = (b - f)\rho + \epsilon \tag{A.1}$$

in which y, resolve, is a function of the product of an individual's risk preferences (ρ, where positive values indicate a greater degree of risk aversion) and the difference between their perception of the riskiness of fighting (f) versus backing down (b). For purposes of simplicity, suppose four different types of actors, each of whom represents a different combination of risk perceptions: a "dovish" profile in which fighting is seen as risky and backing down is not ($b = 0$, $f = 1$), a "hawkish" profile in which backing down is seen as risky and fighting is not ($b = 1$, $f = 0$), an "ambivalent" profile in which both fighting and backing down are seen as risky ($b = 1$, $f = 1$), and a "neutral" profile in which neither fighting nor backing down are seen as risky ($b = 0$, $f = 0$).

For doves, because pressing on in a quagmire is seen as risky, risk aversion will be associated with decreased resolve, and risk acceptance with increased resolve—the traditional way we understand risk preferences in IR. For hawks, because backing down in the face of reputational consequences is seen as risky, risk aversion will be associated with *increased* resolve and risk acceptance with decreased resolve—the opposite of the conventional understanding of risk in the IR literature, which tends to think about risk in relatively dovish ways. For the ambivalent and neutral types, there should be no relationship between risk orientation and resolve, since the two countervailing risk perceptions should cancel one another out.

On average, then, the relationship between risk orientation and resolve in any given population thus depends on two factors that are of particular theoretical interest. First is the distribution of risk perceptions, both in terms of the proportion of ambivalent and neutral types (attenuating the relationship between risk preferences and resolve), and the ratio between doves and hawks (affecting the slope of the effect). In general, given motivated reasoning and the difficulties people have in grappling with tradeoffs, it is plausible to assume that the two different risk perceptions will be negatively correlated with one another, such that believing that fighting is risky decreases the probability of thinking of backing down as risky.[9] In this case, the proportion of ambivalent and neutral types in the population will be relatively low, and our chief interest in the distribution of risk preferences concerns the ratio of doves to hawks.

Second is the correlation between risk perceptions and risk preferences. If risk preferences and risk perceptions are uncorrelated (that is, actors' general comfort toward risk is independent of what they believe to be risky), on average we would expect risk preferences to have a linear relationship with resolve, the precise slope of which will depend on the ratio of doves and hawks. However, if risk preferences and risk perceptions are correlated, the ratio of doves to hawks will shift at different levels of risk aversion, producing a nonlinear relationship between risk preferences and resolve. If hawks in the sample are generally more risk-averse than doves—consistent with conservative foreign policy preferences being linked to decreased tolerance of uncertainty and ambiguity, and lower levels of openness to experience—the relationship between risk and resolve will resemble an inverted bell curve, with relatively risk-averse and relatively risk-acceptant actors displaying more resolve than participants with moderate levels of risk aversion; those with less extreme risk preferences will be more likely to cut and run.[10]

Finally, one of the implications of thinking about these two countervailing sets of risk preferences is that risk aversion should moderate the impact of both the costs of fighting and the costs of backing down: in an experimental context, on average, the effects of casualty treatment T_c should increase with participants' risk aversion (if $y = (b - T_c f)\rho + \epsilon$, $\frac{dy}{dT_c} = -f\rho$, such that resolve should be lower among relatively risk-averse participants than relatively risk-acceptant ones), while the effects of reputation cost treatment T_r should decrease with participants' risk aversion (if $y = (T_r b - f)\rho + \epsilon$, $\frac{dy}{DT_r} = b\rho$, such that resolve should be higher among relatively risk-averse participants than relatively risk-acceptant ones). In both cases, then, risk aversion makes actors relatively more sensitive to the particular type of cost: risk-acceptant actors are more willing to ignore the risks of backing down in the face of reputation costs and the risks of pressing on in a quagmire.

9 Steinbruner 1974; Tetlock 2003.
10 Jost 2003.

APPENDIX B.

Supplementary Empirical Materials

B.1. LABORATORY EXPERIMENT

Instrumentation

The experimental protocol has three components:

(A) The factorial panel experiment
(B) Dispositional questionnaire
(C) Concluding questionnaire measuring political orientations, demographic characteristics, etc.

Participants complete the instrumentation in one of two orderings: ABC, or BAC, varying whether the dispositional questionnaire is administered before or after the intervention experiment, to ensure that the dispositional measures aren't affected by the situational manipulations, and vice versa.

A. Factorial panel experiment

Factorial structure: 2 (Expected costs: low vs. high) × 2 (Actual costs (casualties): low vs. high) × 2 (Reputation: implicated vs. absent)
Panel structure: after the invasion, there are 7 waves in which the subject has the opportunity to terminate the mission.

Pre-intervention Vignette

The following questions are about US relations with other countries around the world. You will read about a situation our country has faced many times in the past and will probably face again. We will describe the situation and ask you for your opinion on what decisions you would make.

United States Considers Deploying Troops

A foreign government has begun a military invasion, sending its troops across the border of a smaller neighboring country.

The United States has a security interest in preserving the regional balance of power, and is a trading partner of the smaller neighboring country.

Best estimates suggest that if the United States intervened, it would [*In low expected cost condition:* only require minimal use of force] [*In high expected cost condition:* require substantial use of force] to protect the smaller country.

[*In reputation condition:* Decision-makers warn of the consequences that failing to stand up to aggression will have on America's reputation.]

1. If the attacker cannot be talked into withdrawing, should our government use our military to push back the invaders, or should we stay out of it?

   - Push back the invaders
   - Stay out of it

2. Do you feel strongly about this, or not very strongly?

   - Strongly
   - Not very strongly

Post-intervention vignette

[Repeat $t = 1 \ldots 7$ times, or until participant advocates withdrawal]

[*In first wave only:* US Marks One-Year Anniversary of Invasion

The United States decided to intervene, and American troops have been sent to push back the invaders. One year has passed.

In the past year, some progress has been made in pushing back the invaders, but the US has suffered casualties, bringing the total loss of American life up to [*In low cost condition:* $72 + \epsilon$] [*In high cost condition:* $1284 + \epsilon$].]

[*In subsequent waves:* US Marks t-Year Anniversary of Invasion

The invasion began t years ago.

In the past year, some progress has been made in pushing back the invaders, but the US has suffered [*In low cost condition:* $72 + \epsilon$] [*In high cost condition:* $1284 + \epsilon$].] casualties, bringing the total loss of American life up to [*casualty total*].]

Pressure [*In first wave only:* is beginning to mount][*In subsequent waves:* continues to mount] in Washington for the US to withdraw its troops, but military commanders urge patience. [*In reputation condition:* Given the consequences that failing to stand up to aggression will have on America's reputation, what would you do?] [*In control condition:* What would you do?]

3. Should the US withdraw its forces?

   • Yes, withdraw
   • No, stay in

[After final stage (either because the participant withdrew, or because the 7 rounds ended)]

4. Do any of the following describe your personal feelings about the intervention? [Yes, no]

   (a) Worried
   (b) Proud
   (c) Frightened
   (d) Angry
   (e) Hopeful

5. If the US stays another year, how many casualties do you expect it will suffer?

6. Explain your answer in the space below.

7. If the US withdraws, on a scale of 1 to 5, how much damage do you expect there will be to the US reputation, with 1 being "no damage," and 5 being "a lot of damage"?

8. Explain your answer in the space below.

B. Dispositional Questionnaire

Now we're interested in your views on a number of different issues. There are no right or wrong answers; please read the questions carefully and choose the responses that best describe your views.

Time preferences

1. Suppose you were given the choice between two different offers:

   A. A payment of $100 now
   B. A payment of $X one year from now

   How much would X have to be to make you want to choose option B over option A?

2. Now, suppose you were given the choice between two different offers:

   A. A payment of $100 now
   B. A payment of $X 10 years from now
      How much would X have to be to make you want to choose option B over option A?

Honor Orientation

To what extent do you agree or disagree with the following statements? [Strongly agree, somewhat agree, neither agree nor disagree, somewhat disagree, strongly disagree]

3. It's always important to be true to your word.

4. I don't care how others think of me.

5. I think many families don't care enough about their reputation.

6. People will take advantage of you if you don't stand up for yourself.

Trait Self-Control

To what extent do you agree or disagree with the following statements? [Strongly agree, somewhat agree, neither agree nor disagree, somewhat disagree, strongly disagree]

7. I generally like to see things through to the end.

8. I tend to give up easily.

9. Unfinished tasks really bother me.

10. Once I start a project, I almost always finish it.

11. I have trouble controlling my impulses.

12. When I am upset I often act without thinking.

13. I have trouble resisting my cravings (for food, cigarettes, etc.).

14. It is hard for me to resist acting on my feelings.

Risk Preferences

How much would you be willing to pay for a lottery ticket for each of the following lotteries?

15. A lottery with a 60% chance to win $100, otherwise nothing

16. A lottery with a 60% chance to win $400, otherwise nothing

C. Demographics

Political Knowledge

Please answer the following questions to the best of your ability. Many people have trouble with these kinds of questions, so you shouldn't worry if you do not know all, or many, of the answers.

1. Who is the current vice president of the United States?

2. How much of a majority is required for the US Senate and House to override a presidential veto?

3. Which political party currently holds the majority (has the most members) in the US House of Representatives?

4. Which political party, Republican or Democratic, is more conservative?

5. Whose responsibility is it to determine whether a law is constitutional or not?
   - Congress
   - President
   - Supreme Court

6. Who is the Speaker of the US House of Representatives?

7. Who is the current majority leader of the US Senate?

8. Who is the Secretary-General of the United Nations?

9. What does NAFTA stand for?

10. What country did Moammar Qadaffi control until this past year?

11. Which five countries are permanent members of the UN Security Council?

General Demographics

1. What is your sex?

2. How old are you?

3. What race do you consider yourself to be? [Black/African American, Hispanic/Latino(a), Asian, White/Caucasian, Other]

4. Generally speaking, do you usually think of yourself as a Republican, Democrat, or as an independent? (Check the option that best applies.) [Strong Republican, Republican, Independent but lean Republican, Independent, Independent but lean Democrat, Democrat, Strong Democrat]

5. Below is a scale on which the political views that people might hold are arranged from "extremely conservative" to "extremely liberal." Where would you place yourself on this scale? [Extremely conservative, conservative, slightly conservative, moderate or "middle of the road," slightly liberal, liberal, extremely liberal]

6. Have you served in the military? [Yes, No]

7. Are you a political science major? [Yes, No]

Manipulation Checks

The main analyses in chapter 3 suggest that the effect of reputation costs differ between participants who initially approved of the intervention and those who did not. There are a number of potential explanations for the divergent effects of the reputation cost manipulation, one stemming from *selection effects*, the other from *escalation effects*. Results at the first stage of the intervention scenario suggest that reputation costs increase the likelihood of initially wanting to intervene, especially among individuals who received the dispositional questionnaire prior to being presented with the intervention scenario. If reputation costs are already taken into account ex ante, it is possible that at the second stage they would no longer appear to exert any effect. If this selection effect argument is true, though, it raises the question of why we do not see the same pattern for the anticipated costs treatment, which instead appears to increase in size among participants who supported the initial intervention. Second, it is also possible that reputation costs are automatically rendered salient by intervening: we know that the costs of backing down increase with the level of escalation, so the act of the United States deploying troops may raise the costs of backing down sufficiently that the reputation manipulation will no longer exert an effect on its own.[1] Third,

1 Fearon 1994.

it is also possible that perceptions of reputation costs are largely a dispositional phenomenon.

Manipulation checks offer a preliminary means of adjudicating between these hypotheses. After participants withdrew, they were presented with two manipulation checks, one of which asked participants about the reputational costs they thought the United States would face for backing down on a scale from 1 to 5, with 1 indicating minimal costs, and 5 indicating very steep costs. If the selection effects explanation is true, we would expect to see two findings:

1. Individuals who initially wanted to intervene should perceive higher reputation costs for withdrawal than those who wanted to stay out, thereby demonstrating that reputational considerations are associated with the initial decision to intervene.

2. The strength of the reputation cost manipulation should vary based on participants' initial degrees of support, since pro-intervention respondents should already have been moved by reputational costs, while anti-intervention respondents should not.

We find support for both of these propositions. First, participants who originally supported the intervention were far more likely to believe the United States would pay higher reputation costs than those who did not ($M = 3.19$ vs. 2.85; Mann-Whitney U Test: $W = 8586$, $p < 0.003$). Second, the strength of the reputation manipulation varies based on the initial decision to intervene. When respondents are studied as a whole, no significant differences were found between those in the reputation cost condition versus the control condition ($M = 3.04$ vs. 3.13; Mann-Whitney U Test: $W = 13362$, $p < 0.324$), but when the manipulation check is re-analyzed based on whether participants initially supported the mission, the two groups diverge. Among participants who supported intervening, the reputation cost manipulation had no effect on the costs participants thought the United States would pay for withdrawing ($M = 3.17$ vs. 3.20; Mann-Whitney U Test: $W = 6120.5$, $p < 0.736$). However, among participants who wanted to stay out, the reputation cost manipulation actually has a negative effect, inducing skepticism that the United States would pay reputational costs for backing down ($M = 2.64$ vs. 3.00; Mann-Whitney U Test: $W = 1401.5$, $p < 0.061$). Note, however, that this latter effect is also consistent with a motivated reasoning argument, in which individuals who do not believe that an intervention is worth prosecuting will therefore underweight criteria that could be used to support it.

If the escalation effects argument is true, perceived reputation costs should increase with the level of American commitment, and thus, the longer the mission continues, the steeper the perceived costs of backing down. An ANOVA confirms that the longer participants support the mission, the steeper the reputation costs, as participants who stayed in longer predicted steeper reputational consequences for withdrawal than those who pulled out earlier ($F = 32.90$, $p < 0.000$). Here too, though, we cannot distinguish an escalation effects argument from a motivated reasoning one, in which individuals justify their support for an intervention by appealing to the costs of backing down.

Indeed, all of the results with the manipulation checks also support a dispositional explanation, in which reminding participants of reputational costs does not affect their beliefs about what these costs will be, because they already have established beliefs about what the costs of backing down are in the first place. Table B.1 displays the results from an OLS regression in which perceived reputation costs are regressed against the experimental treatments as well as a number of individual difference variables and demographic characteristics. Although a number of characteristics are associated with higher perceived reputational consequences of backing down—military service, identifying as a strong Republican, and the casualty manipulation—subscribing to a culture of honor has by far the most substantively significant effect, even when controlling for participants' initial desire to intervene. The third model in the table adds an interaction between honor culture and the reputation manipulation; although the associated p-value ($p < 0.143$) is outside conventional standards of statistical significance,[2] it offers suggestive evidence that the lack of significance of the reputation cost manipulation on the manipulation check is due to individuals low in honor orientation responding negatively to the manipulation, while participants high in honor orientation respond positively. In this respect, we see evidence of the third form of interactionist theorizing discussed in chapter 2, in which dispositional characteristics affect actors' definition of the situation.

Finally, participants were also presented with another manipulation check, in which they were asked to indicate how many casualties they thought the United States would sustain if US troops remained for another year. Unlike with the reputation cost manipulation check, the results here are straightforward: participants in the high casualty condition predicted a higher number of casualties than those in the low casualty condition ($M = 2272.39$ vs. 860; Mann-Whitney U Test: $= 747$, $p < 0.000$).

Demand Characteristics

Since participants remain in the same casualty treatment over time—that is, the experiment manipulates absolute casualty levels, not casualty trends—it is possible that participants become aware of the purpose of the experiment

---

2 In a parsimonious model with just the manipulations, honor orientation, and the reputation cost x honor orientation interaction, the interaction's level of statistical significance is a slightly more comfortable $p < 0.107$.

TABLE B.1. Perceived Reputation Costs

	β	p	β	p	β	p
Anticipated costs	0.128	0.221	0.142	0.171	0.135	0.195
	(0.104)		(0.104)		(0.103)	
Reputation costs	−0.103	0.323	−0.132	0.206	−1.173	0.102
	(0.104)		(0.104)		(0.716)	
Casualties	0.233	0.026	0.246	0.019	0.255	0.014
	(0.104)		(0.104)		(0.104)	
Order	0.013	0.900	0.032	0.758	0.032	0.754
	(0.103)		(0.102)		(0.102)	
Male	−0.144	0.197	−0.153	0.166	−0.155	0.160
	(0.111)		(0.110)		(0.110)	
Age	0.003	0.833	0.002	0.885	0.001	0.937
	(0.012)		(0.012)		(0.012)	
White	−0.053	0.672	−0.055	0.658	−0.050	0.687
	(0.125)		(0.125)		(0.124)	
Party ID	−0.487	0.014	−0.413	0.037	−0.399	0.044
	(0.196)		(0.198)		(0.197)	
Honor culture	1.103	0.025	0.911	0.066	0.259	0.696
	(0.490)		(0.494)		(0.663)	
Knowledge (International)	0.075	0.734	0.130	0.555	0.146	0.507
	(0.221)		(0.220)		(0.220)	
Military	0.361	0.091	0.351	0.097	0.346	0.102
	(0.213)		(0.211)		(0.211)	
Political Science major	−0.135	0.219	−0.25	0.253	−0.125	0.251
	(0.110)		(0.109)		(0.109)	
Stay out			−0.269	0.021	−0.271	
			(0.116)		(0.116)	
Reputation costs × Honor culture					1.367	0.143
					(0.930)	
Intercept	2.424	0.000	2.325	0.000	2.812	0.000
	(0.538)		(0.536)		(0.630)	

OLS coefficients, SEs in parentheses. All variables except age are scaled from 0 to 1.

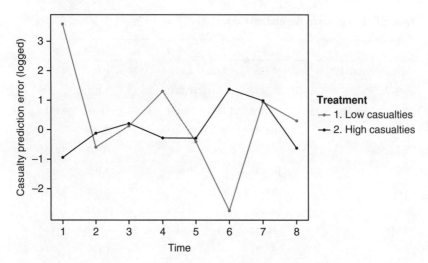

FIGURE B.1. Bootstrapped mean casualty prediction errors. Participants' responses to the casualty manipulation check do not become more accurate the longer they stay in, as measured by the deviation between the bootstrapped mean response to the casualty manipulation check and the casualty treatment level. There is thus little evidence for concerns about demand characteristics.

as time goes on, whereupon their behavior would become less informative in later rounds.[3]

This casualty manipulation check offers the opportunity to test for this possibility: if participants are more accurate in their predictions of future casualties as time goes on, it indicates the existence of a potential demand characteristic problem. Figure B.1 plots how accurate participants' casualty predictions were, as a function of the casualty treatment, and how long they remained in the intervention, as expressed by equation B.1:

$$\widehat{y}_{it} = \log \left(\frac{1}{B-1} \sum_{b=1}^{B} \frac{|\bar{x}_{it}^* - T_i|}{T_i} \right) \tag{B.1}$$

where $B = 1500$ bootstraps, $\bar{x}_{it}^*$ the bootstrapped mean casualty prediction in condition i at time t, and $T =$ the true level of casualties (72 in the low-casualty condition, 1284 in the high-casualty condition).

As figure B.1 illustrates, participants' responses to the casualty manipulation check do not become more accurate the longer they stay in the intervention scenario, thereby mitigating concerns about demand characteristics.

3 On the distinction between casualty levels and casualty trends, see Gartner 2008a.

Demographic Controls

Table B.2 replicates the models estimated in table 3.4, but also controlling for a number of demographic characteristics like age, race, and party ID, and stratifying the baseline hazard on gender.[4] The results from the first model show that the three main situational treatments retain their statistical significance: anticipated costs boost resolve by 22.7% and reputation costs by 21.4%, while casualties lower it by 46.5%. Long-term discounting has a similar effect as without the demographic controls, with a one-unit increase in δ associated with a 74.9% increase in resolve, while present bias continues to lack statistical significance, and is associated with only a 10.9% change in resolve. Risk aversion's significant curvilinear effect also remains the same, as risk aversion initially decreases resolve (by 28.1% as ρ grows from 0 to 0.5), but gradually increases it again at higher levels of risk aversion (-53.5% as ρ increases from 0.5 to 1). The one variable that loses its statistical significance because of the addition of demographic controls (particularly gender and party ID) is honor orientation, illustrating the extent to which honor concerns are heavily gendered, and associated with conservative political ideology.[5] Indeed, it is noteworthy how substantively large an effect partisanship has even when controlling for a number of dispositional variables and situational manipulations: self-described strong Republicans were twice as likely to stay in as self-described strong Democrats. Neither race, age, nor the political science major variable were significant.

Survival Curves

In the main analyses presented in chapter 3, I visually present the substantive effects using coefficient plots of hazard ratios, since they are relatively straightforward to interpret for readers who may be less familiar with event history models. An alternative way to present the results is to directly plot the survival curves, which depict the probability of the intervention "surviving"— that is, of participants continuing to advocate for the presence of US troops at time t; the higher the probability of survival, the more resolve participants

---

4 Residual-based Proportional Hazard tests indicate that gender's effects violate the proportional hazards assumption, so the models stratify the baseline hazard on gender to avoid biasing the coefficient estimates (see Box-Steffensmeier and Zorn, 2001, 975).

5 Indeed, the notion of honor is heavily gendered (masculine honor, family honor, feminine honor, etc.), such that the honor literature in cross-cultural psychology typically relies on questions about female sexual purity, male sexual virility, and so on. (See Rodriguez Mosquera, Manstead, and Fischer 2002). The effect of political ideology is identical to that of party ID: the two variables are highly intercorrelated ($r = 0.835$), so to avoid multicollinearity, I include only party ID in the model.

TABLE B.2. Demographic Characteristics and the Duration of the Intervention

	ALL PARTICIPANTS		PRO-INTERVENTION PARTICIPANTS	
	B	HAZARD RATIO	B	HAZARD RATIO
Anticipated costs	−0.258	−22.7%	−.347	−29.3%
	(0.135)	[−38.1%, −3.5%]	(0.167)	[−46.2%, −7.1%]
Reputation costs	−0.241	−21.4%	−0.222	−19.9%
	(0.138)	[−37.3%, −1.6%]	(0.178)	[−40.2%, 7.2%]
Casualties	0.382	46.5%	0.475	60.7%
	(0.138)	[16.9%, 83.7%]	(0.175)	[20.7%, 114.1%]
Order	0.072	7.4%	0.218	24.4%
	(0.134)	[−13.8%, 33.9%]	(0.174)	[−6.5%, 65.4%]
Discount factor (δ)	−1.382	−74.9%	−1.969	−86.0%
	(0.537)	[−89.6%, −39.4%]	(0.627)	[−95.0%, −61.0%]
Present bias (β)	−0.115	−10.9%	−0.306	−26.4%
	(0.171)	[−32.7%, 18.0%]	(0.217)	[−48.4%, 5.1%]
Honor culture	−0.186	−17.0%	0.643	90.3%
	(0.676)	[−72.6%, 151.4%]	(0.850)	[−53.3%, 652.5%]
Risk aversion	1.508	*	1.430	*
	(1.125)	*	(1.180)	*
Risk aversion^2	−2.026	*	−2.418	*
	(0.915)	*	(1.006)	*
Party ID	1.099	200.2%	1.442	322.9%
	(0.263)	[94.9%, 362.4%]	(0.333)	[144.9%, 630.3%]
Age	−0.016	−1.6%	−0.002	−0.2%
	(0.017)	[−4.3%, 1.1%]	(0.019)	[−3.2%, 2.9%]
White	−0.165	−15.2%	0.029	2.9%
	(0.164)	[−35.2%, 11.0%]	(0.214)	[−27.5%, 46.2%]
Political Science	−0.012	−1.2%	0.023	2.3%
major	(0.139)	[−21.3%, 24.1%]	(0.180)	[−23.8% − 37.4%]
N	289		199	

Main entries are Cox model coefficients; SEs in parentheses; 90% CIs around hazard ratios in brackets. Positive coefficients indicate a greater likelihood of "cutting and running." Baseline hazard stratified by gender.

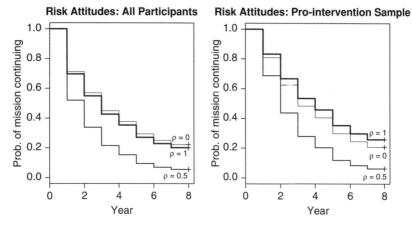

FIGURE B.2. Nonlinear effect of risk preferences survival curves. For both the full sample and pro-intervention subsample, an increase in risk aversion from risk neutrality ($\rho = 0$) to a moderate level of risk aversion ($\rho = 0.5$) is associated with a large drop in participants' tendency to wait things out; as participants become highly risk-averse, however ($\rho = 1$), they become more persistent and less likely to cut and run. Resolve is thus lowest at moderate levels of risk aversion.

display. The substantive conclusions remain the same; an example of this is presented in figure B.2, which uses survival curves to illustrate the quadratic effect of risk aversion in a different manner than the simulations illustrated by figure 3.6.

Results from Fully Crossed Factorial Analyses

Table B.3 and figure B.3 depict the hazard ratios from analyzing the lab experimental results as a fully crossed factorial; to improve legibility given the four-dimensional factorial space, each of the four treatments is referred to by a different letter, based on the order in which they are discussed in the text. The anticipated cost treatment is referred to as A, the reputation cost treatment as B, the casualty treatment as C, and the order manipulation as D. Thus, the -47.12% hazard ratio reported in table B.3 as the effect of B when $A=0$, $C=0$, and $D=1$ means that when anticipated costs and casualties are low, and the dispositional questionnaire was administered first, participants who were told that reputation costs were high displayed 47.12% more resolve than participants who were in the reputation control.

TABLE B.3. Hazard Ratios of Duration of Intervention: Full Factorial Model

	Impact of A: (Higher anticipated costs)			
	D=0		D=1	
	B=0	B=1	B=0	B=1
C=0	+16.95%	−20.05%	−50.05%**	−50.58%**
	[−35.8% −131.5%]	[−60.1% − 26.8%]	[−71.4% − −12.8%]	[−76.7% −4.7%]
C=1	+1.93%	−2.94%	−28.68%	−13.39%
	[−43.2%−82.8%]	[−45.9% −74.1%]	[−65.9%−49.2%]	[−48.5% −45.6%]

	Impact of B: (Reputation costs)			
	D=0		D=1	
	A=0	A=1	A=0	A=1
C=0	+40.58%	−3.9%	−47.12%**	−47.68%**
	[−21.1% − 150.6%]	[−46.2%−71.6%]	[−70.0% −−6.7%]	[−75.1% − 10.1%]
C=1	+1.49%	−3.36%	−43.72%	−31.65%
	[−44.9%−87.6%]	[−44.6% −68.5%]	[−72.8%−16.4%]	[−60.0% −−5.1%]

	Impact of C: (Casualties)			
	D=0		D=1	
	A=0	A=1	A=0	A=1
B=0	+33.76%	+16.58%	+30.72%	+86.6%*
	[−29.9%−155.1%]	[−31.6%−98.9%]	[−36.7%− 170.0%]	[5.4%−230.6%]
B=1	−3.43%	+17.24%	+39.14%	+143.8%**
	[−43.7% − 65.6%]	[−35.6%−113.7%]	[−21.1%−145.2%]	[19.1%−399.2%]

	Impact of D: (Order manipulation)			
	B=0		B=1	
	A=0	A=1	A=0	A=1
C=0	+93.6%*	−17.31%	−27.18%	−54.99%*
	[8.6%−245%]	[−53.7%−47.7%]	[−58.6%−28.4%]	[−78.6%−−5.33%]
C=1	+89.2%E_t	+32.37%	+4.93%	−6.38%
	[−13.3%−313.1%]	[−21.7%−123.8%]	[−38.8%−80.0%]	[−46.8%−64.9%]

90% CIs around hazard ratios in brackets. Positive values indicate a higher likelihood of withdrawal.

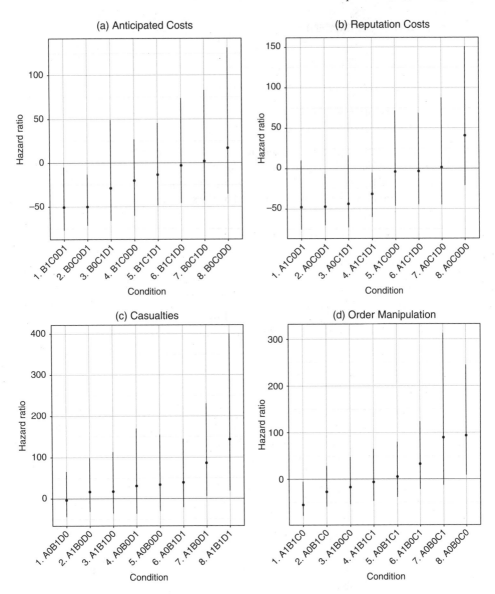

FIGURE B.3. Hazard ratio plots: full factorial analysis. Because the cell sizes are smaller, the confidence intervals around the hazard ratios are far larger when the experiment is re-analyzed with four-way interactions, but the general pattern remains the same: higher anticipated costs tend to prolong the intervention and make withdrawal less likely, as does rendering reputation costs salient. Casualties, though, have the opposite effect, making interventions more likely to end.

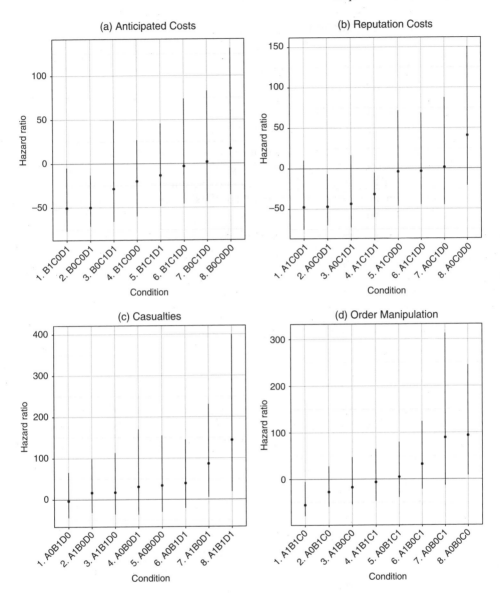

FIGURE B.3. Hazard ratio plots: full factorial analysis. Because the cell sizes are smaller, the confidence intervals around the hazard ratios are far larger when the experiment is re-analyzed with four-way interactions, but the general pattern remains the same: higher anticipated costs tend to prolong the intervention and make withdrawal less likely, as does rendering reputation costs salient. Casualties, though, have the opposite effect, making interventions more likely to end.

B.2. SURVEY EXPERIMENT

The experimental protocol has two components:

(A) Factorial panel experiment
(B) Dispositional questionnaire

Participants complete the instrumentation in one of two orderings: AB, or BA, depending on whether the dispositional questionnaire is administered before or after the intervention experiment, to ensure that the dispositional measures are not affected by the situational manipulations, and vice versa.

A. Factorial Panel Experiment

Factorial structure: 2 (Expected costs: low vs. high) ×2 (Actual costs (casualties): low vs. high) ×2 (Reputation: implicated vs. absent)

Pre-intervention Vignette

The following questions are about US relations with other countries around the world. You will read about a situation our country has faced many times in the past and will probably face again. We will describe the situation and ask you for your opinion on what decisions you would make.

A foreign government has begun a military invasion, sending its troops across the border of a smaller neighboring country. The United States has a security interest in preserving the regional balance of power, and is a trading partner of the smaller neighboring country.

Best estimates suggest that if the United States intervened, it would require [*In low expected cost condition:* only minimal] [*In high expected cost condition:* substantial] use of force to protect the smaller country. [*In reputation condition:* An ally you care a lot about publicly warns that if we don't stand up to aggression now, our allies will doubt our likelihood to stand firm in the future.]

1. On a scale of 1 to 5, how much damage do you think there would be to America's reputation if the US did not intervene on behalf of the smaller country?

B.2. SURVEY EXPERIMENT

> The experimental protocol has two components:
>
> (A) Factorial panel experiment
> (B) Dispositional questionnaire
>
> Participants complete the instrumentation in one of two orderings: AB, or BA, depending on whether the dispositional questionnaire is administered before or after the intervention experiment, to ensure that the dispositional measures are not affected by the situational manipulations, and vice versa.

A. Factorial Panel Experiment

> Factorial structure: 2 (Expected costs: low vs. high) ×2 (Actual costs (casualties): low vs. high) ×2 (Reputation: implicated vs. absent)

Pre-intervention Vignette

The following questions are about US relations with other countries around the world. You will read about a situation our country has faced many times in the past and will probably face again. We will describe the situation and ask you for your opinion on what decisions you would make.

> A foreign government has begun a military invasion, sending its troops across the border of a smaller neighboring country. The United States has a security interest in preserving the regional balance of power, and is a trading partner of the smaller neighboring country.
>
> Best estimates suggest that if the United States intervened, it would require [*In low expected cost condition:* only minimal] [*In high expected cost condition:* substantial] use of force to protect the smaller country. [*In reputation condition:* An ally you care a lot about publicly warns that if we don't stand up to aggression now, our allies will doubt our likelihood to stand firm in the future.]
>
> 1. On a scale of 1 to 5, how much damage do you think there would be to America's reputation if the US did not intervene on behalf of the smaller country?

2. If the attacker cannot be talked into withdrawing, should our government use our military to push back the invaders, or should we stay out of it?

   • Push back the invaders
   • Stay out of it

3. Do you feel strongly about this, or not very strongly?

   • Strongly
   • Not very strongly

Post-intervention Vignette

The United States decided to intervene, sending American troops to push back the invaders. In the first year, some progress has been made in pushing back the invaders, but the US has suffered casualties, bringing the total loss of American life up to [*In low casualty condition:* 72] [*In high casualty condition:* 1284].

Pressure is mounting for the US to withdraw its troops, but military commanders urge [*In reputation condition*: patience, and warn of the consequences that failing to stand up to aggression will have on America's reputation.] [*In reputation control*: patience.]

1. Given the current situation, how many years do you think US troops should stay involved in the mission?

2. If the US stays another year, how many casualties do you expect it will suffer?

B. Dispositional Questionnaire

Time Preferences

1. Suppose you were given the choice between two different offers:

   A. A payment of $100 now
   B. A payment of $X *one year* from now

   How much would X have to be to make you want to choose option B over option A?

2. Now, suppose you were given the choice between two different offers:

   A. A payment of $100 now
   B. A payment of $X *ten years* from now

   How much would X have to be to make you want to choose option B over option A?

Risk Preferences

1. How much would you be willing to pay for a lottery ticket that gave you a 60% chance to win $100, but otherwise nothing?

2. How much would you be willing to pay for a lottery ticket that gave you a 60% chance to win $100, but otherwise nothing?

3. Now, imagine a lottery where you have a 50% chance to lose $25, but a 50% chance to win a sum of money ($X). How much would $X have to be for you to be willing to accept the lottery?

4. Imagine a lottery where you have a 50% chance to lose $100, but a 50% chance to win a sum of money ($X). How much would $X have to be for you to be willing to accept the lottery?

5. In general, people often have to take risks when making financial, career, or other life decisions. Overall, how would you place yourself on the following scale? [1: Extremely comfortable taking risks, 2, 3, 4: Neither comfortable nor uncomfortable taking risks, 5, 6, 7: Extremely uncomfortable taking risks]

Honor Orientation

To what extent do you agree or disagree with the following statements? [Strongly agree, somewhat agree, neither agree nor disagree, somewhat disagree, strongly disagree]

1. A real man never leaves a score unsettled.

2. A real man is seen as tough in the eyes of his peers.

3. A real man should be willing to defend himself if he's insulted in public.

Behavioral Measures

1. Thinking about the past week, how often did you do the following things?

   Avoid foods that are high in fat and/or calories [Rarely or none of the time (less than 1 day), Some or a little of the time (1–2 days), Occasionally or a moderate amount of time (3–4 days), Most or all of the time (5–7 days)

2. During an average week, how often do you exercise? Examples of exercising are aerobics, walking or running, bicycling, playing tennis, lifting weights, calisthenics, etc. [Never, Less than once a week, 1–2 times a week, 3–5 times a week, 6 or more times a week]

3. Do you NOW smoke cigarettes every day, some days, or not at all? [Every day, Some days, Not at all]

Why Do Casualties Fail to Affect Participants' Resolve?

There are at least five potential classes of explanations for the divergent roles of casualties across the lab and survey experiment.

Manipulation Check

First, the manipulations in the survey experiment could have failed. The manipulation check for the casualty treatment rules out this possibility: a Wilcoxon rank-sum test confirms that participants in the high-casualty condition predicted the US would suffer greater casualties the following year than participants in the low-casualty condition ($W = 52829$, $p < 0.000$).

Re-estimating the Results on Compliers

Relatedly, the casualty treatment could have failed because of problems of noncompliance, a common concern in experiments, in which participants may fail to comply with the experimenter's manipulation.[6] For example, in voter turnout field experiments, some voters may be assigned a treatment (e.g., being visited by a canvasser, or receiving a phone call), but not be home to answer the door.[7] However, we can also think of noncompliance as occurring when participants in lab or survey experiments fail to pay sufficient attention to stimuli.[8] One way of gauging the impact of the casualty treatment is thus to use the manipulation check to identify the subset of participants who were the most attentive to the treatment, and estimate the treatment effect for just these compliers.

The challenge, however, is determining who counts as a complier. I employ a sensitivity-based approach. First, note that each individual i either receives the high-casualty treatment ($T_i = 1$) in which the United States experiences $X_0 = 72$ casualties, or the low-casualty treatment ($T_i = 0$), in which the United States experiences $X_1 = 1284$ casualties. Participants also complete a

---

6 Morton and Williams 2010, 48.
7 Imai 2005.
8 Morton and Williams 2010, 156.

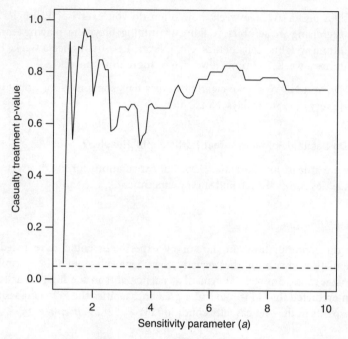

FIGURE B.4. Casualty treatment p-values for compliers. The casualty treatment lacks statistical significance among compliers (defined as those participants whose response to the casualty manipulation check ranged from X_i/a to $X_i(a)$, where X_i is the true number of casualties from manipulation T_i, and a is a sensitivity parameter ranging from 1 to 10). The one exception is when $a = 1$, but as discussed in the text, the sample size is too small here to draw valid inferences. The dashed line indicates $p < 0.05$.

casualty manipulation check, where they indicate Z_i, the number of casualties they expect the US to receive over the next year. To determine the thresholds for who counts as a complier, I re-estimate the first model from table 4.1, but on the subsample of participants for whom $X_i/a \leq Z_i \leq X_i(a)$, where $a = 1 \ldots 10$ is a sensitivity parameter; thus, if $a = 3$, the group of compliers is defined as those participants in the control group whose manipulation check results range from 24 to 216, and those participants in the treatment group whose manipulation check results range from 428 to 3852.

Figure B.4 plots the p-value for the casualty treatment for the compliers, varying a from 1 to 10. The plot shows that the casualty treatment consistently lacks statistical significance, regardless of the level of a, except for when $a = 1$—such that compliers are defined as those participants for whom $X_i = Z_i$ (that is, they predicted an identical number of casualties as the number of casualties the US received in the previous year). Since this stringent threshold reduces the sample size to 25, however (22 participants in the control group and 3 participants in the treatment group), the analysis is severely underpowered, and as soon as sensitivity parameter increases to 1.1, the p-value jumps back up to $p < 0.667$. In other words, it therefore appears that the casualty treatment lacks significance in the survey experiment even among compliers, regardless of whether the parameters defining compliance are relatively strict or relatively relaxed.

A Higher Dosage Reputation Treatment

Third, the casualty treatment's effects could be swamped by the steeper reputation cost treatment: 1,284 casualties a year might not seem particularly costly given the public rebuke by the close ally. If this were the case, however, we should see a statistically significant interaction effect between the casualty and reputation treatments, since the casualty treatment effect would be suppressed for those participants exposed to the reputation treatment, but not the reputation control. However, the lack of a statistically significant interaction effect between the two treatments ($p < 0.826$) suggests this is not the case.

Characteristics of the Sample

Fourth, the lack of a significant casualty treatment could be the result of treatment heterogeneity: if the treatment effect varies with subgroups of the population, a nonsignificant average treatment effect would obscure significant conditional average treatment effects—hence offering a potential explanation for why treatment effects that were significant in a lab experiment on a relatively homogenous sample should lose their significance on a relatively heterogenous one.[9] For example, respondents raised in the era of the Second World War might maintain different "analogies of war" than those who came of age in the war on terror, such that the high casualty treatment might lack sufficient "dosage" for older respondents.[10] Similarly, since college-age participants would be more likely to shoulder the costs of fighting, it is possible that their responses to the casualty treatment would differ from those of older generations.[11]

---

9 Green and Kern 2012. Indeed, Druckman and Kam (2011) note that if a treatment effect is homogenous, results from a convenience sample should generalize easily to a representative one.

10 Khong 1992. Inasmuch as these analogies of war are shaped by previous personal experiences, we can consider them to be "pretreatment effects." See Gaines, Kuklinski, and Quirk 2007; Druckman and Leeper 2012.

11 Horowitz and Levendusky 2011.

To ensure that the nonsignificant casualty treatment effect is not obscuring treatment effect heterogeneity, a series of models were estimated with interactions between the casualty treatment and the demographic characteristics for which the survey experiment sample differs the most from the convenience sample used in the lab experiment, the aggregated results of which are shown in table B.4. The top panel of the table depicts the results from a model with interactions between the casualty treatment and age, disaggregated into a system of dummy variables to avoid linearity assumptions.[12] As the p-values in the fourth column show, there is no evidence that participants in different age cohorts respond differently to the casualty treatment. Since we have specific theoretical reasons to expect that college-age respondents will behave differently from older participants, age was also dichotomized and separate models estimated featuring an interaction between the treatment and whether participants were age 24 or below, but the interaction effect remained insignificant ($p < 0.473$). Likewise, the subsequent panel of the table presents the results from a model where the casualty treatment is interacted with participants' gender, finding the impact of the former is not conditional on the latter ($p < 0.373$). Similarly, the next panels find no significant interactions between the treatment and education, nor with geographic region or income.[13] The only demographic characteristic where treatment heterogeneity is detected is with respect to race, where Hispanics respond to the casualty treatment by becoming 38.1% less likely to withdraw at any given point in time. Given the number of subgroup analyses estimated in the table, we should be wary of false positives, and the relatively small proportion of Hispanics in both the lab and the survey experiment suggest that this difference is unlikely to be driving the results.

Differing Experimental Formats

Since the casualty treatment's effect seems not to stem from manipulation failures, a stronger reputation treatment, or treatment heterogeneity, the most likely explanation stems from the measurement of the dependent variable itself. The lab experiment utilizes a panel structure that presents the casualty information multiple times until the scenario ends or the participants withdraw, whereas the survey experiment uses a one-shot design in which participants only receive casualty information one year into the intervention,

---

12 For table B.4, the p-values reported are for the interaction between the treatment and each dummy variable; the baseline categories are presented in italics, along with the associated p-value and percentage change in the hazard rate for that particular group.

13 Given growing interest in southern cultures of honor (see e.g. Dafoe and Caughey 2016), the mixed results for the South, especially in the more granular analysis using census divisions, is interesting and merits further research.

TABLE B.4. Little Evidence of Heterogeneous Treatment Effects for Casualties

CHARACTERISTIC		CASUALTY TREATMENT EFFECT	
		HR (%)	p-VALUE
Age	*18–24*	7.92	$p < 0.71$
cohort	25–34	−3.93	$p < 0.66$
	35–44	−1.56	$p < 0.72$
	45–54	−7.75	$p < 0.53$
	55–64	−2.35	$p < 0.68$
	65–74	−12.6	$p < 0.42$
	75+	−30.5	$p < 0.18$
Gender	Male	−0.78	$p < 0.37$
	Female	−11.2	$p < 0.18$
Education	Less than High School	16.55	$p < 0.33$
level	High School	−14.43	$p < 0.59$
	Some College	−5.96	$p < 0.96$
	College Graduate	6.72	$p < 0.53$
Region	Northeast	−9.81	$p < 0.39$
	Midwest	6.54	$p < 0.62$
	South	−14.93	$p < 0.17$
	West	−4.29	$p < 0.56$
Region	New England	0.16	$p < 0.93$
(census	Mid-Atlantic	−16.38	$p < 0.51$
divisions)	West-North Central	24.49	$p < 0.37$
	East North Central	−2.51	$p < 0.62$
	South Atlantic	−27.34	$p < 0.17$
	East-South Central	45.17	$p < 0.23$
	West-South Central	−12.97	$p < 0.65$
	Mountain	16.07	$p < 0.54$
	Pacific	−14.12	$p < 0.57$

TABLE B.4. (*continued*)

CHARACTERISTIC		CASUALTY TREATMENT EFFECT	
		HR (%)	p-VALUE
Income level	*Less than $20,000*	−8.73	$p < 0.62$
	$20,000–$39,999	3.03	$p < 0.60$
	$40,000–$59,999	−1.17	$p < 0.74$
	$60,000–$84,999	−18.35	$p < 0.64$
	$85,000–$99,999	44.65	$p < 0.12$
	$100,000–$124,999	−11.13	$p < 0.92$
	$125,000–$149,999	4.17	$p < 0.67$
	$150,000–$174,999	−44.24	$p < 0.21$
	$175,000+	−34.45	$p < 0.32$
Race	Black	9.56	$p < 0.56$
	White, Non-Hispanic	−3.10	$p < 0.66$
	Hispanic	−38.10	$p < 0.04$
	Other	−18.89	$p < 0.53$

Positive HRs = greater probability of withdrawal. P-values are for interaction terms, except for baseline categories (in *italics*), where they represent the p-value for the treatment effect in the baseline category.

which offers little sense of whether the casualties are temporary or part of a broader trend, and instead forces them to extrapolate based on relatively little information.[14]

Figure B.5 uses the results of the casualty manipulation check to plot the distributions of the bootstrapped mean casualty predictions for both the lab and survey experiments, at each level of the treatment; since the lab experiment utilizes a panel structure, the mean casualty predictions are plotted across each wave of the study as well as by casualty treatment condition:

$$\widehat{y}_{it} = \frac{1}{B-1} \sum_{b=1}^{B} \bar{x_{it}}^{*} \tag{B.2}$$

14 See Gartner 2008a.

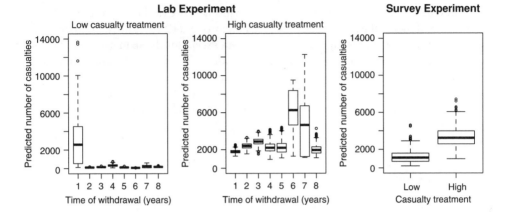

FIGURE B.5. Bootstrapped mean casualty predictions by experiment format. The bootstrapped mean responses (B=1500) to the casualty manipulation checks across each wave of the lab and survey experiment by treatment group show that differences in experiment format may be responsible for the divergent effects of the casualty treatment between the lab and survey experiment: in a one-shot format, participants' uncertainty about casualty trends is relatively high, especially in the high-casualty condition. When the lab experiment results are pooled, bootstrapped calculations indicate that although there is no significant difference between the variance of manipulation check results for the low-casualty treatment in the lab and survey experiment ($p < 0.25$), the variance of the manipulation check results for the high-casualty treatment is significantly greater in the survey experiment than the lab experiment ($p < 0.00$).

Since the survey experiment follows a one-shot design, it only has one wave, so the casualty predictions are plotted solely by treatment condition:

$$\widehat{y}_i = \frac{1}{B-1} \sum_{b=1}^{B} \bar{x}_i^*$$ (B.3)

The boxplots show that the casualty manipulations are successful—that is, that participants predict higher levels of casualties in the high casualty treatment than in the low casualty condition—but more importantly for our purposes, also show changes in the variance of the mean casualty predictions at the time participants withdraw, providing a sense of their uncertainty about casualty trends.[15] The variance in the survey experiment is relatively high,

15 On variance as a measure of uncertainty, see Alvarez and Brehm (1995); Reed (2003); Bas (2012); Mattiacci and Braumoeller (2012).

despite the far larger sample size, whereas the variance in the lab experiment settles down in the low casualty treatment following the first year, and remains relatively small in the high casualty treatment except for the sixth and seventh years, when the sample size has become relatively small; in a dynamic panel setup, it is thus likely that we would see a similar decrease in uncertainty over time, offering suggestive evidence that the divergent effects of casualties across the two setups are at least partially due to differences between the panel- and one-shot designs.

B.3. LARGE-N ANALYSES

A. Great Power Military Interventions, 1945–2003

The backbone of the data used in chapter 5 consist of the Military Interventions by Powerful States (MIPS) dataset, which includes all of the military interventions conducted between 1946 and 2003 by the five permanent members of the UN Security Council.[16] The interventions in the dataset are listed in table B.5. For a complete discussion of the coding rules, see Sullivan and Koch.

B. Logistic Model Estimates

The main analysis in chapter 5 employs a conjunctural Boolean logit model that treats the probability of victory as a function of both dispositional *and* situational sources of resolve. This has the advantage of explicitly using a statistical model consistent with the theory I am interested in testing. Table B.6 replicates these results, but this time using a more traditional (non-Boolean) logistic regression model, in which the effect of dispositional and situational sources of resolve is additive rather than interactive. The general pattern of results remains the same, with no evidence that the costs of fighting shape military outcomes, but relatively more supportive evidence infavor of the costs of backing down as operationalized by proximity, colonial ties, and alliance ties, all of which increase the costs of backing down, and with it, the probability of victory. As before, the strongest evidence comes from leader-level dispositional factors: time horizons (as operationalized by leadership turnover and survival probability) and honor orientations (as operationalized by conservative political ideology) are both associated with increased probabilities of victory, while risk orientations (as operationalized by

16 Sullivan and Koch 2009.

TABLE B.5. Great Power Military Interventions, 1945–2003

MAJOR POWER	LOCATION	START DATE	END DATE	MAJOR POWER	LOCATION	START DATE	END DATE
China	Hainan Island	4/18/1950	5/2/1950	USSR	Afghanistan	12/25/1979	2/15/1989
China	Tibet	5/1/1950	5/19/1951	USSR	Azerbaijan	1/20/1990	2/1/1990
China	N. Korea	10/19/1950	12/24/1950	Russia	Russia/Chechnya	1/1/1994	4/30/1996
China	S. Korea	12/31/1950	7/27/1953	UK	Indonesia	10/1/1945	11/29/1946
China	Burma	1/31/1951	12/31/1953	UK	Br. Honduras	2/26/1948	3/5/1948
China	Taiwan Strait	7/16/1953	7/17/1953	UK	Malaysia	6/16/1948	7/31/1960
China	Taiwan Strait	9/3/1954	5/1/1955	UK	Eritrea	1/3/1950	8/31/1951
China	Taiwan Strait	8/23/1958	12/19/1958	UK	Kenya	10/20/1952	10/19/1956
China	Nepal	4/22/1959	7/31/1960	UK	British Guiana	10/6/1953	5/26/1966
China	India	11/2/1961	11/21/1962	UK	Cyprus	11/26/1955	2/19/1959
China	China	1/15/1974	1/20/1974	UK	Bahrain	3/11/1956	1/1/1957
China	DRV	2/17/1979	3/17/1979	UK	Egypt	10/31/1956	11/6/1956
China	DRV	4/2/1984	7/12/1984	UK	Jordan	7/17/1958	10/29/1958
China	Taiwan Strait	7/21/1995	3/25/1996	UK	Zanzibar	6/3/1961	2/28/1963
China	Taiwan Strait	9/3/1954	5/1/1955	UK	Kuwait	7/1/1961	10/19/1961
China	China	5/1/1969	9/11/1969	UK	Brunei	12/10/1962	5/31/1963

TABLE B.5. (*continued*)

MAJOR POWER	LOCATION	START DATE	END DATE
China	Tibet	4/1/1954	12/31/1973
France	Syria	4/2/1945	4/15/1946
France	Algeria	5/8/1945	5/31/1945
France	Vietnam	10/1/1945	4/1/1946
France	Laos	3/17/1946	10/1/1946
France	Vietnam	11/20/1946	5/7/1954
France	Madagascar	3/29/1947	12/1/1948
France	Tunisia	1/20/1952	6/19/1955
France	Fr. Morocco	12/7/1952	12/31/1952
France	Fr. Morocco	8/15/1953	3/2/1956
France	Algeria	11/1/1954	7/3/1962
France	Tunisia	5/19/1956	10/26/1960
France	Morocco	7/3/1956	9/30/1961
France	Morocco	12/13/1956	2/1/1957
France	Fr. Cameroun	12/15/1957	1/1/1960
France	Spanish Sahara	2/24/1958	5/30/1958

MAJOR POWER	LOCATION	START DATE	END DATE
UK	Malaysia	4/19/1963	5/19/1965
UK	Swaziland	6/13/1963	11/30/1966
UK	Yemen AR	8/3/1963	4/18/1965
UK	Cyprus	12/17/1963	3/27/1964
UK	E. African States	1/25/1964	7/31/1964
UK	Zambia	12/3/1965	4/30/1966
UK	Br. Honduras	1/1/1970	12/31/1973
UK	Br. Honduras	7/7/1977	8/7/1977
UK	Argentina	4/25/1982	6/14/1982
UK	Aden	3/1/1949	10/31/1963
UK	South Arabia	11/25/1964	11/30/1967
UK	N. Ireland	9/1/1969	5/22/1998
USA	Greece	2/28/1948	10/16/1949
USA	S. Korea	6/27/1950	10/1/1950
USA	N. Korea	10/1/1950	7/27/1953
USA	Taiwan	9/4/1954	5/1/1955

TABLE B.5. (*continued*)

MAJOR POWER	LOCATION	START DATE	END DATE	MAJOR POWER	LOCATION	START DATE	END DATE
France	Cameroun	1/12/1960	12/31/1962	USA	Lebanon	7/15/1958	10/24/1958
France	Tunisia	7/18/1961	7/22/1961	USA	Taiwan	8/23/1958	12/31/1958
France	Congo (FR)	8/13/1963	8/17/1963	USA	Dominican Rep	6/3/1961	11/16/1961
France	Gabon	2/19/1964	12/31/1965	USA	Dominican Rep	11/16/1961	1/30/1962
France	Chad	8/28/1968	8/30/1971	USA	Vietnam	2/1/1962	1/27/1973
France	Mauritania	12/12/1977	5/30/1978	USA	Thailand	5/16/1962	7/23/1962
France	Chad	4/28/1978	5/16/1980	USA	Cuba	10/24/1962	10/28/1962
France	Zaire	5/19/1978	6/22/1978	USA	Laos	4/30/1964	8/14/1973
France	CAR/CAE	9/20/1979	9/21/1979	USA	Dominican Rep	4/28/1965	9/20/1966
France	Chad	8/9/1983	11/9/1984	USA	Cambodia	4/30/1970	8/14/1973
France	Chad	2/16/1986	9/11/1987	USA	Turkey	9/10/1970	9/25/1970
France	Chad	12/1/1991	1/7/1992	USA	Lebanon	9/29/1982	2/26/1984
France	Comoros	9/15/1995	10/15/1995	USA	Grenada	10/25/1983	12/12/1983
France	CAR	5/23/1996	6/2/1997	USA	Libya	3/23/1986	3/27/1986
USSR	Iran	12/12/1945	5/9/1946	USA	Honduras	3/17/1988	3/31/1988
USSR	Turkey	3/15/1946	4/5/1946	USA	Panama	5/11/1989	12/20/1989

TABLE B.5. (continued)

MAJOR POWER	LOCATION	START DATE	END DATE	MAJOR POWER	LOCATION	START DATE	END DATE
USSR	E. Germany	6/22/1948	5/30/1949	USA	Panama	12/20/1989	1/31/1990
USSR	E. Germany	6/16/1953	6/17/1953	USA	Saudi Arabia	8/14/1990	2/28/1991
USSR	Poland	6/28/1956	6/29/1956	USA	Kuwait	1/16/1991	2/28/1991
USSR	Poland	10/20/1956	10/24/1956	USA	Somalia	12/3/1992	5/4/1993
USSR	Hungary	10/24/1956	3/31/1958	USA	Somalia	5/4/1993	12/31/1993
USSR	Yemen AR	11/30/1967	3/15/1968	USA	Haiti	9/19/1994	3/31/1995
USSR	Czechoslovakia	8/20/1968	4/17/1969	USA	Kuwait	10/14/1994	12/21/1994
USSR	China	3/2/1969	9/11/1969	USA	Bosnia	8/30/1995	9/21/1995
USSR	Egypt	3/31/1970	8/7/1970	USA	Taiwan	3/8/1996	3/25/1996
USSR	Poland	12/15/1970	12/20/1970	USA	Iraq	2/1/1998	12/20/1998
USSR	Sudan	1/1/1971	8/31/1971	USA	Yugoslavia	3/24/1999	6/10/1999
USSR	Iraq	3/15/1973	3/30/1975	USA	Iraq	4/6/1991	3/19/2003
USSR	Angola	11/14/1975	12/31/1988	USA	Iraq	8/27/1992	3/19/2003
USSR	Ethiopia	12/31/1977	3/9/1978	USA	Kuwait	9/3/1996	3/19/2003
USSR	Vietnam	1/1/1979	6/1/1982	USA	Afghanistan	10/7/2001	3/31/2002

TABLE B.6. Logistic Model Estimates

	(1)		(2)		(3)		(4)	
	$\beta*$	$p*$	$\beta*$	$p*$	$\beta*$	$p*$	$\beta*$	$p*$
Intercept	−3.268	0.001	−3.565	0	−2.474	0.207	−2.783	0.197
	(−1.286)		(−1.290)		(−3.170)		(−3.315)	
Force type	−0.292	0.262	−0.28	0.275	−0.261	0.304	−0.27	0.3
	(−0.483)		(−0.495)		(−0.526)		(−0.542)	
Minimum Distance	−1.056	0.042	−1.029	0.042	−0.866	0.112	−0.86	0.126
	(−0.596)		(−0.618)		(−0.773)		(−0.797)	
Trade	−0.038	0.282	−0.036	0.294	−0.035	0.314	−0.031	0.326
	(−0.075)		(−0.078)		(−0.078)		(−0.078)	
Colony	0.396	0.122	0.413	0.122	0.496	0.106	0.487	0.104
	(−0.338)		(−0.356)		(−0.398)		(−0.388)	
Alliance	0.335	0.136	0.354	0.144	0.36	0.158	0.377	0.154
	(−0.320)		(−0.328)		(−0.378)		(−0.379)	
♛ Leader Culpable			0.23	0.327			0.239	0.294
			(−0.458)				(−0.467)	
♛ Survival probability	2.409	0.003	2.444	0.004	2.369	0.004	2.404	0.004
	(−1.272)		(−1.251)		(−1.297)		(−1.335)	
♛ Military service	−0.642	0.068	−0.701	0.058	−0.681	0.066	−0.716	0.062
	(−0.437)		(−0.451)		(−0.452)		(−0.483)	
♛ Conservative	0.559	0.06	0.573	0.054	0.615	0.044	0.604	0.064
	(−0.348)		(−0.361)		(−0.376)		(−0.402)	
♛ Leadership Turnover	−2.127	0.002	−2.066	0.004	−2.316	0.004	−2.219	0.008
	(−0.808)		(−0.807)		(−0.897)		(−0.944)	
Duration (Months)	−0.495	0.000	−0.46	0.000	−0.482	0.000	−0.45	0.001
	(−0.095)		(−0.113)		(−0.096)		(−0.117)	
Risk (WVS)					−2.974	0.318	−2.527	0.356
					(−6.747)		(−7.083)	
Self-control (WVS)					1.671	0.362	1.17	0.408
					(-4.812)		(−4.977)	

TABLE B.6. (*continued*)

	(1)		(2)		(3)		(4)	
	β*	p*	β*	p*	β*	p*	β*	p*
Conflict-months	2720		2720		2720		2720	
Interventions	109		109		109		109	
AIC	629.90		631.71		633.54		635.58	
BIC	694.90		702.61		710.34		718.10	

♛ denotes leader-level variables. Main entries are coefficient estimates from a traditional logistic regression model; standard errors in parentheses, estimated using 2000 cluster bootstraps.

military service) are associated with a decreased probability of victory. Finally, the country-level dispositional variables show no significant relationship with military outcomes, suggesting once again that country-level situational factors matter more than leader-level situational ones, and leader-level dispositional variables play a larger role than country-level dispositional ones.

BIBLIOGRAPHY

Achen, Christopher H. 1977. "Measuring Representation: Perils of the Correlation Coefficient." *American Journal of Political Science* 21 (4): 805–815.

Achen, Christopher H. 2002. "Toward a New Political Methodology: Microfoundations and ART." *Annual Review of Political Science* 5: 423–450.

Ackerman, Joshua M., Noah J. Goldstein, Jenessa R. Shapiro, and John A. Bargh. 2009. "You Wear Me Out: The Vicarious Depletion of Self-Control." *Psychological Science* 20 (3): 326–332.

Ainslie, George. 1992. *Picoeconomics: The Strategic Interaction of Successive Motivational States within the Person.* Cambridge: Cambridge University Press.

Ainslie, George. 2001. *Breakdown of Will.* Cambridge: Cambridge University Press.

Alford, John R., Carolyn L. Funk, and John R. Hibbing. 2005. "Are Political Orientations Genetically Transmitted?" *American Political Science Review* 99 (2): 153–167.

Alicke, Mark D., M. L. Klotz, David L. Brietenbecher, Tricia J. Yurak, and Debbie S. Vredenburg. 1995. "Personal Contact, Individuation, and the Better-Than-Average Effect." *Journal of Personality and Social Psychology* 68 (5): 804–825.

Allison, Graham. 1971. *Essence of Decision.* Boston: Little Brown and Company.

Almond, Gabriel A. 1950. *The American People and Foreign Policy.* New York: Harcourt, Brace and Company.

Alt, James E., Randall L. Calvert, and Brian Humes. 1988. "Reputation and Hegemonic Stability: A Game-Theoretic Analysis." *American Political Science Review* 82 (2): 445–466.

Althaus, Scott L., and Kevin Coe. 2011. "Social Identity Processes and the Dynamics of Public Support for War." *Public Opinion Quarterly* 75 (1): 65–88.

Alvarez, R. Michael, and John Brehm. 1995. "American Ambivalence Towards Abortion Policy: Development of a Heteroskedastic Probit Model of Competing Values." *American Journal of Political Science* 39 (4): 1055–1082.

Ameriks, John, Andrew Caplin, John Leahy, and Tom Tyler. 2007. "Measuring Self-Control Problems." *American Economic Review* 97 (3): 966–972.

Arendt, Hannah. 1971. *The Life of the Mind, Vol. II: Willing.* Orlando, FL: Harcourt.

Arkes, Hal R., and Catherine Blumer. 1985. "The Psychology of Sunk Cost." *Organizational Behavior and Human Decision Processes* 35 (1): 124–140.

Arneklev, Bruce J., Harold G. Grasmick, and Robert J. Bursik. 1999. "Evaluating the Dimensionality and Invariance of 'Low Self-Control'." *Journal of Quantitative Criminology* 15 (3): 307–331.

Arreguín-Toft, Ivan. 2001. "How the Weak Win Wars: A Theory of Asymmetric Conflict." *International Security* 26 (1): 93–128.

Atran, Scott. 2010. "A Question of Honour: Why the Taliban Fight and What to Do About It." *Asian Journal of Social Science* 38 (3): 343–363.

Atran, Scott, Robert Axelrod, and Richard Davis. 2007. "Sacred Barriers to Conflict Resolution." *Science* 317 (5841): 1039–1040.

Atran, Scott, Hammad Sheikh, and Angel Gomez. 2014. "Devoted Actors Sacrifice for Close Comrades and Sacred Cause." *Proceedings of the National Academy of Sciences* 111 (50): 17702–17703.

Avant, Deborah, and Lee Sigelman. 2010. "Private Security and Democracy: Lessons from the US in Iraq." *Security Studies* 19 (2): 230–265.

Axelrod, Robert. 1973. "Schema Theory: An Information Processing Model of Perception and Cognition." *American Political Science Review* 67 (4): 1248–1266.

Axelrod, Robert. 1984. *The Evolution of Cooperation.* New York: Basic Books.

Axelrod, Robert. 1997. *The Complexity of Cooperation: Agent-Based Models of Cooperation and Collaboration.* Princeton, NJ: Princeton University Press.

Azam, Jean-Paul. 2005. "Suicide-Bombing as Inter-generational Investment." *Public Choice* 122 (1–2): 177–198.

Bak, Daehee, and Glenn Palmer. 2010. "Testing the Biden Hypotheses: Leader Tenure, Age, and International Conflict." *Foreign Policy Analysis* 6 (3): 257–273.

Baldwin, David. 1979. "Power Analysis and World Politics: New Trends versus Old Tendencies." *World Politics* 31 (2): 161–194.

Barabas, Jason, and Jennifer Jerit. 2010. "Are Survey Experiments Externally Valid?" *American Political Science Review* 104 (2): 226–242.

Barkin, J. Samuel. 2004. "Time Horizons and Multilateral Enforcement in International Cooperation." *International Studies Quarterly* 48 (2): 363–382.

Baron, Reuben M., and David A. Kenny. 1986. "The Moderator-Mediator Variable Distinction in Social Psychological Research: Conceptual, Strategic, and Statistical Considerations." *Journal of Personality and Social Psychology* 51 (6): 1173–1182.

Bartone, Paul T. 2006. "Resilience Under Military Operational Stress: Can Leaders Influence Hardiness?" *Military Psychology* 18: 131–148.

Bartram, Dave. 2013. "Scalar Equivalence of OPQ32: Big Five Profiles of 31 Countries." *Journal of Cross-Cultural Psychology* 44 (1): 61–83.

Bas, Muhammet A. 2012. "Measuring Uncertainty in International Relations: Heteroskedastic Strategic Models." *Conflict Management and Peace Science* 29 (5): 490–520.

Bassin, Mark. 1993. "Turner, Solov'ev, and the 'Frontier Hypothesis'." *Journal of Modern History* 65 (3): 473–511.

Bauer, Daniel J. 2011. "Explaining Individual Differences in Psychological Processes." *Current Directions in Psychological Science* 20 (2): 115–118.

Baum, Matthew A. 2002. "The Constituent Foundations of the Rally-Round-the-Flag Phenomenon." *International Studies Quarterly* 46 (2): 263–298.

Baum, Matthew A. 2004. "Going Private: Public Opinion, Presidential Rhetoric, and the Domestic Politics of Audience Costs in U.S. Foreign Policy Crises." *Journal of Conflict Resolution* 48 (5): 603-631.

Baumeister, Roy F., and Julie Juola Exline. 1999. "Virtue, Personality, and Social Relations: Self-Control as the Moral Muscle." *Journal of Personality* 67 (6): 1165–1194.

Baumeister, Roy F., and Kathleen D. Vohs. 2004. *Handbook of Self-Regulation: Research, Theory, and Applications.* New York: Guilford Press.

Baumeister, Roy F., Kathleen D. Vohs, and Dianne M. Tice. 2007. "The Strength Model of Self-Control." *Current Directions in Psychological Science* 16 (6): 351–355.

Baynes, John. 1967. *Morale: A Study of Men and Courage*. New York: Frederick A. Praeger.

Beardsley, Kyle. 2008. "Agreement without Peace? International Mediation and Time Inconsistency Problems." *American Journal of Political Science* 52 (4): 723–740.

Beaver, Kevin M., Matt DeLisi, Michael G. Vaughn, and John Paul Wright. 2010. "The Intersection of Genes and Neuropsychological Deficits in the Prediction of Adolescent Delinquency and Low Self-Control." *International Journal of Offender Therapy and Comparative Criminology* 54 (1): 22–42.

Becker, Howard S. 1961. "Notes on the Concept of Commitment." *American Journal of Sociology* 66 (1): 32–40.

Beisner, Robert L. 1990. "History and Henry Kissinger." *Diplomatic History* 14 (4): 511–528.

Bem, Daryl J. 1967. "Self-Perception: An Alternative Interpretation of Cognitive Dissonance Phenomena." *Psychological Review* 74 (3): 183–200.

Bénabou, Roland, and Jean Tirole. 2002. "Self-Confidence and Personal Motivation." *Quarterly Journal of Economics* 117 (3): 871–915.

Bénabou, Roland, and Jean Tirole. 2004. "Willpower and Personal Rules." *Journal of Political Economy* 112 (4): 848–886.

Benhabib, Jess, and Alberto Bisin. 2005. "Modelling Internal Commitment Mechanisms and Self-Control: A Neuroeconomics Approach to Consumption-Saving Decisions." *Games and Economic Behavior* 52 (2): 460–492.

Benjamin, Daniel J., James J. Choi, and A. Joshua Strickland. 2010. "Social Identity and Preferences." *American Economic Review* 100 (4): 1913–1928.

Bennett, D. Scott. 1999. "Parametric Models, Duration Dependence, and Time-Varying Data Revisited." *American Journal of Political Science* 43 (1): 256–270.

Bennett, D. Scott, and Allan C Stam. 1998. "The Declining Advantages of Democracy: A Combined Model of War Outcomes and Duration." *Journal of Conflict Resolution* 42 (3): 344–366.

Bennett, D. Scott, and Allan C Stam. 2000. "EUGene: A conceptual manual." *International Interactions* 26 (2): 179–204.

Berejikian, Jeffrey. 1997. "The Gains Debate: Framing State Choice." *American Political Science Review* 91 (4): 789–805.

Berinsky, Adam J. 2007. "Assuming the Costs of War: Events, Elites, and American Public Support for Military Conflict." *Journal of Politics* 69 (4): 975–997.

Berinsky, Adam J., Michele F. Margolis, and Michael W. Sances. 2014. "Separating the Shirkers from the Workers?" *American Journal of Political Science* 58 (3): 739–753.

Bernile, Gennaro, Vineet Bhagwat, and P. Raghavendra Rau. Forthcoming. "What Doesn't Kill You Will Only Make You More Risk-Loving: Early-Life Disasters and CEO Behavior." *Journal of Finance*.

Besley, Timothy, and Marta Reynal-Querol. 2011. "Do Democracies Select More Educated Leaders?" *American Political Science Review* 105 (3): 552–566.

Betts, Richard K. 1980. "Comment on Mueller: Interests, Burdens, and Persistence: Asymmetries Between Washington and Hanoi." *International Studies Quarterly* 24 (4): 520–524.

Bially Mattern, Janice. 2005. "Why Soft Power Isn't So Soft: Representational Force and the Sociolinguistic Construction of Attraction in World Politics." *Millennium: Journal of International Studies* 33 (3): 583–612.

Bilmes, Linda J., and Joseph E. Stiglitz. 2008. *The Three Trillion Dollar War: The True Cost of the Iraq Conflict*. New York: W.W. Norton.

Blainey, Geoffrey. 1973. *The Causes of War*. New York: Free Press.

Boettcher, William A. III. 1995. "Context, Methods, Numbers, and Words: Prospect Theory in International Relations." *Journal of Conflict Resolution* 39 (3): 561–583.

Boettcher, William A. III, and Michael D. Cobb. 2006. "Echoes of Vietnam? Casualty Framing and Public Perceptions of Success and Failure in Iraq." *Journal of Conflict Resolution* 50 (6): 831–854.

Boettcher, William A. III, and Michael D. Cobb. 2009. "'Don't Let Them Die in Vain': Casualty Frames and Public Tolerance for Escalating Commitment in Iraq." *Journal of Conflict Resolution* 53 (5): 677–697.

Bollen, Kenneth, A. 1989. *Structural Equations with Latent Variables*. New York: John Wiley & Sons.

Bouchard, Thomas J., Jr. 1994. "Genes, Environment, and Personality." *Science* 264 (5166): 1700–1701.

Bourbeau, Philippe. 2013. "Resiliencism: Premises and Promises in Securitisation Research." *Resilience: International Politics, Practices and Discourses* 1 (1): 3–17.

Boutwell, Brian B., and Kevin M. Beaver. 2010. "The Intergenerational Transmission of Low Self-control." *Journal of Research in Crime and Delinquency* 47 (2): 174–209.

Box-Steffensmeier, Janet M., and Bradford S. Jones. 2004. *Event History Modeling: A Guide for Social Scientists*. New York: Cambridge University Press.

Box-Steffensmeier, Janet M., and Christopher Zorn. 2001. "Duration Models and Proportional Hazards in Political Science." *American Journal of Political Science* 45 (4): 972–988.

Braumoeller, Bear F. 2003. "Causal Complexity and the Study of Politics." *Political Analysis* 11 (3): 209–233.

Braumoeller, Bear F., and Austin Carson. 2011. "Political Irrelevance, Democracy, and the Limits of Militarized Conflict." *Journal of Conflict Resolution* 55 (2): 292–320.

Brehm, John. 1993. *The Phantom Respondents. Opinion Surveys and Political Representation*. Ann Arbor: University of Michigan Press.

Brody, Richard. 1969. "The Study of International Politics Qua Science." In *Contending Approaches to International Politics*, ed. Klaus Knorr and James N. Rosenau. Princeton University Press.

Brunner, H. G., M. Nelen, X. O. Breakefield, H. H. Ropers, and B. A. van Ooost. 1993. "Abnormal Behavior Associated with a Point Mutation in the Structural Gene for Monoamine Oxidase A." *Science* 262 (5133): 578–580.

Bueno de Mesquita, Bruce. 1985. "Toward a Scientific Understanding of International Conflict." *International Studies Quarterly* 29: 121–136.

Bueno de Mesquita, Bruce, James D. Morrow, Randolph M. Siverson, and Alastair Smith. 1999. "An Institutional Explanation of the Democratic Peace." *American Political Science Review* 93 (4): 791–808.

Bueno de Mesquita, Bruce, and Randolph M. Siverson. 1995. "War and the Survival of Political Leaders: A Comparative Study of Regime Types and Political Accountability." *American Political Science Review* 89 (4): 841–855.

Callen, Michael, Mohammad Isaqzadeh, James D. Long, and Charles Sprenger. 2014. "Violence and Risk Preference: Experimental Evidence from Afghanistan." *American Economic Review* 104 (1): 123–148.

Carlsnaes, Walter. 1992. "The Agent-Structure Problem in Foreign Policy Analysis." *International Studies Quarterly* 36 (3): 245–270.

Caro, Robert A. 1990. *The Years of Lyndon Johnson: Means of Ascent.* New York: Vintage Books.

Caspi, Avshalom. 2000. "The Child Is Father of the Man: Personality Continuities from Childhood to Adulthood." *Journal of Personality and Social Psychology* 78 (1): 158–172.

Caspi, Avshalom, and Terrie E. Moffitt. 2006. "Gene–Environment Interactions in Psychiatry: Joining Forces with Neuroscience." *Nature Reviews Neuroscience* 7 (7): 583–590.

Castles, Francis G., and Peter Mair. 1984. "Left-Right Political Scales: Some 'Expert' Judgments." *European Journal of Political Research* 12 (1): 73–88.

Caverley, Jonathan D. 2009/10. "The Myth of Military Myopia: Democracy, Small Wars, and Vietnam." *International Security* 34 (3): 119–157.

Cederman, Lars-Erik. 1997. *Emergent Actors in World Politics: How States & Nations Develop & Dissolve.* Princeton, NJ: Princeton University Press.

Cederman, Lars-Erik. 2003. "Modeling the Size of Wars: From Billiard Balls to Sandpiles." *American Political Science Review* 97 (1): 135–150.

Chait, Jonathan. 2011. "Paul Ryan's Norquistian-Churchillian Foreign Policy." *The New Republic.* http://www.newrepublic.com/blog/jonathan-chait/89382/paul-ryan-foreign-policy-american-exceptionalism-obama.

Chambers, John R., Nicholas Epley, Kenneth Savitsky, and Paul D. Windschitl. 2008. "Knowing Too Much: Using Private Knowledge to Predict How One Is Viewed by Others." *Psychological Science* 19 (6): 542–548.

Chandler, David. 2013. "International Statebuilding and the Ideology of Resilience." *Politics* 33 (4): 276–286.

Chandler, David G. 1966. *The Campaigns of Napoleon.* New York: MacMillan.

Charlesworth, James C. 1967. "National Character in the Perspective of Political Science." *Annals of the American Academy of Political and Social Science* 370: 23–29.

Charney, Evan, and William English. 2012. "Candidate Genes and Political Behavior." *American Political Science Review* 106 (1): 1–34.

Chiozza, Giacomo, and H. E. Goemans. 2004. "International Conflict and the Tenure of Leaders: Is War Still Ex Post Inefficient?" *American Journal of Political Science* 48 (3): 604–619.

Chiozza, Giacomo, and H. E. Goemans. 2011. *Leaders and International Conflict.* Cambridge, UK: Cambridge University Press.

Christiansen, Bjorn. 1959. *Attitudes Towards Foreign Affairs as a Function of Personality.* Oslo: Oslo University Press.

Churchill, Winston. 1934. "Penny-in-the-slot Politics, 1934." https://www.national churchillmuseum.org/penny-in-the-slot-politics.html.

Clark, David H., and Patrick M. Regan. 2003. "Opportunities to Fight : A Statistical Technique for Modeling Unobservable Phenomena." *Journal of Conflict Resolution* 47 (1): 94–115.

Clarkson, Joshua J., John R. Chambers, Edward R. Hirt, Ashley S. Otto, Frank R. Kardes, and Christopher Leone. 2015. "The Self-Control Consequences of Political Ideology." *Proceedings of the National Academy of Sciences* 112 (27): 8250–8253.

Cline, Ray S. 1975. *World Power Assessment: A Calculus of Strategic Drift.* Boulder, CO: Westview Press.

Cline, Ray S. 1994. *The Power of Nations in the 1990s.* Lanham, MD: University Press of America.

CNN Larry King Live. 2009. "Interview with President and Mrs. George W. Bush." http://transcripts.cnn.com/TRANSCRIPTS/0901/13/lkl.01.html.

Converse, Philip E. 1964. "The Nature and Origin of Belief Systems in Mass Publics." In *Ideology and Discontent*, ed. David E. Apter. New York: Free Press.

Copeland, Dale C. 1997. "Do Reputations Matter?" *Security Studies* 7 (1): 33–71.

Copeland, Dale C. 2000. *The Origins of Major War.* Ithaca, NY: Cornell University Press.

Copeland, Dale C. 2001. "Theory and History in the Study of Major War." *Security Studies* 10 (4): 212–239.

Crescenzi, Mark J. C., Jacob D. Kathman, Katja B. Kleinberg, and Reed M. Wood. 2012. "Reliability, Reputation, and Alliance Formation." *International Studies Quarterly* 56 (2): 259–274.

Croco, Sarah E. 2011. "The Decider's Dilemma: Leader Culpability, War Outcomes, and Domestic Punishment." *American Political Science Review* 105 (August 2011): 457–477.

C-Span. 2015. "Army Chief of Staff Confirmation Hearing." http://www.c-span.org/video/?327238-1/army-chief-staff-nominee-general-mark-milley-confirmation-hearing.

Dafoe, Allan, and Devin M. Caughey. 2016. "Honor and War: Southern Presidents and the Effects of Concern for Reputation." *World Politics* 68 (2): 341–381.

Dafoe, Allan, and Jessica Chen Weiss. 2015. "Authoritarian Audiences in International Crises: Evidence from China." Unpublished manuscript, Yale University.

Dahl, Robert A. 1957. "The Concept of Power." *Systems Research* 2 (3): 201–215.

Dauber, Cori. 2001. "Image as Argument: The Impact of Mogadishu on U.S. Military Intervention." *Armed Forces & Society* 27 (2): 205–229.

Davenport, John. 2007. *Will as Commitment and Resolve: An Existential Account of Creativity, Love, Virtue, and Happiness.* New York: Fordham University Press.

de Ridder, Denise T. D., Gerty Lensvelt-Mulders, Catrin Finkenauer, F. Marijn Stok, and Roy F. Baumeister. 2012. "Taking Stock of Self-Control: A Meta-Analysis of How Trait Self-Control Relates to a Wide Range of Behaviors." *Personality and Social Psychology Review* 16 (1): 76–99.

Dean, Robert D. 1998. "Masculinity as Ideology: John F. Kennedy and the Domestic Politics of Foreign Policy." *Diplomatic History* 22 (1): 29–62.

Dehghani, Morteza, Scott Atran, Rumen Iliev, Sonya Sachdeva, Douglas Medin, and Jeremy Ginges. 2010. "Sacred Values and Conflict over Iran's Nuclear Program." *Judgment and Decision Making* 5 (7): 540–546.

Dehghani, Morteza, Rumen Iliev, Sonya Sachdeva, Scott Atran, Jeremy Ginges, and Douglas Medin. 2009. "Emerging Sacred Values: Iran's Nuclear Program." *Judgment and Decision Making* 4 (7): 930–933.

Dennett, Daniel C. 1987. *The Intentional Stance.* Cambridge, MA: MIT Press.

Desch, Michael C. 2008. *Power and Military Effectiveness: The Fallacy of Democratic Triumphalism.* Baltimore, MD: Johns Hopkins University Press.

Dessler, David. 1989. "What's At Stake in the Agent-Structure Debate?" *International Organization* 43 (3): 441–473.

Diamantopoulos, Adamantios, and Heidi M. Winklhofer. 2001. "Index Construction with Formative Indicators: An Alternative to Scale Development." *Journal of Marketing Research* 38 (2): 269–277.

Dickson, Eric S. 2009. "Do Participants and Observers Assess Intentions Differently During Bargaining and Conflict?" *American Journal of Political Science* 53 (4): 910–930.

Dorfleitner, Gregor, and Michael Krapp. 2007. "On Multiattributive Risk Aversion: Some Clarifying Results." *Review of Managerial Science* 1 (1): 47–63.

Döring, Holger, and Philip Manow. 2012. "Parliament and Government Composition Database (ParlGov): An Infrastructure for Empirical Information on Parties, Elections and Governments in Modern Democracies." www.parlgov.org.

Doty, Roxanne Lynn. 1997. "Aporia: A Critical Exploration of the Agent-Structure Problematique in International Relations Theory." *European Journal of International Relations* 3 (3): 365–392.

Downs, George W., and David M. Rocke. 1995. *Optimal Imperfection? Domestic Uncertainty and Institutions in International Relations.* Princeton, NJ: Princeton University Press.

Dreher, Axel, Michael J. Lamla, Sarah M. Lein, and Frank Somogyi. 2009. "The Impact of Political Leaders' Profession and Education on Reforms." *Journal of Comparative Economics* 37 (1): 169–193.

Druckman, James N., Donald P. Green, James H. Kuklinski, and Arthur Lupia. 2006. "The Growth and Development of Experimental Research in Political Science." *American Political Science Review* 100 (4): 627–635.

Druckman, James N., and Cindy D. Kam. 2011. "Students as Experimental Participants: A Defense of the 'Narrow Data Base'." In *Cambridge Handbook of Experimental Political Science*, ed. James N. Druckman, Donald P. Green, James H. Kuklinski, and Arthur Lupia. New York: Cambridge University Press.

Druckman, James N., and Thomas J. Leeper. 2012. "Learning More from Political Communication Experiments: Pretreatment and Its Effects." *American Journal of Political Science* 56 (4): 875–896.

Duckworth, Angela Lee, and Margaret L. Kern. 2011. "A Meta-Analysis of the Convergent Validity of Self-Control Measures." *Journal of Research in Personality* 45 (3): 259–268.

Dueck, Colin. 2015. *The Obama Doctrine: American Grand Strategy Today.* New York: Oxford University Press.

Dunn, Robert. 1987. *The Possibility of Weakness of Will.* Indianapolis: Hackett.

Dunning, David, Chip Heath, and Jerry M. Suls. 2004. "Flawed Self-Assessment: Implications for Health, Education, and the Workplace." *Psychological Science in the Public Interest* 5 (3): 69–106.

Dyson, Stephen Benedict. 2007. "Alliances, Domestic Politics, and Leader Psychology: Why Did Britain Stay Out of Vietnam and Go into Iraq?" *Political Psychology* 28 (6): 647–666.

Eckles, David L., and Brian F. Schaffner. 2011. "Risk Tolerance and Support for Potential Military Interventions." *Public Opinion Quarterly* 75 (3): 533–544.

Edwards, Jeffrey R., and Richard P. Bagozzi. 2000. "On the Nature and Direction of Relationships Between Constructs and Measures." *Psychological Methods* 5 (2): 155–174.

Ehrlich, Sean, and Cherie Maestas. 2010. "Risk Orientation, Risk Exposure, and Policy Opinions: The Case of Free Trade." *Political Psychology* 31 (5): 657–684.

Eliades, George C. 1993. "Once More unto the Breach: Eisenhower, Dulles, and Public Opinion during the Offshore Islands Crisis of 1958." *Journal of American-East Asian Relations* 2 (4): 343–367.

Elias, Norbert. 2000. *The Civilizing Process*. Revised ed. Oxford: Blackwell.

Elster, Jon. 1979. *Ulysses and the Sirens*. Cambridge: Cambridge University Press.

Elster, Jon. 1982. "The Case for Methodological Individualism." *Theory and Society* 11 (4): 453–482.

Elster, Jon. 1985. *Making Sense of Marx*. Cambridge: Cambridge University Press.

Elster, Jon. 1986. *The Multiple Self*. Cambridge: Cambridge University Press.

Elster, Jon. 1989. *Nuts and Bolts for the Social Sciences*. Cambridge: Cambridge University Press.

Elster, Jon. 2000. *Ulysses Unbound: Studies in Rationality, Precommitment, and Constraints*. Cambridge: Cambridge University Press.

Elster, Jon. 2006. "Weakness of Will and Preference Reversals." In *Understanding Choice, Explaining Behavior: Essays in Honour of Ole-Jørgen Skog*, ed. Jon Elster, Gjelsvik, Aanund Hylland, and Karl Moene. Oslo: Unipub Forlag.

Endler, Norman S., and David Magnusson. 1976. "Toward an Interactional Psychology of Personality." *Psychological Bulletin* 83 (5): 956–974.

Epley, Nicholas, and David Dunning. 2000. "Feeling 'Holier Than Thou': Are Self-Serving Assessments Produced by Errors in Self- or Social Prediction?" *Journal of Personality and Social Psychology* 79 (6): 861–875.

Etheredge, Lloyd S. 1978. "Personality Effects on American Foreign Policy, 1898–1968: A Test of Interpersonal Generalization Theory." *American Political Science Review* 72 (2): 434–451.

Etzioni, Amitai. 1986. "The Case for a Multiple-Utility Conception." *Economics and Philosophy* 2 (2): 159–183.

Eyal, Tal, Nira Liberman, Yaacov Trope, and Eva Walther. 2004. "The Pros and Cons of Temporally Near and Distant Action." *Journal of Personality and Social Psychology* 86 (6): 781–795.

Fearon, James. 1995. "Rationalist Explanations for War." *International Organization* 49 (3): 379–414.

Fearon, James. 1997. "Tying Hands versus Sinking Costs: Signaling Foreign Policy Interests." *Journal of Conflict Resolution* 41 (1): 68–90.

Fearon, James D. 1994. "Domestic Political Audiences and the Escalation of International Disputes." *American Political Science Review* 88 (3): 577–592.

Fearon, James D. 2002. "Selection Effects and Deterrence." *International Interactions* 28 (1): 5–29.

Feaver, Peter D., and Christopher Gelpi. 2005. *Choosing Your Battles: American Civil-Military Relations and the Use of Force*. Princeton, NJ: Princeton University Press.

Feinerer, Ingo, Kurt Hornik, and David Meyer. 2008. "Text Mining Infrastructure in R." *Journal of Statistical Software* 25 (5): 1–54.

Fennell, Jonathan. 2011. *Combat and Morale in the North African Cmpaign: The Eighth Army and the Path to el Alamein*. New York: Cambridge University Press.

Fennell, Lee Anne. 2009. "Willpower and Legal Policy." *Annual Review of Law and Social Science* 5: 91–113.

Fessler, Daniel M.T., and Katinka Quintelier. 2013. "Suicide Bombers, Weddings, and Prison Tattoos: An Evolutionary Perspective on Subjective Commitment and Objective Commitment." In *Cooperation and Its Evolution, Vol. 2: Agents and Mechanisms*, ed. Kim Sterelny, Richard Joyce, Brett Calcott, and Ben Fraser. Cambridge MA: MIT Press.

Fettweis, Christopher J. 2007. "Credibility and the War on Terror." *Political Science Quarterly* 122 (4): 607–633.

Fey, Mark, and Kristopher W. Ramsay. 2006. "The Common Priors Assumption: A Comment on 'Bargaining and the Nature of War'." *Journal of Conflict Resolution* 50 (4): 607–613.

Fey, Mark, and Kristopher W. Ramsay. 2007. "Mutual Optimism and War." *American Journal of Political Science* 51 (4): 738–754.

Fey, Mark, and Kristopher W. Ramsay. 2011. "Uncertainty and Incentives in Crisis Bargaining: Game-Free Analysis of International Conflict." *American Journal of Political Science* 55 (1): 149–169.

Fiedler, Fred E. 1965. "A Contingency Model of Leadership Effectiveness." In *Advances in Experimental Social Psychology, Vol. 1*, ed. Leonard Berkowitz. New York: Academic Press.

Field, Christopher, and Alan H. Welsh. 2007. "Bootstrapping Clustered Data." *Journal of the Royal Statistical Society: Series B* 69 (3): 369–390.

Filson, Darren, and Suzanne Werner. 2002. "A Bargaining Model of War and Peace: Anticipating the Onset, Duration, and Outcome of War." *American Journal of Political Science* 46 (4): 819–838.

Filson, Darren, and Suzanne Werner. 2004. "Bargaining and Fighting: The Impact of Regime Type on War Onset, Duration, and Outcomes." *American Journal of Political Science* 48 (2): 296–313.

Filson, Darren, and Suzanne Werner. 2007a. "The Dynamics of Bargaining and War." *International Interactions* 33 (1): 31–50.

Filson, Darren, and Suzanne Werner. 2007b. "Sensitivity to Costs of Fighting versus Sensitivity to Losing the Conflict." *Journal of Conflict Resolution* 51 (5): 691–714.

Finkenauer, Catrin, Rutger C.M.E. Engels, and Roy F. Baumeister. 2005. "Parenting Behaviour and Adolescent Behavioural and Emotional Problems: The Role of Self-Control." *International Journal of Behavioral Development* 29 (1): 58–69.

Fischer, David Hackett. 1989. *Albion's Seed: Four British Folkways in America*. New York: Oxford University Press.

Fleeson, William. 2001. "Toward a Structure- and Process-Integrated View of Personality: Traits as Density Distributions of States." *Journal of Personality and Social Psychology* 80 (6): 1011–1027.

Fleeson, William. 2004. "Moving Personality Beyond the Person-Situation Debate." *Current Directions in Psychological Science* 13 (2): 83–87.

Flores, Thomas Edward, and Irfan Nooruddin. 2009. "Financing the Peace: Evaluating World Bank Post-Conflict Assistance Programs." *Review of International Organizations* 4 (1): 1–27.

Fordham, Benjamin O. 2009. "The Limits of Neoclassical Realism: Additive and Interactive Approaches to Explaining Foreign Policy Preferences." In *Neoclassical Realism, The State, and Foreign Policy*, ed. Steven E. Lobell, Norrin M. Ripsman, and Jeffrey W. Taliaferro. New York: Cambridge University Press.

Fowler, James H., and Christopher T. Dawes. 2008. "Two Genes Predict Voter Turnout." *Journal of Politics* 70 (3): 579–594.

Foyle, Douglas C. 1999. *Counting the Public In: Presidents, Public Opinion, and Foreign Policy.* New York: Columbia University Press.

Frankfurt, Harry G. 1971. "Freedom of the Will and the Concept of a Person." *Journal of Philosophy* 68 (1): 5–20.

Frederick, Shane. 2006. "Valuing Future Life and Future Lives: A Framework for Understanding Discounting." *Journal of Economic Psychology* 27 (5): 667–680.

French, David. 2015. "Why America Has Lost the Will to Win Wars." *National Review.* http://www.nationalreview.com/article/419278/why-america-has-lost-will-win-wars-david-french.

Friedman, Milton. 1953. "The Methodology of Positive Economics." In *Essays in Positive Economics.* Chicago: University of Chicago Press.

Fudenberg, Drew, and David K. Levine. 2006. "A Dual-Self Model of Impulse Control." *American Economic Review* 96 (5): 1449–1476.

Fujita, Kentaro, and Joseph C. Roberts. 2010. "Promoting Prospective Self-Control through Abstraction." *Journal of Experimental Social Psychology* 46 (6): 1049–1054.

Gaines, Brian J., James H. Kuklinski, and Paul J. Quirk. 2007. "The Logic of the Survey Experiment Reexamined." *Political Analysis* 15 (1): 1–20.

Galliot, Matthew T., and Roy F. Baumeister. 2007. "The Physiology of Willpower: Linking Blood Glucose to Self-Control." *Personality and Social Psychology Review* 11 (4): 303–327.

Galliot, Matthew T., Roy F. Baumeister, C. Nathan DeWall, Jon K. Maner, Ashby Plant, Dianne M. Tice, Lauren E. Brewer, and Brandon J. Schmeichel. 2007. "Self-Control Relies on Glucose as a Limited Energy Source: Willpower Is More Than a Metaphor." *Journal of Personality and Social Psychology* 92 (2): 325–336.

Gartner, Scott Sigmund. 1997. *Strategic Assessment in War.* New Haven, CT: Yale University Press.

Gartner, Scott Sigmund. 2008a. "The Multiple Effects of Casualties on Public Support for War: An Experimental Approach." *American Political Science Review* 102 (1): 95–106.

Gartner, Scott Sigmund. 2008b. "Secondary Casualty Information: Casualty Uncertainty, Female Casualties, and Wartime Support." *Conflict Management and Peace Science* 25 (2): 98–111.

Gartner, Scott Sigmund, and Gary M. Segura. 1998. "War, Casualties, and Public Opinion." *Journal of Conflict Resolution* 42 (3): 278–300.

Gartner, Scott Sigmund, Gary M. Segura, and Michael Wilkening. 1997. "All Politics Are Local: Local Losses and Individual Attitudes toward the Vietnam War." *Journal of Conflict Resolution* 41 (5): 669–694.

Gartzke, Eric. 1999. "War Is in the Error Term." *International Organization* 53 (3): 567–587.

Gartzke, Eric. 2001. "Democracy and the Preparation for War: Does Regime Type Affect States' Anticipation of Casualties?" *International Studies Quarterly* 45 (3): 467–484.

Gartzke, Eric, Quan Li, and Charles Boehmer. 2001. "Investing in the Peace: Economic Interdependence and International Conflict." *International Organization* 55 (2): 391–438.

Gelman, Andrew. 2007. "Struggles with Survey Weighting and Regression Modeling." *Statistical Science* 22 (2): 153–164.

Gelpi, Christopher, Peter D. Feaver, and Jason Reifler. 2005/06. "Success Matters: Casualty Sensitivity and the War in Iraq." *International Security* 30 (3): 7–46.

Gelpi, Christopher, Peter D. Feaver, and Jason Reifler. 2009. *Paying the Human Costs of War*. Princeton, NJ: Princeton University Press.

Gelpi, Christopher, and Joseph M. Grieco. 2001. "Attracting Trouble: Democracy, Leadership Tenure, and the Targeting of Militarized Challenges, 1918–1992." *Journal of Conflict Resolution* 45 (6): 794–817.

Gelpi, Christopher, and Joseph M. Grieco. 2014. "Competency Costs in Foreign Affairs: Presidential Performance in International Conflicts and Domestic Legislative Success, 1953–2001." *American Journal of Political Science* 59 (2): 440–456.

Gelpi, Christopher F., and Michael Griesdorf. 2001. "Winners or Losers? Democracies in International Crisis, 1918–94." *American Political Science Review* 95 (3): 633–647.

George, Alexander L. 1969. "The 'Operational Code': A Neglected Approach to the Study of Political Leaders and Decision Making." *International Studies Quarterly* 13 (2): 190–222.

George, Alexander L., and Juliette L. George. 1956. *Woodrow Wilson and Colonel House: A personality study*. New York: John Day.

George, Alexander L., and William E. Simons. 1994. *The Limits of Coercive Diplomacy.* 2nd ed. Boulder, CO: Westview Press.

Gerring, John. 2007. "The Mechanistic Worldview: Thinking Inside the Box." *British Journal of Political Science* 38 (1): 161–179.

Geys, Benny. 2010. "Wars, Presidents and Popularity: The Political Cost(s) of War Re-examined." *Public Opinion Quarterly* 74 (2): 357–374.

Gibbs, John J., Dennis Giever, and Jamie S. Martin. 1998. "Parental Management and Self-Control: An Empirical Test of Gottfredson and Hirschi's General Theory." *Journal of Research in Crime and Delinquency* 35 (1): 40–70.

Gibler, Douglas M. 2007. "Bordering on Peace: Democracy, Territorial Issues, and Conflict." *International Studies Quarterly* 51 (3): 509–532.

Gibler, Douglas M. 2010. "Outside-In: The Effects of External Threat on State Central-ization." *Journal of Conflict Resolution* 54 (4): 519–542.

Gifford, Adam, Jr. 2002. "Emotion and Self-Control." *Journal of Economic Behavior & Organization* 49 (1): 113–130.

Gilbert, Daniel T. 1998. "Ordinary Personology." In *The Handbook of Social Psychology*, ed. Daniel T. Gilbert, Susan T. Fiske, and Gardner Lindzey. New York: McGraw-Hill.

Ginges, Jeremy, and Scott Atran. 2011. "War as a Moral Imperative (not just Practical Politics by Other Means)." *Proceedings of the Royal Society B: Biological Sciences* 278 (February 16, 2011): 1–9.

Gleditsch, Kristian Skrede. 2002. "Expanded Trade and GDP Data." *Journal of Conflict Resolution* 46 (5): 712–724.

Goddard, Stacie E. 2006. "Uncommon Ground: Indivisible Territory and the Politics of Legitimacy." *International Organization* 60 (1): 35–68.

Goemans, H. E., Kristian Skrede Gleditsch, and Giacomo Chiozza. 2009. "Introducing Archigos: A Data Set of Political Leaders." *Journal of Peace Research* 46 (2): 269–283.

Goemans, Hein. 2000. *War and Punishment: The Causes of War Termination and the First World War*. Princeton, NJ: Princeton University Press.

Gottfredson, Michael, and Travis Hirschi. 1990. *A General Theory of Crime*. Stanford: Stanford University Press.

Gourevitch, Peter. 1978. "The Second Image Reversed: The International Sources of Domestic Politics." *International Organization* 32 (4): 881–912.

Grasmick, Harold G., Charles R. Tittle, Robert J. Bursik, and Bruce J. Arneklev. 1993. "Testing the Core Empirical Implications of Gottfredson and Hirschi's General Theory of Crime." *Journal of Research in Crime and Delinquency* 30 (1): 5–29.

Grauer, Ryan. 2014. "Why Do Soldiers Give Up? A Self-Preservation Theory of Surrender." *Security Studies* 23 (3): 622–655.

Gray, Colin S. 1981. "National Style in Strategy: the American Example." *International Security* 6 (2): 21–47.

Green, Donald P., and Holger L. Kern. 2012. "Modeling Heterogeneous Treatment Effects in Survey Experiments with Bayesian Additive Regression Trees." *Public Opinion Quarterly* 76 (3): 491–511.

Green, Donald P., Soo Yeon Kim, and David H. Yoon. 2001. "Dirty Pool." *International Organization* 55 (2): 441–468.

Green, Leonard, and Jr. Fisher, Edwin B. 1988. "Self-Control in Context." *Behavioral and Brain Sciences* 11 (4): 684–685.

Grimmer, Justin, and Brandon M. Stewart. 2013. "Text as Data: The Promise and Pitfalls of Automatic Content Analysis Methods for Political Texts." *Political Analysis* 21 (3): 267–297.

Grynaviski, Eric. 2014. *Constructive Illusions: Misperceiving the Origins of International Cooperation*. Ithaca, NY: Cornell University Press.

Gul, Faruk, and Wolfgang Pesendorfer. 2001. "Temptation and Self-Control." *Econometrica* 69 (6): 1403–1435.

Hafner-Burton, Emilie M., Brad L. LeVeck, David G. Victor, and James H. Fowler. 2014. "Decision Makers' Preferences for International Legal Cooperation." *International Organization* 68 (4): 845–876.

Hagger, Martin S., Chantelle Wood, Chris Stiff, and Nikos L. D. Chatzisarantis. 2010. "Ego Depletion and the Strength Model of Self-Control: A Meta-Analysis." *Psychological Bulletin* 136 (4): 495–525.

Haglund, David G., and Joshua D. Kertzer. 2008. "From Geo to Neo: A Speculative Inquiry into the Unusual 'Geo-Ethnic' Roots of Neoconservatism in U.S. Foreign Policy." *Geopolitics* 13 (3): 519–544.

Hall, Todd H. 2015. *Emotional Diplomacy: Official Emotion on the International Stage*. Ithaca, NY: Cornell University Press.

Harrigan, Anthony. 1965. "We Can Win in Southeast Asia." *National Review,* March 9, 1965: 187–188.

Harrison, Glenn W., and John A. List. 2004. "Field Experiments." *Journal of Economic Literature* 42 (4): 1009–1055.

Hartog, Joop, Ada Ferrer-i Carbonell, and Nicole Jonker. 2002. "Linking Measured Risk Aversion to Individual Characteristics." *Kyklos* 55 (1): 3–26.

Hassner, Ron E. 2003. "'To Halve and to Hold': Conflicts over Sacred Space and the Problem of Indivisibility." *Security Studies* 12 (4): 1–33.

Hassner, Ron E. 2006/2007. "The Path to Intractability: Time and the Entrenchment of Territorial Disputes." *International Security* 31 (3): 107–138.

Hatemi, Peter K. and Rose McDermott, eds. 2011. *Man Is By Nature a Political Animal: Evolution, Biology, and Politics.* Chicago: University of Chicago Press.

Hayward, Steven. 1997. *Churchill on Leadership: Executive Success in the Face of Adversity.* New York: Crown Publishing.

Hedström, Peter, and Petri Ylikoski. 2010. "Causal Mechanisms in the Social Sciences." *Annual Review of Sociology* 36: 49–67.

Heider, Fritz. 1958. *The Psychology of Interpersonal Relations.* New York: Wiley.

Henrich, Joseph, Steven J. Heine, and Ana Norenzayan. 2010. "The Weirdest People in the World?" *Behavioral and Brain Sciences* 33 (2–3): 1–75.

Herbert, Bob. 2010. "Resolve Among the Ruins." *New York Times,* January 15, p. A21. http://www.nytimes.com/2010/01/16/opinion/16herbert.html.

Hermann, Margaret G. 1977. "Introduction: A Statement of Issues." In *A Psychological Examination of Political Leaders,* ed. Margaret G. Hermann and Thomas W. Milburn. New York: Free Press.

Hermann, Margaret G., Thomas Preston, Baghat Korany, and Timothy M. Shaw. 2001. "Who Leads Matters: The Effects of Powerful Individuals." *International Studies Review* 3 (2): 88–131.

Herrmann, Richard. 1988. "The Empirical Challenge of the Cognitive Revolution: A Strategy for the Drawing Inferences about Perceptions." *International Studies Quarterly* 32 (2): 175–203.

Herrmann, Richard K., and Michael P. Fischerkeller. 1995. "Beyond the Enemy Image and Spiral Model: Cognitive-Strategic Research After the Cold War." *International Organization* 49 (3): 415–450.

Herrmann, Richard K., and Vaughn P. Shannon. 2001. "Defending International Norms: The Role of Obligation, Material Interest, and Perception in Decision Making." *International Organization* 55 (3): 621–654.

Herrmann, Richard K., Philip E. Tetlock, and Penny S. Visser. 1999. "Mass Public Decisions to Go to War: A Cognitive-Interactionist Framework." *American Political Science Review* 93 (3): 553–573.

Herrmann, Richard K., James F. Voss, Tonya Y. E. Schooler, and Joseph Ciarrochi. 1997. "Images in International Relations: An Experimental Test of Cognitive Schemata." *International Studies Quarterly* 41 (3): 403–433.

Herrnstein, Richard J. 1970. "On the Law of Effect." *Journal of the Experimental Analysis of Behavior* 13 (2): 243–266.

Hilfrich, Fabian. 2004. "Manliness and 'Realism:' The Use of Gendered Tropes in the Debates on the Philippine-American and on the Vietnam Wars." In *Culture and International History*, ed. Jessica C. E. Gienow-Hecht and Frank Schumacher. New York: Berghahn Publishers.

Hoebel, E. Adamson. 1967. "Anthropological Perspectives on National Character." *Annals of the American Academy of Political and Social Science* 370: 1–7.

Hoffman, Aaron M., Christopher R. Agnew, Justin J. Lehmiller, and Natasha T. Duncan. 2009. "Satisfaction, Alternatives, Investments, and the Microfoundations of Audience Cost Models." *International Interactions* 35 (4): 365–389.

Hoffmann, Tobias. 2008. *Weakness of Will From Plato to the Present.* Washington, DC: Catholic University of America Press.

Hofmann, Wilhelm, Malte Friese, and Fritz Strack. 2009. "Impulse and Self-Control From a Dual-Systems Perspective." *Perspectives on Psychological Science* 4 (2): 162–176.

Hollis, Martin, and Steve Smith. 1990. *Explaining and Understanding International Relations.* Oxford: Oxford University Press.

Holmes, Marcus, and David Traven. 2015. "Acting Rationally Without Really Thinking: The Logic of Rational Intuitionism for International Relations Theory." *International Studies Review* 17 (3): 414–440.

Holmes, Richard. 2005. *In the Footsteps of Churchill: A Study in Character.* New York: Basic Books.

Holsti, Ole R. 2004. *Public Opinion and American Foreign Policy.* Revised ed. Ann Arbor: University of Michigan Press.

Hopf, Ted. 1991a. "Polarity, the Offense Defense Balance, and War." *American Political Science Review* 85 (2): 475–493.

Hopf, Ted. 1991b. "Soviet Inferences from Their Victories in the Periphery: Visions of Resistance or Cumulating Gains?" In *Dominoes and Bandwagons: Strategic Beliefs and Great Power Competition in the Eurasian Rimland*, ed. Robert Jervis and Jack Snyder. Oxford: Oxford University Press.

Hopf, Ted. 1998. "The Promise of Constructivism in International Relations Theory." *International Security* 23 (1): 171–200.

Hopf, Ted. 2002. *Social Construction of International Politics: Identities & Foreign Policies, Moscow, 1955 & 1999.* Ithaca, NY: Cornell University Press.

Hopf, Ted. 2010. "The Logic of Habit in International Relations." *European Journal of International Relations* 16 (4): 539–561.

Hopf, Ted. 2013. "Common-sense Constructivism and Hegemony in World Politics." *International Organization* 67 (2): 317–354.

Hopkins, Daniel, and Gary King. 2010. "A Method of Automated Nonparametric Content Analysis for Social Science." *American Journal of Political Science* 54 (1): 229–247.

Horowitz, Michael, Rose McDermott, and Allan C Stam. 2005. "Leader Age, Regime Type, and Violent International Relations." *Journal of Conflict Resolution* 49 (5): 661–685.

Horowitz, Michael C., and Matthew S. Levendusky. 2011. "Drafting Support for War: Conscription and Mass Support for Warfare." *Journal of Politics* 73 (2): 524–534.

Horowitz, Michael C., and Allan C Stam. 2014. "How Prior Military Experience Influences The Future Militarized Behavior of Leaders." *International Organization* 68 (3): 527–559.

Hsee, Christopher K., and Elke U. Weber. 1999. "Cross-National Differences in Risk Preference and Lay Predictions." *Journal of Behavioral Decision Making* 12 (2): 165–179.

Huntington, Samuel P. 1957. *The Soldier and the State: The Theory and Politics of Civil-Military Relations.* Cambridge, MA: Belknap/Harvard University Press.

Huntington, Samuel P. 1993. "The Clash of Civilizations?" *Foreign Affairs* 72: 22–49.

Huth, Paul K. 1997. "Reputations and Deterrence: A Theoretical and Empirical Assessment." *Security Studies* 7 (1): 72–99.

Hyde, Susan D. 2015. "Experiments in International Relations: Lab, Survey, and Field." *Annual Review of Political Science* 18: 403–424.

Iklé, Fred Charles. 1964. *How Nations Negotiate.* New York: Harper & Row.

Imai, Kosuke. 2005. "Do Get-Out-the-Vote Calls Reduce Turnout? The Importance of Statistical Methods for Field Experiments." *American Political Science Review* 99 (2): 283–300.

Imai, Kosuke, Luke Keele, Dustin H. Tingley, and Teppei Yamamoto. 2011. "Unpacking the Black Box of Causality: Learning about Causal Mechanisms from Experimental and Observational Studies." *American Political Science Review* 105 (November 2011): 765–789.

Iyengar, Radha, and Jonathan Monten. 2008. "Is There an 'Emboldenment' Effect? Evidence from the Insurgency in Iraq." *NBER Working Paper* 13839.

Izjerman, Hans, and Dov Cohen. 2011. "Grounding Cultural Syndromes: Body Comportment and Values in Honor and Dignity Cultures." *European Journal of Social Psychology* 41 (4): 456–467.

Jentleson, Bruce W. 1992. "The Pretty Prudent Public: Post Post-Vietnam American Opinion on the Use of Military Force." *International Studies Quarterly* 36 (1): 49–74.

Jervis, Robert. 1972. "Bargaining and Bargaining Tactics." In *Nomos, vol. 14, Coercion*, ed. J. Roland Pennock and John W. Chapman. Vol. 14. Chicago: Aldine Atherton.

Jervis, Robert. 1976. *Perception and Misperception in International Politics.* Princeton, NJ: Princeton University Press.

Jervis, Robert. 1979. "Deterrence Theory Revisited." *World Politics* 31 (2): 289–324.

Jervis, Robert. 1985a. "Introduction: Approach and Assumptions." In *Psychology and Deterrence*, ed. Robert Jervis, Richard Ned Lebow, and Janice Gross Stein. Baltimore, MD: Johns Hopkins University Press.

Jervis, Robert. 1985b. "Perceiving and Coping with Threat." In *Psychology and Deterrence*, ed. Robert Jervis, Richard Ned Lebow, and Janice Gross Stein. Baltimore, MD: Johns Hopkins University Press.

Jervis, Robert. 2013. "Do Leaders Matter and How Would We Know?" *Security Studies* 22 (2): 153–179.

Job, Veronika, Carol S. Dweck, and Gregory M. Walton. 2010. "Ego Depletion—Is It All in Your Head? : Implicit Theories About Willpower Affect Self-Regulation." *Psychological Science* 21 (11): 1686–1693.

Johnson, Dominic D. P., Rose McDermott, Emily S. Barrett, Jonathan Cowden, Richard Wrangham, Matthew H. McIntyre, and Stephen Peter Rosen. 2006. "Overconfidence in Wargames: Experimental Evidence on Expectations, Aggression, Gender and Testosterone." *Proceedings of the Royal Society B: Biological Sciences* 273 (1600): 2513–2520.

Johnson, Dominic D. P., and Dominic Tierney. 2006. *Failing to Win: Perceptions of Victory and Defeat in International Politics*. Cambridge, MA: Harvard University Press.

Johnson, Dominic D. P., Richard W. Wrangham, and Stephen Peter Rosen. 2002. "Is Military Incompetence Adaptive? An Empirical Test with Risk-Taking Behaviour in Modern Warfare." *Evolution and Human Behavior* 23 (4): 245–264.

Johnston, Alastair Iain. 1995. *Cultural Realism: Strategic Culture and Grand Strategy in Chinese History*. Princeton, NJ: Princeton University Press.

Joll, James. 1968. *1914: The unspoken assumptions; an inaugural lecture delivered 25 April 1968*. London: London School of Economics and Political Science; Weidenfeld & Nicolson.

Jolls, Christine, Cass R. Sunstein, and Richard Thaler. 1998. "A Behavioral Approach to Law and Economics." *Stanford Law Review* 50 (5): 1471–1550.

Joseph, Jonathan. 2013. "Resilience in UK and French Security Strategy: An Anglo-Saxon Bias?" *Politics* 33 (4): 253–264.

Joseph, Jonathan, and Colin Wight. 2010. *Scientific Realism and International Relations*. New York: Palgrave Macmillan.

Jost, John T., Jack Glaser, Arie W. Kruglanski, and Frank Sulloway. 2003. "Political Conservatism as Motivated Social Cognition." *Psychological Bulletin* 129 (3): 339–375.

Kagel, John H., and Alvin E. Roth. 1995. *The Handbook of Experimental Economics*. Princeton, NJ: Princeton University Press.

Kahneman, Daniel, and Amos Tversky. 2000. *Choices, Values and Frames*. Cambridge: Cambridge University Press.

Kalis, Annemarie, Andreas Mojzisch, T. Sophie Schweizer, and Stefan Kaiser. 2008. "Weakness of Will, Akrasia, and the Neuropsychiatry of Decision Making: An Interdisciplinary Perspective." *Cognitive, Affective & Behavioral Neuroscience* 8 (4): 402–417.

Kam, Cindy D., and Jennifer M. Ramos. 2008. "Joining and Leaving the Rally: Understanding the Surge and Decline in Presidential Approval Following 9/11." *Public Opinion Quarterly* 72 (4): 619–650.

Kam, Cindy D., and Elizabeth N. Simas. 2010. "Risk Orientations and Policy Frames." *Journal of Politics* 72 (2): 381–396.

Keele, Luke J. 2010. "Proportionally Difficult: Testing for Nonproportional Hazards in Cox Models." *Political Analysis* 18 (2): 189–205.

Kelman, Herbert C. 1981. "Reflections on the History and Status of Peace Research." *Conflict Management and Peace Science* 5 (2): 95–110.

Kennan, George F. 1951. *American Diplomacy, 1900–1950*. Chicago: University of Chicago Press.

Kennedy, Paul. 1987. *The Rise and Fall of the Great Powers*. New York: Vintage Books.

Keohane, Robert O., and Jr. Nye, Joseph S. 1977. *Power and Interdependence*. New York: HarperCollins.

Kertzer, Joshua D. 2013. "Making Sense of Isolationism: Foreign Policy Mood as a Multilevel Phenomenon." *Journal of Politics* 75 (1): 225–240.

Kertzer, Joshua D., and Ryan Brutger. 2016. "Decomposing Audience Costs: Bringing the Audience Back into Audience Cost Theory." *American Journal of Political Science* 60 (1): 234–249.

Kertzer, Joshua D., and Kathleen M. McGraw. 2012. "Folk Realism: Testing the Microfoundations of Realism in Ordinary Citizens." *International Studies Quarterly* 56 (2): 245–258.

Kertzer, Joshua D., and Brian C. Rathbun. 2015. "Fair is Fair: Social Preferences and Reciprocity in International Politics." *World Politics* 67 (4): 613–655.

Khong, Yuen Foong. 1992. *Analogies at War: Korea, Munich, Dien Bien Phu and the Vietnam Decision of 1965*. Princeton, NJ: Princeton University Press.

Kim-Cohen, J, A Caspi, A Taylor, B Williams, R Newcombe, IW Craig, and TE Moffitt. 2006. "MAOA, Maltreatment, and Gene-Environment Interaction Predicting Children's Mental Health: New Evidence and a Meta-Analysis." *Molecular Psychiatry* 11 (10): 903–913.

King, Gary, Jennifer Pan, and Margaret E. Roberts. 2013. "How Censorship in China Allows Government Criticism but Silences Collective Expression." *American Political Science Review* 107 (2): 1–18.

King, Gary, and Langche Zeng. 2001. "Explaining Rare Events in International Relations." *International Organization* 55 (3): 693–715.

King, Gary, and Langche Zeng. 2007. "When Can History Be Our Guide? The Pitfalls of Counterfactual Inference." *International Studies Quarterly* 51 (1): 183–210.

King, Lynda A., Daniel W. King, John A. Fairbank, Terence M. Keane, and Gary A. Adams. 1998. "Resilience–Recovery Factors in Post–Traumatic Stress Disorder Among Female and Male Vietnam Veterans: Hardiness, Postwar Social Support, and Additional Stressful Life Events." *Journal of Personality and Social Psychology* 74 (2): 420–434.

Kirshner, Jonathan. 2000. "Rationalist Explanations for War?" *Security Studies* 10 (1): 143–150.

Kivetz, Ran, and Anat Keinan. 2006. "Repenting Hyperopia: An Analysis of Self-Control Regrets." *Journal of Consumer Research* 33 (2): 273–282.

Kivetz, Ran, and Itamar Simonson. 2002. "Self-Control for the Righteous: Toward a Theory of Precommitment to Indulgence." *Journal of Consumer Research* 29 (2): 199–217.

Klarevas, Louis. 2002. "The 'Essential Domino' of Military Operations: American Public Opinion and the Use of Force." *International Studies Perspectives* 3 (4): 417–437.

Klein, William M., and Ziva Kunda. 1993. "Maintaining Self-Serving Social Comparisons: Biased Reconstruction of One's Past Behaviors." *Personality and Social Psychology Bulletin* 19 (6): 732–739.

Klingberg, Frank L. 1952. "The Historical Alternation of Moods in American Foreign Policy." *World Politics* 4 (2): 239–273.

Knight, Frank H. 1921. *Risk, Uncertainty and Profit*. Boston: Houghton Mifflin.

Koch, Michael, and Scott Sigmund Gartner. 2005. "Casualties and Constituencies: Democratic Accountability, Electoral Institutions, and Costly Conflicts." *Journal of Conflict Resolution* 49 (6): 874–894.

Koch, Michael T., and Patricia L. Sullivan. 2010. "Should I Stay or Should I Go Now? Partisanship, Approval, and the Duration of Major Power Democratic Military Interventions." *Journal of Politics* 72 (3): 616–629.

Kohn, Alfie. 2008. "Why Self-Discipline is Overrated: The (Troubling) Theory and Practice of Control from Within." *Phi Delta Kappan* 90 (3): 168–176.

Kowert, Paul A., and Margaret G. Hermann. 1997. "Who Takes Risks? Daring and Caution in Foreign Policy Making." *Journal of Conflict Resolution* 41 (5): 611–637.

Krauthammer, Charles. 2009. "Decline Is a Choice: The New Liberalism and the End of American Ascendancy." *Weekly Standard* 15 (October 19).

Krebs, Ronald R., and Patrick Thaddeus Jackson. 2007. "Twisting Tongues and Twisting Arms: The Power of Political Rhetoric." *European Journal of International Relations* 13 (1): 35–66.

Krebs, Ronald R., and Aaron Rapport. 2012. "International Relations and the Psychology of Time Horizons." *International Studies Quarterly* 56 (3): 530–543.

Kreps, Sarah. 2008. "When Does the Mission Determine the Coalition? The Logic of Multilateral Intervention and the Case of Afghanistan." *Security Studies* 17 (3): 531–567.

Kroenig, Matthew. 2013. "Nuclear Superiority and the Balance of Resolve: Explaining Nuclear Crisis Outcomes." *International Organization* 67 (1): 141–171.

Kuhl, Julius. 1988. "Functional Characteristics of Human Self-Control." *Behavioral and Brain Sciences* 11 (4): 688.

Kunda, Ziva. 1990. "The Case for Motivated Reasoning." *Psychological Bulletin* 108 (3): 480–498.

Kydd, Andrew. 2003. "Which Side Are You On? Bias, Credibility, and Mediation." *American Journal of Political Science* 47 (4): 597–611.

Kydland, Finn E., and Edward C. Prescott. 1977. "Rules Rather than Discretion: The Inconsistency of Optimal Plans." *Journal of Political Economy* 85 (3): 473–492.

Lake, David A. 1992. "Powerful Pacifists: Democratic States and War." *American Political Science Review* 86 (1): 24–37.

Lake, David A. 2010/11. "Two Cheers for Bargaining Theory: Assessing Rationalist Explanations of the Iraq War." *International Security* 35 (3): 7–52.

Lake, David A. 2011. "Why 'isms' Are Evil: Theory, Epistemology, and Academic Sects as Impediments to Understanding and Progress." *International Studies Quarterly* 55 (2): 465–480.

Lake, David A., and Robert Powell. 1999. "International Relations: A Strategic-Choice Approach." In *Strategic Choice and International Relations*, ed. David A. Lake and Robert Powell. Princeton, NJ: Princeton University Press.

Langlois, Catherine C., and Jean-Pierre P. Langlois. 2009. "Does Attrition Behavior Help Explain the Duration of Interstate Wars? A Game Theoretic and Empirical Analysis." *International Studies Quarterly* 53 (4): 1051–1073.

Lanoszka, Alexander, and Michael A. Hunzeker. 2015. "Rage of Honor: Entente Indignation and the Lost Chance for Peace in the First World War." *Security Studies* 24 (4): 662–695.

Larson, Eric V. 2000. "Putting Theory to Work: Diagnosing Public Opinion on the U.S. Intervention in Bosnia." In *Being Useful: Policy Relevance and International Relations Theory*, ed. Miroslav Nincic and Joseph Lepgold. Ann Arbor: University of Michigan Press.

Lau, Ursula, and Ashley van Niekerk. 2011. "Restorying the Self: An Exploration of Young Burn Survivors' Narratives of Resilience." *Qualitative Health Research* 21 (9): 1165–1181.

Lebow, Richard Ned. 1998. "Beyond Parsimony: Rethinking Theories of Coercive Bargaining." *European Journal of International Relations* 4 (1): 31–66.

Leeds, Brett Ashley, Jeffrey M. Ritter, Sara McLaughlin Mitchell, and Andrew G. Long. 2002. "Alliance Treaty Obligations and Provisions, 1815–1944." *International Interactions* 28 (3): 237–260.

Leites, Nathan. 1951. *The Operational Code of the Politburo.* New York: McGraw-Hill.

Lemke, Thomas. 2001. "'The Birth of Bio-Politics': Michel Foucault's Lecture at the College de France on Neo-liberal Governmentality." *Economy and Society* 30 (2): 190–207.

Lentz, Harris M. 1994. *Heads of States and Governments: A Worldwide Encyclopedia of Over 2,300 Leaders, 1945 through 1992.* Jefferson, NC: McFarland & Company.

Leung, Angela K.-Y., and Dov Cohen. 2011. "Within- and Between-Culture Variation: Individual Differences and the Cultural Logics of Honor, Face, and Dignity Cultures." *Journal of Personality and Social Psychology* 100 (3): 507–526.

LeVeck, Brad L., Alex Hughes, James H. Fowler, Emilie M. Hafner-Burton, and David G. Victor. 2014. "The role of self-interest in elite bargaining." *Proceedings of the National Academy of Sciences* 111 (52): 18536–18541.

Levendusky, Matthew S., and Michael C. Horowitz. 2012. "When Backing Down Is the Right Decision: Partisanship, New Information, and Audience Costs." *Journal of Politics* 74 (2): 323–338.

Levy, Charles S. 1999. "Implementing TRIPS—A Test of Political Will." *Law and Policy in International Business* 31: 789–795.

Levy, Jack S. 1997. "Prospect Theory, Rational Choice, and International Relations." *International Studies Quarterly* 41 (1): 87–112.

Levy, Jack S., and William F. Mabe Jr. 2004. "Politically Motivated Opposition to War." *International Studies Review* 6 (1): 65–83.

Levy, Yagil. 2006. "The War of the Peripheries: A Social Mapping of IDF Casualties in the Al-Aqsa Intifada." *Social Identities* 12 (3): 309–324.

Lewin, Eyal. 2012. *National Resilience During War: Refining the Decision-Making Model.* Plymouth, UK: Lexington Books.

Lieberman, Joseph. 2011. "A Decade of Resolve." *Foreign Policy*, September 9. http://www.foreignpolicy.com/articles/2011/09/09/a_decade_of_resolve.

Loehlin, John C. 1992. *Genes and Environment in Personality Development.* Newbury Park, CA: Sage.

Loewen, Peter John, Lior Sheffer, Stuart N. Soroka, Stefaan Walgrave, and Tamir Shaefer. 2014. "Are Politicians Better Risky Decision Makers? Evidence from Experiments with Members of Parliament in Belgium, Canada, and Israel." Working paper.

Loewenstein, George, and Jon Elster. 1992. *Choice Over Time.* New York: Russell Sage Foundation.

Logue, A. W. 1988. "Research on Self-Control: An Integrating Framework." *Behavioral and Brain Sciences* 11 (4): 665–709.

Logue, A. W. 1998. "Self-Control." In *Learning and Behavior Therapy*, ed. William O'Donohue. Boston: Allyn and Bacon.

Lupovici, Amir. 2010. "The Emerging Fourth Wave of Deterrence Theory—Toward a New Research Agenda." *International Studies Quarterly* 54 (3): 705–732.

Lyall, Jason. 2010. "Do Democracies Make Inferior Counterinsurgents? Reassessing Democracy's Impact on War Outcomes and Duration." *International Organization* 64 (1): 167–192.

Lyall, Jason, Graeme Blair, and Kosuke Imai. 2013. "Explaining Support for Combatants during Wartime: A Survey Experiment in Afghanistan." *American Political Science Review* 107 (4): 679–705.

MacCrimmon, Kenneth R., Donald A. Wehrung, and W. T. Stanbury. 1986. *Taking Risks: The Management of Uncertainty.* New York: Free Press.

Mack, Andrew. 1974. "Why Big Nations Lose Small Wars: The Politics of Asymmetric Conflict." *World Politics* 27 (2): 175–200.

MacKinnon, David P., Jennifer L. Krull, and Chondra M. Lockwood. 2000. "Equivalence of the Mediation, Confounding and Suppression Effect." *Prevention Science* 1 (4): 173–181.

Mader, Matthias. 2015. "Citizens' Perceptions of Policy Objectives and Support for Military Action: Looking for Prudence in Germany." *Journal of Conflict Resolution.*

Magaletta, Philip R., and J.M. Oliver. 1999. "The Hope Construct, Will, and Ways: Their Relations with Self-Efficacy, Optimism, and General Well-Being." *Journal of Clinical Psychology* 55 (5): 539–551.

Malmendier, Ulrike, and Stefan Nagel. 2011. "Depression Babies: Do Macroeconomic Experiences Affect Risk Taking?" *Quarterly Journal of Economics* 126 (1): 373–416.

Manley, John, Derek H. Burney, Jake Epp, Paul Tellier, and Pamela Wallin. 2008. Independent Panel on Canada's Future Role in Afghanistan. Technical Report, Minister of Public Works.

Mansfield, Edward D., and Jack Snyder. 1995. "Democratization and the Danger of War." *International Security* 20 (1): 5–38.

Maoz, Zeev. 1983. "Resolve, Capabilities, and the Outcomes of Interstate Disputes, 1816–1976." *Journal of Conflict Resolution* 27 (2): 195–229.

Maoz, Zeev, and Randolph M. Siverson. 2008. "Bargaining, Domestic Politics, and International Context in the Management of War: A Review Essay." *Conflict Management and Peace Science* 25 (2): 171–189.

March, James G. 1966. "The Power of Power." In *Varieties of Political Theory*, ed. David Easton. Englewood Cliffs, NJ: Prentice-Hall.

March, James G., and Johan P. Olsen. 1998. "The Institutional Dynamics of International Political Orders." *International Organization* 52 (4): 943–969.

Marinov, Nikolay, William G. Nomikos, and Josh Robbins. 2015. "Does Electoral Proximity Affect Security Policy?" *Journal of Politics* 77 (3): 762–773.

Martin, Lisa L. 1999. "The Contributions of Rational Choice: A Defense of Pluralism." *International Security* 24 (2): 74–83.

Mattes, Michaela, and T. Clifton Morgan. 2004. "When Do They Stop? Modeling the Termination of War." *Conflict Management and Peace Science* 21 (3): 179–193.

Mattiacci, Eleonora, and Bear F. Braumoeller. 2011. "The Fog of Peace." Unpublished manuscript, Ohio State University.

May, Ernest R. 1961. *Imperial Diplomacy: The Emergence of America as a Great Power.* New York: Harcourt, Brace and Company.

May, Joshua, and Richard Holton. 2012. "What in the World Is Weakness of Will?" *Philosophical Studies* 157 (3): 341–360.

McCrae, Robert R., and Costa, Paul T. Jr., 1987. "Validation of the Five-Factor Model of Personality Across Instruments and Observers." *Journal of Personality and Social Psychology* 52 (1): 81–90.

McCrae, Robert R., and Antonio Terracciano. 2005. "Personality Profiles of Cultures: Aggregate Personality Traits." *Journal of Personality and Social Psychology* 89 (3): 407–425.

McDermott, Rose. 1998. *Risk-Taking in International Politics: Prospect Theory in American Foreign Policy*. Ann Arbor: University of Michigan Press.

McDermott, Rose. 2002. "Experimental Methods in Political Science." *Annual Review of Political Science* 5: 31–61.

McDermott, Rose. 2004. "The Feeling of Rationality: The Meaning of Neuroscience for Political Science." *Perspectives on Politics* 2 (4): 691–706.

McDermott, Rose. 2011a. "Internal and External Validity." In *Cambridge Handbook of Experimental Political Science*, ed. James N. Druckman, Donald P. Green, James H. Kuklinski, and Arthur Lupia. New York: Cambridge University Press.

McDermott, Rose. 2011b. "New Directions for Experimental Work in International Relations." *International Studies Quarterly* 55 (2): 503–520.

McDermott, Rose, and Jonathan A. Cowden. 2001. "The Effects of Uncertainty and Sex in a Crisis Simulation Game." *International Interactions* 27 (4): 353–380.

McDermott, Rose, Dustin Tingley, Jonathan Cowden, Giovanni Frazzetto, and Dominic D. P. Johnson. 2009. "Monoamine oxidase A gene (MAOA) Predicts Behavioral Aggression Following Provocation." *Proceedings of the National Academy of Sciences* 106 (7): 2118–2123.

McGarry, Ross, Sandra Walklate, and Gabe Mythen. 2015. "A Sociological Analysis of Military Resilience: Opening Up the Debate." *Armed Forces & Society* 41 (2): 352–378.

McManus, Roseanne W. 2014. "The Role of Statements of Resolve in International Conflict." Doctoral dissertation.

Mead, Walter Russell. 2002. *Special Providence: American Foreign Policy and How It Changed the World*. New York: Routledge.

Mearsheimer, John J. 2001. *The Tragedy of Great Power Politics*. New York: W.W. Norton.

Mebane, Walter R., Jr., and Jasjeet S. Sekhon. 2011. "Genetic Optimization Using Derivatives: The rgenoud package for R." *Journal of Statistical Software* 42 (11): 1–26.

Meirowitz, Adam, and Anne E. Sartori. 2008. "Strategic Uncertainty as a Cause of War." *Quarterly Journal of Political Science* 3 (4): 327–352.

Mercer, Jonathan. 1996. *Reputation and International Politics*. Ithaca, NY: Cornell University Press.

Mercer, Jonathan. 2005. "Rationality and Psychology in International Politics." *International Organization* 59 (1): 77–106.

Mercer, Jonathan. 2010. "Emotional Beliefs." *International Organization* 64 (1): 1–31.

Mercer, Jonathan. 2012. "Audience Costs are Toys." *Security Studies* 21 (3): 398–404.

Merom, Gil. 2003. *How Democracies Lose Small Wars: State, Society, and the Failures of France in Algeria, Israel in Lebanon, and the United States in Vietnam*. Cambridge: Cambridge University Press.

Merton, Robert K. 1968. *Social Theory and Social Structure*. New York: Free Press.

Michaels, Jim, and Theodore May. 2011. "Protesters' Resolve 'Unshakable': Many Promise to Continue Demonstrations until Mubarak Has Left Office." *USA Today*,

February 2. p. 5A. http://usatoday30.usatoday.com/printedition/news/20110202/egyptinside02_st.art.htm.

Miller, Holly C., Kristina F. Pattison, C. Nathan DeWall, Rebecca Rayburn-Reeves, and Thomas R. Zentall. 2010. "Self-Control Without a 'Self'?" *Psychological Science* 21 (4): 534–538.

Miller, John H., and Scott E. Page. 2007. *Complex Adaptive Systems: An Introduction to Computational Models of Social Life*. Princeton, NJ: Princeton University Press.

Mintz, Alex, Steven B. Redd, and Arnold Vedlitz. 2006. "Can We Generalize from Student Experiments to the Real World in Political Science, Military Affairs, and International Relations?" *Journal of Conflict Resolution* 50 (5): 757–776.

Mischel, Walter. 1968. *Personality and Assessment*. New York: John Wiley & Sons.

Mischel, Walter. 2004. "Toward an Integrative Science of the Person." *Annual Review of Psychology* 55: 1–22.

Mischel, Walter, and Joan Grusec. 1967. "Waiting for Rewards and Punishments: Effects of Time and Probability on Choice." *Journal of Personality and Social Psychology* 5 (1): 24–31.

Mischel, Walter, Yuichi Shoda, and Monica L. Rodriguez. 1989. "Delay of Gratification in Children." *Science* 244 (4907): 933–938.

Mitzen, Jennifer, and Randall L. Schweller. 2011. "Knowing the Unknown Unknowns: Misplaced Certainty and the Onset of War." *Security Studies* 20 (1): 2–35.

Mondak, Jeffrey J. 2010. *Personality and the Foundations of Political Behavior*. Cambridge: Cambridge University Press.

Moore, Jay. 1988. "Evolution and Impulsiveness." *Behavioral and Brain Sciences* 11 (4): 691.

Moravscik, Andrew. 1997. "Taking Preferences Seriously: A Liberal Theory of International Politics." *International Organization* 51 (4): 513–553.

Morgan, T. Clifton. 1990. "Power, Resolve and Bargaining in International Crises: A Spatial Theory." *International Interactions* 15 (3/4): 279–302.

Morgan, T. Clifton. 1994. *Untying the Knot of War: A Bargaining Theory of International Crises*. Ann Arbor: University of Michigan Press.

Morgenthau, Hans J. 1951. *In Defense of the National Interest*. New York: Alfred A. Knopf.

Morgenthau, Hans J. 1985. *Politics Among Nations: The Struggle for Power and Peace*. Brief ed. Boston, MA: McGraw-Hill.

Morrow, James D. 1985. "A Continuous-Outcome Expected Utility Theory of War." *Journal of Conflict Resolution* 29 (3): 473–502.

Morrow, James D. 1987. "On the Theoretical Basis of a Measure of National Risk Attitudes." *International Studies Quarterly* 31 (4): 423–438.

Morrow, James D. 1988. "Social Choice and System Structure in World Politics." *World Politics* 41 (1): 75–97.

Morrow, James D. 1989. "Capabilities, Uncertainty, and Resolve: A Limited Information Model of Crisis Bargaining." *American Journal of Political Science* 33 (4): 941–972.

Morsella, Ezequiel, John A. Bargh, and Peter M. Gollwitzer. 2009. *Oxford Handbook of Human Action*. Oxford: Oxford University Press.

Morton, Rebecca B., and Kenneth C. Williams. 2010. *Experimental Political Science and the Study of Causality*. New York: Cambridge University Press.

Most, Benjamin A., and Harvey Starr. 1984. "International Relations Theory, Foreign Policy Substitutability, and "Nice" Laws." *World Politics* 36 (3): 383–406.

Mueller, John E. 1971. "Trends in Popular Support for the Wars in Korea and Vietnam." *American Political Science Review* 65 (2): 358–375.

Mueller, John E. 1980. "The Search for the "Breaking Point" in Vietnam: The Statistics of a Deadly Quarrel." *International Studies Quarterly* 24 (4): 497–519.

Müller, Harald. 2004. "Arguing, Bargaining and All That: Communicative Action, Rationalist Theory and the Logic of Appropriateness in International Relations." *European Journal of International Relations* 10 (3): 395–435.

Muraven, Mark, R. Lorraine Collins, Saul Shiffman, and Jean A. Paty. 2005. "Daily Fluctuations in Self-Control Demands and Alcohol Intake." *Psychology of Addictive Behaviors* 19 (2): 140–147.

Murray, Shoon Kathleen. 1996. *Anchors Against Change: American Opinion Leaders' Beliefs After the Cold War*. Ann Arbor: University of Michigan Press.

Mutz, Diana C. 2011. *Population-Based Survey Experiments*. Princeton, NJ: Princeton University Press.

Nelson, Alan. 1984. "Some Issues Surrounding the Reduction of Macroeconomics to Microeconomics." *Philosophy of Science* 51 (4): 573–594.

Nelson, Stephen C., and Peter J. Katzenstein. 2014. "Uncertainty, Risk, and the Financial Crisis of 2008." *International Organization* 68 (2): 361–392.

Neustadt, Richard E., and Ernest R. May. 1986. *Thinking in Time: The Uses of History for Decision-Makers*. New York: Free Press.

Nincic, Miroslav. 1997. "Domestic Costs, the U.S. Public, and the Isolationist Calculus." *International Studies Quarterly* 41 (4): 593–610.

Nisbett, Richard E., and Dov Cohen. 1996. *Culture of Honor: The Psychology of Violence in the South*. Boulder, CO: Westview Press.

Noonan, Peggy. 2002. *When Character Was King: A Story of Ronald Reagan*. New York: Penguin.

Noyes, Richard. 1980. "The Time Horizon of Planned Social Change: I. Why Utopian Movements Always Promise Amelioration in the Future." *American Journal of Economics and Sociology* 39 (1): 65–77.

Offer, Avner. 2006. *The Challenge of Affluence: Self-Control and Well-Being in the United States and Britain since 1950*. Oxford: Oxford University Press.

O'Neill, Barry. 1999. *Honor, Symbols and War*. Ann Arbor: University of Michigan Press.

O'Neill, Barry. 2001. "Risk Aversion in International Relations Theory." *International Studies Quarterly* 45 (4): 617–649.

Ong, Anthony D., C.S. Bergeman, Toni L. Bisconti, and Kimberly A. Wallace. 2006. "Psychological Resilience, Positive Emotions, and Successful Adaptation to Stress in Later Life." *Journal of Personality and Social Psychology* 91 (4): 730–749.

Onuf, Nicholas. 1995. "Levels." *European Journal of International Relations* 1 (1): 35–58.

Organski, A.F.K. 1968. *World Politics*. 2nd ed. New York: Alfried A. Knopf.

Orne, Martin T. 1962. "On the Social Psychology of the Psychological Experiment: With Particular Reference to Demand Characteristics and Their Implications." *American Psychologist* 17 (11): 776–783.

Osterman, Lindsey L., and Ryan P. Brown. 2011. "Culture of Honor and Violence Against the Self." *Personality and Social Psychology Bulletin* 37 (12): 1611–1623.

Owen, John M., IV. 2010. *The Clash of Ideas in World Politics: Transnational Networks, States, and Regime Change, 1510–2010.* Princeton, NJ: Princeton University Press.

Oye, Kenneth A. 1985. "Explaining Cooperation Under Anarchy: Hypotheses and Strategies." *World Politics* 38 (1): 1–24.

Page, Benjamin I., and Robert Y. Shapiro. 1992. *The Rational Public: Fifty Years of Trends in Americans' Policy Preferences.* Chicago: University of Chicago Press.

Palacios-Huerta, Ignacio. 2003. "Time-Inconsistent Preferences in Adam Smith and David Hume." *History of Political Economy* 35 (2): 241–268.

Palmer, Glenn, Tamar London, and Patrick Regan. 2004. "What's Stopping You? The Sources of Political Constraints on International Conflict Behavior in Parliamentary Democracies." *International Interactions* 30 (1): 1–24.

Pape, Robert A. 1996. *Bombing to Win: Air Power and Coercion in War.* Ithaca, NY: Cornell University Press.

Pape, Robert A. 2003. "The Strategic Logic of Suicide Terrorism." *American Political Science Review* 97 (3): 343–361.

Papies, Esther K., Wolfgang Stroebe, and Henk Aarts. 2008. "Healthy Cognition: Processes of Self-Regulatory Success in Restrained Eating." *Personality and Social Psychology Bulletin* 34 (9): 1290–1300.

Parfit, Derek. 1971. "Personal Identity." *The Philosophical Review* 80 (1): 3–27.

Payne, Rodger A. 2001. "Persuasion, Frames and Norm Construction." *European Journal of International Relations* 7 (1): 37–61.

Pearson, John. 1991. *The Private Lives of Winston Churchill.* New York: Simon & Schuster.

Perri, Michael G., C. Steven Richards, and Karen R. Schultheis. 1977. "Behavioral Self-Control and Smoking Reduction: A Study of Self-initiated Attempts to Reduce Smoking." *Behavior Therapy* 8 (3): 360–365.

Petersen, Michael Bang, Daniel Sznycer, Aaron Sell, Leda Cosmides, and John Tooby. 2013. "The Ancestral Logic of Politics: Upper-Body Strength Regulates Men's Assertion of Self-Interest Over Economic Redistribution." *Psychological Science* 24 (7): 1098–1103.

Polsky, Andrew J. 2010. "Staying the Course: Presidential Leadership, Military Stalemate, and Strategic Inertia." *Perspectives on Politics* 8 (1): 127–139.

Posner, Richard A. 1997. "Are We One Self or Multiple Selves? Implications for Law and Public Policy." *Legal Theory* 3 (1): 23–35.

Post, Jerrold M. 2015. *Narcissism and Politics: Dreams of Glory.* Cambridge, UK: Cambridge University Press.

Powell, Robert. 1987. "Crisis Bargaining, Escalation, and MAD." *American Political Science Review* 81 (3): 717–735.

Powell, Robert. 1988. "Nuclear Brinkmanship with Two-Sided Incomplete Information." *American Political Science Review* 82 (1): 155–177.

Powell, Robert. 2003. "Nuclear Deterrence Theory, Nuclear Proliferation, and National Missile Defense." *International Security* 27 (4): 86–118.

Powell, Robert. 2004. "Bargaining and Learning While Fighting." *American Journal of Political Science* 48 (2): 344–361.

Powell, Robert. 2006. "War as a Commitment Problem." *International Organization* 60 (1): 169–203.

Power, Samantha. 2002. *"A Problem from Hell": America and the Age of Genocide.* New York: Basic Books.

Pratt, Travis C., Michael G. Turner, and Alex R. Piquero. 2004. "Parental Socialization and Community Context: A Longitudinal Analysis of the Structural Sources of Low Self-Control." *Journal of Research in Crime and Delinquency* 41 (3): 219–243.

Press, Daryl G. 2005. *Calculating Credibility: How Leaders Assess Military Threats.* Ithaca, NY: Cornell University Press.

Presser, Stanley, and Howard Schuman. 1981. *Questions and Answers in Attitude Surveys: Experiments on Question Form, Wording, and Context.* San Diego: Academic Press.

Przeworski, Adam, and James Raymond Vreeland. 2000. "The Effect of IMF Programs on Economic Growth." *Journal of Development Economics* 62 (2): 385–421.

Putnam, Robert D. 1988. "Diplomacy and Domestic Politics: the Logic of Two-Level Games." *International Organization* 42 (3): 427–460.

Rachlin, Howard, and Leonard Green. 1972. "Commitment, Choice and Self-Control." *Journal of the Experimental Analysis of Behavior* 17 (1): 15–22.

Ramsay, Kristopher W. 2008. "Settling It on the Field: Battlefield Events and War Termination." *Journal of Conflict Resolution* 52 (6): 850–879.

Rathbun, Brian C. 2012. "Politics and Paradigm Preferences: The Implicit Ideology of International Relations Scholars." *International Studies Quarterly* 56 (3): 607–622.

Rathbun, Brian C. 2014. *Diplomacy's Value: Creating Security in 1920s Europe and the Contemporary Middle East.* Ithaca, NY: Cornell University Press.

Rathbun, Brian C., Joshua D. Kertzer, Jason Reifler, Paul Goren, and Thomas J. Scotto. 2016. "Taking Foreign Policy Personally: Personal Values and Foreign Policy Attitudes." *International Studies Quarterly* 60 (1): 124–137.

Rathbun, Brian C., Joshua D. Kertzer, and Mark Paradis. 2014. "Homo Diplomaticus: Mixed-Method Evidence of Variation in Strategic Rationality." Working paper.

Rauchhaus, Robert W. 2006. "Asymmetric Information, Mediation, and Conflict Management." *World Politics* 58 (2): 207–241.

Ray, James Lee, and Ayse Vural. 1986. "Power Disparities and Paradoxical Conflict Outcomes." *International Interactions* 12 (4): 315–342.

Recouly, Raymond. 1920. *Foch: The Winner of the War.* New York: Charles Scribner's Sons.

Reed, William. 2000. "A Unified Statistical Model of Conflict Onset and Escalation." *American Journal of Political Science* 44 (1): 84–93.

Reed, William. 2003. "Information, Power, and War." *American Political Science Review* 97 (4): 633–641.

Reiter, Dan, and Allan C. Stam III. 1998a. "Democracy and Battlefield Military Effectiveness." *Journal of Conflict Resolution* 42 (3): 259–277.

Reiter, Dan, and Allan C. Stam III. 1998b. "Democracy, War Initiation, and Victory." *American Political Science Review* 92 (2): 377–389.

Reiter, Dan, and Allan C. Stam. 2002. *Democracies at War.* Princeton, NJ: Princeton University Press.

Renshon, Jonathan. 2009. "When Public Statements Reveal Private Beliefs: Assessing Operational Codes at a Distance." *Political Psychology* 30 (4): 649–661.

Renshon, Jonathan. 2015. "Losing Face and Sinking Costs: Experimental Evidence on the Judgment of Political and Military Leaders." *International Organization* 69 (3): 659–695.

Renshon, Jonathan, and Arthur Spirling. 2015. "Modeling 'Effectiveness' in International Relations." *Journal of Conflict Resolution* 59 (2): 207–238.

Rentfrow, Peter J., Samuel D. Gosling, and Jeff Potter. 2008. "A Theory of the Emergence, Persistence, and Expression of Geographic Variation in Psychological Characteristics." *Perspectives on Psychological Science* 3 (5): 339–369.

Reus-Smit, Christian. 2003. "Politics and International Legal Obligation." *European Journal of International Relations* 9 (4): 591–625.

Reynolds, Katherine J., John C. Turner, Nyla R. Branscombe, Kenneth I. Mavor, Boris Bizumic, and Emina Subašić. 2010. "Interactionism in Personality and Social Psychology: An Integrated Approach to Understanding the Mind and Behaviour." *European Journal of Personality* 24 (5): 458–482.

Richardson, Lewis F. 1948. "Variation of the Frequency of Fatal Quarrels with Magnitude." *Journal of the American Statistical Association* 43 (244): 523–546.

Roberts, Brent W., Oleksandr S. Chernyshenko, Stephen Stark, and Lewis R. Goldberg. 2005. "The Structure of Conscientiousness: An Empirical Investigation Based on Seven Major Personality Questionnaires." *Personnel Psychology* 58 (1): 103–139.

Rodriguez Mosquera, Patricia M., Antony S. R. Manstead, and Agneta H. Fischer. 2002. "The Role of Honour Concerns in Emotional Reactions to Offences." *Cognition and Emotion* 16 (1): 143–163.

Rogers, Alan R. 1994. "Evolution of Time Preference by Natural Selection." *American Economic Review* 84 (3): 460–481.

Rosato, Sebastian. 2003. "The Flawed Logic of Democratic Peace Theory." *American Political Science Review* 97 (4): 585–602.

Rosen, Stephen. 1972. "War Power and the Willingness to Suffer." In *Peace, War, and Numbers*, ed. Bruce M. Russett. Beverly Hills, CA: Sage Publications.

Rosen, Stephen Peter. 2005. *War and Human Nature*. Princeton, NJ: Princeton University Press.

Rosenau, James N. 1980. "Thinking Theory Thoroughly." In *The Scientific Study of Foreign Policy*. Revised & enlarged ed. London: Frances Pinter Publishers.

Ross, Lee. 1977. "The Intuitive Psychologist and His Shortcomings: Distortions in the Attribution Process." In *Advances in Experimental Social Psychology, Vol. 10*, ed. Leonard Berkowitz. New York: Academic Press.

Rothkopf, David. 2014. "Why the U.S. Can't Beat an Army the Size of a Junior College." Time, October 3. http://time.com/3547026/us-army-match-for-isis/

Rousseau, David L. 2006. *Identifying Threats and Threatening Identities: The Social Construction of Realism and Liberalism*. Stanford, CA: Stanford University Press.

Rubenzer, Steven J., and Thomas R. Faschingbauer. 2004. *Personality, Character, and Leadership in the White House: Psychologists Assess the Presidents*. Dulles, VA: Potomac Books.

Rubinstein, Ariel. 1982. "Perfect Equilibrium in a Bargaining Model." *Econometrica* 50 (1): 97–109.

Rucker, Phillip. 2015. "Scott Walker calls Reagan's Bust of Air Traffic Controller Strike 'most significant foreign policy decision'." Washington Post, February 28, 2015, https://www.washingtonpost.com/news/post-politics/wp/2015/02/28/scott-walker-calls-reagans-bust-of-air-traffic-controller-strike-most-significant-foreign-policy-decision/

Rummel, Rudolph J. 1975a. *Understanding Conflict and War: Vol. 1, The Dynamic Psychological Field.* Beverly Hills, CA: Sage Publications.

Rummel, Rudolph J. 1975b. *Understanding Conflict and War: Vol. 4, War, Power, Peace.* Beverly Hills, CA: Sage Publications.

Russett, Bruce, Jonathan Cowden, David Kinsella, and Shoon Murray. 1994. "Did Americans' Expectations of Nuclear War Reduce Their Savings?" *International Studies Quarterly* 38 (4): 587–603.

Ryan, Richard M., and Edward L. Deci. 2006. "Self-Regulation and the Problem of Human Autonomy: Does Psychology Need Choice, Self-Determination, and Will?" *Journal of Personality* 74 (6): 1557–1586.

Ryle, Gilbert. 1949. *The Concept of Mind.* Chicago: University of Chicago Press.

Samuelson, Paul. 1937. "A Note on Measurement of Utility." *Review of Economic Studies* 4 (2): 155–161.

Sartori, Anne E. 2002. "The Might of the Pen: A Reputational Theory of Communication in International Disputes." *International Organization* 56 (1): 121–149.

Sartori, Anne E. 2005. *Deterrence by Diplomacy.* Princeton, NJ: Princeton University Press.

Sartori, Giovanni. 1970. "Concept Misformation in Comparative Politics." *American Political Science Review* 64 (4): 1033–1053.

Saunders, Elizabeth N. 2011. *Leaders at War: How Presidents Shape Military Interventions.* Ithaca, NY: Cornell University Press.

Schaller, Mark, and Damian R. Murray. 2008. "Pathogens, Personality, and Culture: Disease Prevalence Predicts Worldwide Variability in Sociosexuality, Extraversion, and Openness to Experience." *Journal of Personality and Social Psychology* 95 (1): 212–221.

Schelling, Thomas C. 1960. *The Strategy of Conflict.* Cambridge, MA: Harvard University Press.

Schelling, Thomas C. 1966. *Arms and Influence.* New Haven, CT: Yale University Press.

Schelling, Thomas C. 1978. *Micromotives and Macrobehavior.* New York: W.W. Norton.

Schelling, Thomas C. 1984. "Self-Command in Practice, in Policy, and in a Theory of Rational Choice." *American Economic Review* 74 (2): 1–11.

Schultz, Kenneth. 1998. "Domestic Opposition and Signaling in International Crises." *American Political Science Review* 92 (4): 829–844.

Schultz, Kenneth A. 1999. "Do Democratic Institutions Constrain or Inform? Contrasting Two Institutional Perspectives on Democracy and War." *International Organization* 53 (2): 233–266.

Schultz, Kenneth A. 2001. *Democracy and Coercive Diplomacy.* New York: Cambridge University Press.

Schuman, Howard. 1992. "Historical Analogies, Generational Effects, and Attitudes Toward War." *American Sociological Review* 57 (3): 315–326.

Schwartz, Shalom H. 1992. "Universals in the Content and Structure of Values: Theoretical Advances and Empirical Tests in 20 Countries." In *Advances in Experimental Social Psychology, Vol. 25,* ed. Mark P. Zanna. San Diego: Academic Press.

Schweller, Randall L. 1994. "Bandwagoning for Profit: Bringing the Revisionist State Back In." *International Security* 19 (1): 72–107.

Schweller, Randall L. 1996. "Neorealism's Status-Quo Bias: What Security Dilemma?" *Security Studies* 5 (3): 90–121.

Schweller, Randall L. 2003. "The Progressiveness of Neoclassical Realism." In *Progress in International Relations Theory: Appraising the Field*, ed. Colin Elman and Miriam Fendius Elman. Cambridge, MA: MIT Press.

Sechser, Todd S. 2004. "Are Soldiers Less War-Prone than Statesmen?" *Journal of Conflict Resolution* 48 (5): 746–774.

Sechser, Todd S., and Matthew Fuhrmann. 2013. "Crisis Bargaining and Nuclear Blackmail." *International Organization* 67 (1): 173–195.

Sell, Aaron, John Tooby, and Leda Cosmides. 2009. "Formidability and the Logic of Human Anger." *Proceedings of the National Academy of Sciences* 106 (35): 15073–15078.

Shadish, William R., Thomas D. Cook, and Donald T. Campbell. 2002. *Experimental and Quasi-Experimental Designs for Generalized Causal Inference*. Boston: Houghton-Mifflin.

Shannon, Vaughn P., and Michael Dennis. 2007. "Militant Islam and the Futile Fight for Reputation." *Security Studies* 16 (2): 287–317.

Sheeran, Paschal. 2002. "Intention-Behavior Relations: A Conceptual and Empirical Review." In *European Review of Social Psychology*, ed. Wolfgang Stroebe and Miles Hewstone. Vol. 12. London: John Wiley & Sons.

Shils, Edward A., and Morris Janowitz. 1948. "Cohesion and Disintegration in the Wehrmacht in World War II." *Public Opinion Quarterly* 12 (2): 280–315.

Simon, Herbert A. 1957. *Models of Man*. New York: Wiley.

Simon, Herbert A. 1985. "Human Nature in Politics: The Dialogue of Psychology with Political Science." *American Political Science Review* 79 (2): 293–304.

Singer, J. David. 1961. "The Level-of-Analysis Problem in International Relations." *World Politics* 14 (1): 77–92.

Singer, J. David, Stuart Bremer, and John Stuckey. 1972. "Capability Distribution, Uncertainty, and Major Power War, 1820–1965." In *Peace, War, and Numbers*, ed. Bruce M. Russett. Beverly Hills, CA: Sage Publications.

Siverson, Randolph M. 1995. "Democracies and War Participation: In Defense of the Institutional Constraints Argument." *European Journal of International Relations* 1 (4): 481–489.

Slantchev, Branislav L. 2003. "The Power to Hurt: Costly Conflict with Completely Informed States." *American Political Science Review* 97 (1): 123–133.

Slantchev, Branislav L. 2005. "Military Coercion in Interstate Crises." *American Political Science Review* 99 (4): 533–547.

Slantchev, Branislav L. 2010. "Feigning Weakness." *International Organization* 64 (3): 357–388.

Slovic, Paul. 1987. "Perception of Risk." *Science* 236 (4799): 280–285.

Smith, Alastair. 1998. "Fighting Battles, Winning Wars." *Journal of Conflict Resolution* 42 (3): 301–320.

Smith, Alastair, and Allan C Stam. 2004. "Bargaining and the Nature of War." *Journal of Conflict Resolution* 48 (6): 783–813.

Smith, Anthony D. 2001. "Will and Sacrifice: Images of National Identity." *Millennium: Journal of International Studies* 30 (3): 571–584.

Smith, Hugh. 2005. "What Costs Will Democracies Bear? A Review of Popular Theories of Casualty Aversion." *Armed Forces & Society* 31 (4): 487–512.

Snidal, Duncan. 2002. "Rational Choice and International Relations." In *Handbook of International Relations*, ed. Walter Carlsnaes, Thomas Risse, and Beth A. Simmons. London: Sage.

Sniehotta, Falko F., Urte Scholz, and Ralf Schwarzer. 2005. "Bridging the Intention–Behaviour gap: Planning, Self-efficacy, and Action Control in the Adoption and Maintenance of Physical exercise." *Psychology & Health* 20 (2): 143–160.

Snyder, Glenn H., and Paul Diesing. 1977. *Conflict Among Nations: Bargaining, Decision Making, and System Structure in International Crises*. Princeton, NJ: Princeton University Press.

Snyder, Jack. 1978. "Rationality at the Brink: The Role of Cognitive Processes in Failures of Deterrence." *World Politics* 30 (3): 345–365.

Snyder, Jack, and Erica D. Borghard. 2011. "The Cost of Empty Threats: A Penny, Not a Pound." *American Political Science Review* 105 (August 2011): 437–456.

Spirling, Arthur. 2012. "US Treaty-making with American Indians: Institutional Change and Relative Power, 1784-1911." *American Journal of Political Science* 56 (1): 84–97.

Sprout, Harold, and Margaret Sprout. 1957. "Environmental Factors in the Study of International Politics." *Journal of Conflict Resolution* 1 (4): 309–328.

Stam, Allan C III. 1996. *Win, Lose, or Draw: Domestic Politics and the Crucible of War*. Ann Arbor: University of Michigan Press.

Stanley, Elizabeth A. 2009. *Paths to Peace: Domestic Coalition Shifts, War Termination and the Korean War*. Stanford: Stanford University Press.

Starr, Harvey. 1978. "'Opportunity' and 'Willingness' as Ordering Concepts in the Study of War." *International Interactions* 4 (4): 363–387.

Steinbruner, John D. 1974. *The Cybernetic Theory of Decision*. Princeton, NJ: Princeton University Press.

Stiglitz, Joseph E., and Linda J. Bilmes. 2012. "Estimating the Costs of War: Methodological Issues, with Applications to Iraq and Afghanistan." In *Oxford Handbook of the Economics of Peace and Conflict*. New York: Oxford University Press.

Streich, Philip, and Jack S. Levy. 2007. "Time Horizons, Discounting, and Intertemporal Choice." *Journal of Conflict Resolution* 51 (2): 199–226.

Stroud, Sarah, and Christine Tappolet. 2003. *Weakness of Will and Practical Irrationality*. Oxford: Clarendon Press.

Sullivan, Patricia L. 2007. "War Aims and War Outcomes." *Journal of Conflict Resolution* 51 (3): 496–524.

Sullivan, Patricia L. 2008. "Sustaining the Fight: A Cross-Sectional Time-Series Analysis of Public Support for Ongoing Military Interventions." *Conflict Management and Peace Science* 25 (2): 112–135.

Sullivan, Patricia L., and Michael T. Koch. 2009. "Military Interventions by Powerful States, 1945-2003." *Journal of Peace Research* 46 (5): 707–718.

Swann Jr., William B., Ángel Gómez, D. Conor Seyle, J. Francisco Morales, and Carmen Huici. 2009. "Identity Fusion: The Interplay of Personal and Social Identities in

Extreme Group Behavior." *Journal of Personality and Social Psychology* 96 (5): 995–1011.

Tang, Shiping. 2005. "Reputation, Cult of Reputation, and International Conflict." *Security Studies* 14 (1): 34–62.

Tang, Shiping. 2008. "Fear in International Politics: Two Positions." *International Studies Review* 10 (3): 451–471.

Tangney, June P., Roy F. Baumeister, and Angie Luzio Boone. 2004. "High Self-Control Predicts Good Adjustment, Less Pathology, Better Grades, and Interpersonal Success." *Journal of Personality* 72 (2): 273–324.

Terracciano, A., A. M. Abdel-Khalek, N. Ádám, L. Adamovová, C.-k. Ahn, H.-n. Ahn, B. M. Alansari, L. Alcalay, J. Allik, A. Angleitner, M. D. Avia, L. E. Ayearst, C. Barbaranelli, A. Beer, M. A. Borg-Cunen, D. Bratko, M. Brunner-Sciarra, L. Budzinski, N. Camart, D. Dahourou, F. De Fruyt, M. P. de Lima, G. E. H. del Pilar, E. Diener, R. Falzon, K. Fernando, E. Ficková, R. Fischer, C. Flores-Mendoza, M. A. Ghayur, S. Gülgöz, B. Hagberg, J. Halberstadt, M. S. Halim, M. Hřebíčková, J. Humrichouse, H. H. Jensen, D. D. Jocic, F. H. Jónsson, B. Khoury, W. Klinkosz, G. Knežević, M. A. Lauri, N. Leibovich, T. A. Martin, I. Marušić, K. A. Mastor, D. Matsumoto, M. McRorie, B. Meshcheriakov, E. L. Mortensen, M. Munyae, J. Nagy, K. Nakazato, F. Nansubuga, S. Oishi, A. O. Ojedokun, F. Ostendorf, D. L. Paulhus, S. Pelevin, J.-M. Petot, N. Podobnik, J. L. Porrata, V. S. Pramila, G. Prentice, A. Realo, N. Reátegui, J.-P. Rolland, J. Rossier, W. Ruch, V. S. Rus, M. L. Sánchez-Bernardos, V. Schmidt, S. Sciculna-Calleja, A. Sekowski, J. Shakespeare-Finch, Y. Shimonaka, F. Simonetti, T. Sineshaw, J. Siuta, P. B. Smith, P. D. Trapnell, K. K. Trobst, L. Wang, M. Yik, A. Zupančič, and R. R. McCrae. 2005. "National Character Does Not Reflect Mean Personality Trait Levels in 49 Cultures." *Science* 310 (5745): 96–100.

Tetlock, Philip E. 2003. "Thinking the Unthinkable: Sacred Values and Taboo Cognitions." *Trends in Cognitive Sciences* 7 (7): 320–324.

Tett, Robert P., and Dawn D. Burnett. 2003. "A Personality Trait-Based Interactionist Model of Job Performance." *Journal Of Applied Psychology* 88 (3): 500–517.

Tett, Robert P., and Hal A. Gutterman. 2000. "Situation Trait Relevance, Trait Expression, and Cross-situational Consistency: Testing a Principle of Trait Activation." *Journal of Research in Personality* 36 (4): 397–423.

Thaler, Richard. 1985. "Mental Accounting and Consumer Choice." *Marketing Science* 4 (3): 199–214.

Thaler, Richard, and H.M. Shefrin. 1981. "An Economic Theory of Self-Control." *Journal of Political Economy* 89 (2): 392–406.

Thompson, William R. 2003. "A Streetcar Named Sarajevo: Catalysts, Multiple Causation Chains, and Rivalry Structures." *International Studies Quarterly* 47 (3): 453–474.

Thucydides. 1998. *The Landmark Thucydides: A Comprehensive Guide to the Peloponnesian War.* Trans. Richard Crawley and Ed. Robert B. Strassler. New York: Simon & Schuster.

Tingley, Dustin H., and Barbara F. Walter. 2011. "The Effect of Repeated Play on Reputation Building: An Experimental Approach." *International Organization* 65 (2): 343–365.

Tingley, Dustin, Teppei Yamamoto, Kentaro Hirose, Luke Keele, and Kosuke Imai. 2014. "mediation: R Package for Causal Mediation Analysis." *Journal of Statistical Software* 59 (5): 1–38.

Tittle, Charles R., David A. Ward, and Harold G. Grasmick. 2003. "Self-control and Crime/Deviance: Cognitive vs. Behavioral Measures." *Journal of Quantitative Criminology* 19 (4): 333–365.

Tobin, Henry, and A.W. Logue. 1994. "Self-Control Across Species (*Columba livia, Homo sapiens*, and *Rattus norvegicus*)." *Journal of Comparative Psychology* 108 (2): 126–133.

Todd, Peter M., and Gerd Gigerenzer. 2003. "Bounding Rationality to the World." *Journal of Economic Psychology* 24 (2): 143–165.

Toft, Monica Duffy. 2006. "Issue Indivisibility and Time Horizons as Rationalist Explanations for War." *Security Studies* 15 (1): 34–69.

Tomz, Michael. 2007a. "Domestic Audience Costs in International Relations: An Experimental Approach." *International Organization* 61 (4): 821–840.

Tomz, Michael. 2007b. *Reputation and International Cooperation: Sovereign Debt across Three Centuries*. Princeton, NJ: Princeton University Press.

Trager, Robert F. 2011. "Multidimensional Diplomacy." *International Organization* 65 (3): 469–506.

Trager, Robert F., and Lynn Vavreck. 2011. "The Political Costs of Crisis Bargaining: Presidential Rhetoric and the Role of Party." *American Journal of Political Science* 55 (3): 526–545.

Travers, T.H.E. 1979. "Technology, Tactics, and Morale: Jean de Bloch, the Boer War, and British Military Theory, 1900–1914." *Journal of Modern History* 51 (2): 264–286.

Treier, Shawn, and Simon Jackman. 2008. "Democracy as a Latent Variable." *American Journal of Political Science* 52 (1): 201–217.

Trivedi, Ranak B., Hayden B. Bosworth, and George L. Jackson. 2011. "Resilience in Chronic Illness." In *Resilience in Aging: Concepts, Research, and Outcomes*, ed. Barbara Resnick, Lisa P. Gwyther, and Karen A. Roberto. New York: Springer.

Trope, Yaacov, and Nira Liberman. 2003. "Temporal Construal." *Psychological Review* 110 (3): 403–421.

Turner, Frederick Jackson. 1956. "The Significance of the Frontier in American History." In *The Turner Thesis: Concerning the Role of the Frontier in American History*, ed. George Rogers Taylor. Boston: D.C. Heath and Company.

Udehn, Lars. 2001. *Methodological Individualism: Background, History and Meaning*. London: Routledge.

Ungar, Michael. 2004. "A Constructionist Discourse on Resilience: Multiple Contexts, Multiple Realities among At-Risk Children and Youth." *Youth & Society* 35 (3): 341–365.

Valentino, Benjamin A., Paul K. Huth, and Sarah E. Croco. 2010. "Bear Any Burden? How Democracies Minimize the Costs of War." *Journal of Politics* 72 (2): 528–544.

Van de Vliert, Evert, Huadong Yang, Yongli Wang, and Xiao-peng Ren. 2013. "Climato-Economic Imprints on Chinese Collectivism." *Journal of Cross-Cultural Psychology* 44 (4): 589–605.

Van Evera, Stephen. 1984. "The Cult of the Offensive and the Origins of the First World War." *International Security* 9 (1): 58–107.

Van Evera, Steven. 1999. *Causes of War: Power and the Roots of Conflict.* Ithaca, NY: Cornell University Press.

Vasquez, Joseph Paul III. 2005. "Shouldering the Soldiering : Democracy, Conscription, and Military Casualties." *Journal of Conflict Resolution* 49 (6): 849–873.

Velleman, J. David. 2007. "What Good Is a Will?" In *Action in Context,* ed. Anton Leist. Berlin: Walter de Gruyter.

Viscusi, W. Kip, and Joseph E. Aldy. 2003. "The Value of a Statistical Life: A Critical Review of Market Estimates Throughout the World." *Journal of Risk and Uncertainty* 27 (1): 5–76.

Voeten, Erik. 2000. "Clashes in the Assembly." *International Organization* 54 (2): 185–215.

von Neumann, John, and Oskar Morgenstern. 1944. *Theory of Games and Economic Behavior.* Princeton, NJ: Princeton University Press.

Wagner, R. Harrison. 2000. "Bargaining and War." *American Journal of Political Science* 44 (3): 469–484.

Walker, Stephen G., Mark Schafer, and Michael D. Young. 1999. "Presidential Operational Codes and Foreign Policy Conflicts in the Post–Cold War World." *Journal of Conflict Resolution* 43 (5): 610–625.

Walt, Stephen M. 1985. "Alliance Formation and the Balance of World Power." *International Security* 9 (4): 3–43.

Walt, Stephen M. 1999. "Rigor or Rigor Mortis?: Rational Choice and Security Studies." *International Security* 23 (4): 5–48.

Walter, Barbara F. 1997. "The Critical Barrier to Civil War Settlement." *International Organization* 51 (3): 335–364.

Walter, Barbara F. 2006. "Building Reputation: Why Governments Fight Some Separatists but Not Others." *American Journal of Political Science* 50 (2): 313–330.

Waltz, Kenneth N. 1959. *Man, The State, and War: A Theoretical Analysis.* New York: Columbia University Press.

Waltz, Kenneth N. 1979. *Theory of International Politics.* Boston: McGraw-Hill.

Waltz, Kenneth N. 1986. "Reflections on *Theory of International Politics*: A Response to My Critics." In *Neorealism and Its Critics,* ed. Robert O. Keohane. New York: Columbia University Press.

Wang, Mei, Marc Oliver Rieger, and Thorsten Hens. 2016. "How Time Preferences Differ: Evidence from 53 Countries." *Journal of Economic Psychology* 52 (1): 115–135.

Wansbeek, Tom, and Erik Meijer. 2000. *Measurement Error and Latent Variables in Econometrics.* Amsterdam: North-Holland.

Warren, Michael. 2011. "Paul Ryan Embraces American Exceptionalism, Rejects Isolationism in Foreign Policy Speech." *The Weekly Standard,* June 2. http://www.weeklystandard.com/blogs/ryan-embraces-exceptionalism-rejects-isolationism-foreign-policy-speech_573194.html.

Watson, Alexander. 2008. *Enduring the Great War: Combat, Morale and Collapse in the German and British Armies, 1914–1918.* Cambridge: Cambridge University Press.

Watson, Carl B., Martin M. Chemers, and Natalya Preiser. 2001. "Collective Efficacy: A Multilevel Analysis." *Personality and Social Psychology Bulletin* 27 (8): 1057–1068.

Watson, P. J., Stephanie O. Grisham, Marjorie V. Trotter, and Michael D. Biderman. 1984. "Narcissism and Empathy: Validity Evidence for the Narcissistic Personality Inventory." *Journal of Personality Assessment* 48 (3): 301–305.

Weber, Elke U., and Christopher K. Hsee. 1998. "What Folklore Tells Us about Risk and Risk Taking: Cross-Cultural Comparisons of American, German, and Chinese Proverbs." *Organizational Behavior and Human Decision Processes* 75 (2): 170–186.

Weber, Max. 1904/1984. *The Protestant Ethic and the Spirit of Capitalism*. Winchester, MA: Allen & Unwin.

Wedeen, Lisa. 2002. "Conceptualizing Culture: Possibilities for Political Science." *American Political Science Review* 96 (4): 713–728.

Weeks, Jessica L. 2008. "Autocratic Audience Costs: Regime Type and Signaling Resolve." *International Organization* 62 (1): 35–64.

Weeks, Jessica L. P. 2014. *Dictators at War and Peace*. Ithaca, NY: Cornell University Press.

Weidmann, Nils B., Doreen Kuse, and Kristian Skrede Gleditsch. 2010. "The Geography of the International System: The CShapes Dataset." *International Interactions* 36 (1): 86–106.

Weinberger, Caspar W. 1984. "Remarks Prepared for Delivery by the Hon. Caspar W. Weinberger, Secretary of Defense, to the National Press Club, Washington D.C." http://www.pbs.org/wgbh/pages/frontline/shows/military/force/weinberger.html.

Weiss, Jessica Chen. 2014. *Powerful Patriots: Nationalist Protest in China's Foreign Relations*. Oxford: Oxford University Press.

Wendt, Alexander. 1987. "The Agent-Structure Problem in International Relations Theory." *International Organization* 41 (3): 335–369.

Wendt, Alexander. 1992. "Anarchy is what States Make of It: the Social Construction of Power Politics." *International Organization* 46 (2): 391–425.

Wendt, Alexander. 1998. "On Constitution and Causation in International Relations." *Review of International Studies* 24 (5): 101–117.

Wendt, Alexander. 1999. *Social Theory of International Politics*. Cambridge, UK: Cambridge University Press.

Wendt, Alexander. 2004. "The State as Person in International Theory." *Review of International Studies* 30 (2): 289–316.

White, Jeffrey. 2011. The Grinding War in Libya Favors Qadhafi, *Policywatch 1801*. Washington Institute for Near East Policy, April 21. http://www.washington institute.org/policy-analysis/view/the-grinding-war-in-libya-favors-qadhafi

Whiteside, Stephen P., and Donald R. Lynam. 2001. "The Five Factor Model and Impulsivity: Using a Structural Model of Personality to Understand Impulsivity." *Personality and Individual Differences* 30 (4): 669–689.

Wight, Martin. 1966. "Why Is There No International Theory?" In *Diplomatic Investigations: Essays in the Theory of International Politics*, eds. Herbert Butterfield and Martin Wight. London, UK: Allen and Unwin.

Williams, Vanessa. 2015. "Defense Secretary Carter: Iraq's Forces Showed 'no will to fight' Islamic State." *Washington Post*.

Wilson, Timothy D., and Daniel T. Gilbert. 2003. "Affective Forecasting." In *Advances in Experimental Social Psychology, Vol. 35*, ed. Mark P. Zanna. San Deigo: Academic Press.

Winship, Christopher, and Larry Radbill. 1994. "Sampling Weights and Regression Analysis." *Sociological Methods & Research* 23 (2): 230–257.

Wittkopf, Eugene R. 1990. *Faces of internationalism: Public Opinion and American foreign policy*. Durhum, NC: Duke University Press.

Wolfers, Arnold. 1962. *Discord and Collaboration: Essays on International Politics*. Baltimore, MD: Johns Hopkins University Press.

Wolford, Scott. 2007. "The Turnover Trap: New Leaders, Reputation, and International Conflict." *American Journal of Political Science* 51 (4): 772–788.

World Values Survey Association. 2009. "World Values Survey 1981–2008 Official Aggregate v. 20090901." http://www.wvsevsdb.com.

Wright, Quincy. 1964. *A Study of War*. Abridged ed. Chicago: University of Chicago Press.

Xiang, Jun. 2010. "Relevance as a Latent Variable in Dyadic Analysis of Conflict." *Journal of Politics* 72 (2): 484–498.

Yarhi-Milo, Keren. 2014. *Knowing the Adversary: Leaders, Intelligence, and Assessment of Intentions in International Relations*. Princeton, NJ: Princeton University Press.

Yglesias, Matthew. 2006. "The Green Lantern Theory of Geopolitics." In *TPM Cafe*. http://www.smirkingchimp.com/thread/845.

Young, Oran R. 1968. *The Politics of Force: Bargaining During International Crises*. Princeton, NJ: Princeton University Press.

Zaller, John R. 1992. *The Nature and Origins of Mass Public Opinion*. Cambridge: Cambridge University Press.

Zeiler, Michael D. 1988. "Evolution Is Not Rational Banking." *Behavioral and Brain Sciences* 11 (4): 696–697.

INDEX

Achen, Christopher, 111n1
affective forecasting, 149
Afghanistan, Soviet invasion of, 119
Afghanistan War, 2, 32, 50
agent-based modeling, 112
agent-structure problem, 20–21, 156. *See also* person-situation debate
Ainslie, George, 39
Akrasia, 8n24. *See also* weakness of will
Archigos, 121–122
Asian disease experiment, 69n52, 161
asymmetric conflict, 2, 11, 113
attribution theory, 152
audience costs, 10, 13, 35–37, 55n23, 112, 120–21, 148n19

Bak, Daehee 134
behavioral economics, 6, 15, 26, 52, 56, 57, 68, 81, 104, 109, 143, 152, 154; libertarian paternalist tradition in, 154
behavioral genetics, 159
behaviorism, 15–16
Bénabou, Roland, 39, 148
Bennett, Scott, 67
Berinsky, Adam, 88
Bilmes, Linda, 35
Boehmer, Charles, 155
Bonaparte, Napoleon, 2, 7, 18, 146, 167
Borghard, Erica, 13
Box-Steffensmeier, Janet, 60n38
Bradley-Terry models, 113
Braumoeller, Bear, 116n23, 131
Breivik, Anders, 158
Brown, Ryan, 89n16, 116n23
Burghley, Lord, 12
Bush, George W., 50, 83
Burma, intervention in, 152

capabilities, 3, 10, 11–15, 22, 23, 113n10, 142, 146, 150–51, 153, 165, 167–68
Carson, Austin, 116, 131
Carter, Ashton, 1

Carter, Jimmy, 45
Castlereagh, Viscount, 161
Castles, Francis, 125
casualties, 27, 33, 30, 35, 38, 40, 49, 51, 53, 58, 61–64, 75, 79, 80, 91–96, 99, 102, 103, 105–8, 115, 119, 120, 144, 170, 173–75, 180–82, 184–89, 191–98. *See also* cost of fighting
Ceausescu, Nicolae, 161
Chait, Jonathan, 25
Cheney, Richard, 83
Chiozza, Giacomo, 37, 123
Churchill, Winston, 25, 45, 123, 163
climate change, 147
Cline, Ray, 115, 134
Clinton, Bill, 50
Cold War, 10, 43, 45
commitment devices, 10, 15, 21, 25, 155; commitment problems, 10, 21
constructivism, 5, 30, 33n26, 41, 42n65, 46, 163n89
Copeland, Dale, 160
Correlates of War (COW), 151
cost sensitivity, 19, 34, 38, 47, 61, 83, 94–95, 104, 106, 120
costs of backing down, 6, 26, 27, 33–38, 40–44, 46, 48, 49, 55, 58, 61, 72, 77–79, 81, 83, 85, 86, 95, 96, 98, 103, 104, 101, 105–6, 108, 111, 120, 121, 123, 126, 131, 134, 138, 139, 143, 144, 147, 165, 171, 127, 178–80; reputational, 6, 9, 10, 17, 23, 25, 34–37, 40–44, 49, 51, 53–55, 58, 61–67, 69, 70, 73–77, 79–83, 85–89, 91–99, 102–8, 118, 120–22, 131, 134, 139, 144, 163, 165, 166, 170–76, 178–89, 193, 194
costs of fighting: anticipated costs, 61, 62, 64, 66, 70, 75, 76, 91–95, 96, 97, 99, 102, 105, 106–7, 120, 139, 181, 185–87; costs of personal political fortune, 34; dilution of, 106–7; economic costs, 34, 35n35, 170; opportunity costs, 34, 170; sunk costs, 34, 91, 59, 144
counterinsurgency, 11, 43